SERVE AND GROW RICHLY

SERVE AND GROW RICHLY

How Serving Others Unlocks Success, Fulfillment, And Spiritual Growth

PAUL KELLEY

Please visit the *Serve And Grow Richly* book website at:

www.serveandgrowrichly.com

Copyright © 2025 by Paul Kelley Publishing

ISBN : 979-8-9931537-0-4

Independently Self-Published

The author/self-publisher supports copyright. Copyright fuels creativity, encourages diverse voices, promotes free speech, and creates a vibrant culture. Thank you for buying an authorized edition of this book and for complying with copyright laws by not reproducing, scanning, or distributing any part of it in any form without permission. You are supporting writers and allowing this author self-publisher to continue to publish books for every reader.

To my Heavenly Father Jehovah God

And His Son, my Lord and Savior Jesus Christ.

To my aunt Zena.

To my mom Rebekah.

To my children Katie, Kathryn, and David.

To my son-in-law Troy and his mom Lori.

Thank you for your love and support.

Contents

1	Mindset & Attitude	1
2	Action & Persistence	11
3	Goal Setting & Vision	23
4	Overcoming Fear & Adversity	37
5	Habits & Daily Practice	51
6	Purpose & Meaning	65
7	Self-Discovery & Identity	81
8	Change & Growth	97
9	Resilience & Endurance	115
10	Relationships & Influence	133
11	Love & Compassion	151
12	Responsibility & Ownership	167
13	Faith & Spiritual Strength	185
14	Gratitude & Application	201
15	Learning & Growth Mindset	219

1
Mindset & Attitude

There is a quiet, powerful truth at the heart of every meaningful transformation: the way we see the world shapes the world we see.

OUR MINDSET IS THE LENS through which we interpret challenges, opportunities, and even our own potential. Attitude, as many have said, is not just a small thing—it is everything. It determines how we show up, how we serve, and ultimately, how richly we grow.

Consider this: two people can face the same circumstance, yet one sees a setback, while the other sees a setup for something greater. The difference is not in the situation, but in the story they tell themselves about it. This is the gift—and the responsibility—of mindset. When we choose to cultivate an attitude of possibility, gratitude, and resilience, we unlock doors that others may never even notice.

In business and in life, those who serve with a positive spirit not only lift others, but also elevate themselves. A generous mindset is magnetic; it attracts collaboration, trust, and new opportunities. This is why some of the world's most successful leaders and entrepreneurs spend as much time nurturing their inner world as they do building their outer one. They understand that true richness begins in the mind and radiates outward through every action.

Faith traditions have long taught the power of renewing the mind and guarding the heart. While this book is not a sermon, it is worth remembering the timeless wisdom: "For as he thinketh in his heart, so is he." When we align our thoughts with hope, purpose, and service, we become architects of abundance—not just for ourselves, but for everyone we encounter.

The Science of Mindset

Modern neuroscience has confirmed what ancient wisdom has always known: our thoughts literally reshape our brains. Dr. Carol Dweck's groundbreaking research on growth mindset versus fixed mindset has revolutionized how we understand human potential. Those with a growth mindset—the belief that abilities can be developed through dedication and hard work—consistently outperform those who believe their talents are fixed traits.

But here's what makes this particularly relevant for those who seek to serve and grow richly: mindset doesn't just affect our personal success; it profoundly impacts our capacity to serve others. When we approach challenges with curiosity rather than defensiveness, when we see setbacks as learning opportunities rather than failures, we model resilience for those around us. We become beacons of hope in a world that desperately needs it.

Consider the story of a small business owner who faced bankruptcy during the economic downturn. Instead of focusing on what he had lost, he chose to see the crisis as an opportunity to serve his community in new ways. He transformed his struggling restaurant into a community food bank, feeding families in need while finding innovative ways to sustain his business. His mindset shift didn't just save his enterprise—it transformed an entire neighborhood. This is the power of a service-oriented mindset: it turns personal challenges into community solutions.

The Biblical Foundation of Transformed Thinking

The apostle Paul understood the transformative power of mindset long before modern psychology gave it a name. In Romans 12:2, he writes, "And be not conformed to this world: but be ye transformed by the renewing of your mind, that ye may prove what is that good, and acceptable, and perfect, will of God." This isn't just spiritual advice—it's practical wisdom for anyone seeking to live with purpose and impact.

The Hebrew word for "think" in Proverbs 23:7—"For as he thinketh in his heart, so is he"—comes from the root word "sha'ar," which means to calculate, estimate, or reckon. It suggests that our thoughts are not passive observations but active calculations that determine our reality. When we choose to calculate our lives in terms of possibility, gratitude, and service, we literally become different people.

This biblical understanding of mindset goes beyond positive thinking. It's about aligning our thoughts with divine purpose. When Jesus taught his disciples to pray, "Thy will be done on earth as it is in heaven," he was teaching them to cultivate a mindset that seeks God's perspective on earthly circumstances. This is the foundation of a service-oriented life: seeing situations not just as they are, but as they could be when viewed through the lens of divine love and purpose.

The Magnetic Power of Positive Service

There's something almost mystical about the way positive, service-oriented people attract opportunities and relationships. It's not just that they're pleasant to be around—though they certainly are. It's that their mindset creates a gravitational pull that draws resources, partnerships, and possibilities toward them.

Zig Ziglar captured this principle perfectly: "You can have everything in life you want, if you will just help other people get what they want." This isn't just motivational speaking; it's a practical formula for abundance. When our mindset is focused on adding value to others, we position ourselves at the center of networks of reciprocity and goodwill.

Consider the difference between two sales professionals. The first focuses on meeting quotas and closing deals. The second focuses on understanding customer needs and providing genuine solutions. Both may have similar skills and knowledge, but the second consistently outperforms the first. Why? Because their mindset shapes their approach. The service-oriented salesperson builds trust, creates loyalty, and generates referrals. Their positive mindset becomes a business advantage.

This principle extends beyond business into every area of life. Parents who approach child-rearing with a service mindset—seeing themselves as stewards of their children's potential rather than controllers of their behavior—tend to raise more confident, capable children. Leaders who view their role as serving their teams rather than directing them often see higher engagement and performance. The mindset of service creates a positive feedback loop that enriches everyone involved.

Overcoming the Mindset Barriers

Of course, cultivating a positive, service-oriented mindset isn't always easy. We live in a world that often rewards cynicism, competition, and self-protection. Our brains are wired to notice threats and problems—a survival mechanism that once kept our ancestors alive but now often keeps us trapped in negative thinking patterns.

The first step in overcoming these barriers is awareness. We must learn to observe our thoughts without being controlled by them. This is where the practice of mindfulness intersects with biblical wisdom. When we take captive "every thought to the obedience of Christ" (2 Corinthians 10:5), we're practicing a form of spiritual mindfulness that helps us choose our responses rather than react automatically.

One practical technique is what psychologists call "cognitive reframing." Instead of asking "Why is this happening to me?" we can learn to ask "What is this here to teach me?" or "How can I use this experience to serve others better?" This simple shift in questioning can transform our relationship with adversity.

Another powerful tool is gratitude practice. When we actively look for things to appreciate—even in difficult circumstances—we literally rewire our brains to notice opportunities rather than obstacles. This isn't about denying problems; it's about maintaining hope and perspective in the midst of challenges.

The Leadership Advantage of Positive Mindset

In today's business environment, leadership isn't about position or authority—it's about influence. And influence flows most naturally from those who combine competence with a positive, service-oriented mindset. These leaders don't just achieve better results; they create cultures where others thrive.

Research by the Harvard Business Review shows that teams led by positive leaders show 31% higher productivity, 37% better sales performance, and 3x higher levels of creativity. But here's what's even more significant: these leaders report higher levels of personal satisfaction and meaning in their work. They're not just more effective; they're more fulfilled.

This creates what we might call the "servant leadership advantage." When leaders approach their role with a mindset of service—seeing themselves as resources for their teams rather than directors of their teams—they unlock discretionary effort and innovation. People don't just work for these leaders; they work with them toward shared goals.

Consider the example of a manufacturing plant manager who inherited a facility with low morale and declining productivity. Instead of implementing stricter controls, he began each week by asking his team members what they needed to do their jobs better. He instituted regular "listening sessions" where employees could share ideas and concerns. His mindset shift from controller to servant leader resulted in a 40% increase in productivity and a 60% reduction in turnover within 18 months.

Mindset as Ministry

For those who embrace faith as part of their worldview, mindset becomes a form of ministry. When we choose to respond to challenges with hope, to treat difficult people with kindness, and to serve others with joy, we become living demonstrations of spiritual truth. Our attitude becomes our testimony.

This doesn't mean we ignore problems or pretend everything is perfect. Rather, it means we approach difficulties with faith that there is purpose in our struggles and that even our challenges can become opportunities to serve others. Joseph in the Old Testament exemplified this mindset when he told his brothers, "But as for you, ye thought evil against me; but God meant it unto good, to bring to pass, as it is this day, to save much people alive." (Genesis 50:20).

When we adopt this perspective, our setbacks become setups for service. Our tests become testimonies. Our mess becomes our message. This is the transformative power of a faith-based mindset: it allows us to find meaning and purpose even in difficult circumstances.

The Ripple Effect of Positive Mindset

Perhaps the most compelling reason to cultivate a positive, service-oriented mindset is its ripple effect. Our attitude doesn't just affect us—it influences everyone around us. Families, teams, communities, and organizations all reflect the collective mindset of their members.

When we choose to approach life with optimism, gratitude, and a desire to serve, we give others permission to do the same. We become what psychologists call "emotional contagion" agents—people who spread positive emotions and attitudes simply by embodying them.

Think about the people in your life who have had the greatest positive impact on you. Chances are, they weren't just skilled or intelligent—they had a quality of spirit that lifted you up. They saw potential in you that you might not have seen in yourself. They approached challenges with a combination of realism and hope that made difficult things seem possible.

This is the legacy of a transformed mindset: it doesn't just change our own lives; it changes the lives of everyone we touch. When we serve and grow richly, we create an expanding circle of positive influence that continues long after our direct involvement ends.

PRACTICAL APPLICATIONS
Daily Mindset Practices:
Building Your Mental Foundation

Transforming your mindset isn't a one-time event—it's a daily practice that requires intention and consistency. Just as physical fitness requires regular exercise, mental fitness requires regular habits that strengthen your capacity for positive, service-oriented thinking.

The Morning Mindset Ritual. Begin each day with what we call the «Serve and Grow» morning practice. Before checking your phone or diving into your to-do list, spend five minutes in quiet reflection. Ask yourself three questions:

1. "How can I serve someone today?"
2. "What opportunity for growth will I embrace today?"
3. "What am I grateful for in this moment?"

Write your answers down. This simple practice primes your brain to notice service opportunities and growth possibilities throughout the day. One business executive who adopted this practice reported that it transformed not just her productivity, but her relationships with colleagues and clients.

The Reframe Technique. When you encounter a challenging situation, practice the «reframe technique.» Instead of your first reaction, pause and ask:

- "What is this situation here to teach me?"
- "How might this challenge serve a greater purpose?"
- "What would someone I admire do in this situation?"
- "How can I use this experience to better serve others?"

For example, if you're stuck in traffic, instead of frustration, you might reframe it as an opportunity for prayer, reflection, or planning. If a project fails, you might reframe it as valuable feedback that will improve your next effort.

The Service Lens Exercise. Throughout your day, practice viewing situations through what we call the «service lens.» In every interaction, ask yourself: «How can I add value to this person or situation?» This doesn›t mean becoming a people-pleaser or saying yes to everything. It means looking for genuine opportunities to contribute positively.

A customer service representative who adopted this practice found that difficult customers became opportunities to demonstrate patience and problem-solving skills. Complaints became chances to improve systems. Her mindset shift led to increased job satisfaction and recognition from management.

Weekly Mindset Strengthening

The Weekly Reflection Practice. Set aside 20-30 minutes each week for mindset reflection. Review your week and identify:

- Three moments when your mindset served you well
- Two situations where you could have reframed your thinking
- One person you served through your positive attitude
- One lesson you learned about growth or service

This practice helps you recognize patterns in your thinking and celebrate progress in your mindset development.

The Gratitude Inventory. Each week, create a comprehensive gratitude inventory. List:

- Three people who made your week better
- Two challenges that taught you something valuable
- One way you were able to serve someone else

- One improvement you noticed in your own attitude or behavior

Research shows that people who practice weekly gratitude exercises experience increased happiness, better relationships, and improved physical health.

The Growth Goal Setting. Each week, set one specific goal for mindset growth. Examples might include:

- "I will reframe one negative thought each day"
- "I will compliment one person daily"
- "I will look for service opportunities in routine interactions"
- "I will practice patience in one challenging situation"

Make your goals specific, measurable, and achievable. Track your progress and celebrate small victories.

Monthly Mindset Challenges

The Service Challenge. Each month, commit to a specific service challenge that stretches your mindset. This might include:

- Volunteer for a cause you care about
- Mentor someone in your field
- Practice random acts of kindness
- Write thank-you notes to people who have influenced you
- Offer to help a colleague with a difficult project

The key is to choose something that requires you to think beyond yourself and your immediate needs.

The Learning Challenge. Commit to learning something new each month that expands your perspective. This could be:

- Reading a book outside your usual genre
- Taking an online course in a new field
- Attending a workshop or seminar
- Learning from someone with a different background or viewpoint
- Practicing a new skill that requires patience and persistence

The goal is to keep your mind flexible and open to new possibilities.

Building Your Mindset Support System

The Accountability Partnership. Find someone who shares your commitment to developing a positive, service-oriented mindset. Meet weekly or bi-weekly to:

- Share your mindset goals and progress

- Discuss challenges and how you're handling them
- Celebrate victories and lessons learned
- Hold each other accountable for growth

The Mindset Library. Create a collection of resources that support your mindset development:

- Books that inspire positive thinking and service
- Podcasts that reinforce growth mindset principles
- Scripture verses that encourage faith-based thinking
- Quotes that remind you of your commitment to serve
- Stories of people who exemplify servant leadership

Review these resources regularly, especially during challenging times.

The Influence Audit. Regularly evaluate the influences in your life. Ask yourself:

- Which people, media, and activities support my positive mindset?
- Which influences tend to pull me toward negativity or selfishness?
- What changes do I need to make to protect and nurture my mindset?
- How can I be a more positive influence on others?

Emergency Mindset Reset

The 5-Minute Reset. When you find yourself in a negative mindset spiral, use this 5-minute reset:

1. Pause - Stop what you're doing and take three deep breaths
2. Acknowledge - Name the negative thoughts without judgment
3. Reframe - Ask "What would love do in this situation?"
4. Gratitude - Identify three things you're grateful for right now
5. Serve - Think of one person you can help or encourage today

The Scripture Meditation. Keep a few favorite Bible verses readily available for mindset challenges:

- "I can do all things through Christ which strengtheneth me" (Philippians 4:13)
- "Finally, brethren, whatsoever things are true... think on these things" (Philippians 4:8)
- "For as he thinketh in his heart, so is he" (Proverbs 23:7)

Meditate on these verses, allowing their truth to replace negative thought patterns.

CHAPTER CONCLUSION
Your Mindset, Your Ministry

As we close this first chapter, take a moment to reflect on the profound truth we've explored: your mindset is not just a personal asset—it's a gift you offer to the world. Every thought you choose, every attitude you cultivate, and every perspective you embrace becomes part of your service to others. When you decide to see possibilities instead of problems, hope instead of despair, and opportunities instead of obstacles, you become a beacon of light in a world that desperately needs it.

The journey of serving and growing richly begins in the quiet moments when you choose your thoughts. It starts when you wake up each morning and decide to approach the day with gratitude rather than anxiety. It continues when you encounter difficult people and choose patience over frustration. It deepens when you face setbacks and choose to see them as setups for something greater.

Remember, you are not just developing a positive mindset for your own benefit—though you will certainly benefit. You are cultivating a way of thinking that will enable you to serve others more effectively, lead with greater influence, and create positive change in every environment you enter. Your transformed mindset becomes a tool for ministry, a weapon against despair, and a bridge to authentic abundance.

The Ripple Effect Begins

As you implement the practices we've discussed in this chapter, you'll begin to notice something remarkable: your positive mindset becomes contagious. Colleagues will comment on your resilience. Friends will seek your perspective during challenging times. Family members will be inspired by your hope. This is the beginning of your legacy—not just what you achieve, but how you help others achieve their potential.

The most successful leaders, entrepreneurs, and servant-hearted individuals all share this common trait: they understand that their mindset is their most valuable asset and their greatest gift to others. They invest in it daily, protect it carefully, and share it generously.

Your Next Steps

As you move forward, carry with you the practical exercise from our opening: continue to notice your inner dialogue. When you face challenges or difficult people, pause and ask yourself: "What story am I telling myself about this?" Then consciously choose a story that serves not just you, but everyone involved.

Remember the words of Scripture: "Let this mind be in you, which was also in Christ Jesus" (Philippians 2:5). The mind of Christ is a mind focused on service, sacrifice, and love. When you align your thoughts with this divine perspective, you begin to see the world—and your place in it—differently.

Looking Ahead

In our next chapter, we'll explore how to transform your positive mindset into purposeful action. Because while attitude determines altitude, action determines destination. You'll discover how to move beyond good intentions and into the consistent behaviors that turn dreams into reality and service into impact.

But for now, your task is simple: begin today. Choose one mindset practice from this chapter and commit to it for the next week. Notice how it changes not just your inner experience, but your outer influence. Watch how your transformed thinking begins to transform your world.

The journey to serve and grow richly has begun. It starts with a single thought, chosen with intention and offered with love. Your mindset is your ministry. Use it well.

2
Action & Persistence

*If mindset is the lens through which we see the world,
action is the step that moves us forward, and persistence is the engine
that keeps us going when the journey gets long.*

IN EVERY STORY OF SERVICE AND SUCCESS, there is a moment when someone chooses to do more than just dream—they decide to act, and to keep acting, even when the results are slow or setbacks appear. This is the quiet, relentless power that separates wishful thinking from lasting impact.

In business and in life, ambition alone is never enough. As Bill Bradley said, "Ambition is the path to success. Persistence is the vehicle you arrive in." The world is full of talented dreamers, but it is those who consistently take action—who show up, try again, and refuse to quit—who build something that lasts. "Success seems to be connected to action. Successful people keep moving. They make mistakes, but they don't quit," reminds Conrad Hilton. Walt Disney put it simply: "The way to get started is to quit talking and begin doing." The truth is, opportunities rarely fall into our laps; more often, we create them through steady effort, learning from both our wins and our failures.

Persistence is not about stubbornly repeating the same approach, but about adapting, learning, and pressing on. "Energy and persistence conquer all things," wrote Benjamin Franklin. When we serve others, the results may not be immediate. Sometimes, the seeds we plant today take time to grow, and it is only through faith and perseverance that we see the harvest. The Bible echoes this wisdom: "And let us not be weary in well doing: for in due season we shall reap, if we faint not" (Galatians 6:9). Even when progress feels invisible, every small act of service and every step forward builds momentum.

Action is also the antidote to fear and doubt. "Inaction breeds doubt and fear. Action breeds confidence and courage," said Dale Carnegie. When you choose to move, to serve, to persist, you become a living example of hope for those around you. You show that setbacks are not dead ends, but stepping stones. As the old saying goes, "Rome wasn't built in a day," and neither are the lives or businesses that truly matter.

The Paradox of Perfect Timing

One of the greatest enemies of action is the myth of perfect timing. How many dreams have died in the waiting room of "someday"? How many opportunities for service have been missed because we were waiting for the ideal moment, the perfect plan, or the complete skill set? The truth is, there is no perfect time to begin anything meaningful. There is only now, and the choice to start where you are with what you have.

Reid Hoffman, founder of LinkedIn, captured this beautifully: "If you are not embarrassed by the first version of your product, you've launched too late." This principle applies not just to business ventures, but to every act of service and growth. The person who waits until they feel fully qualified to mentor someone may never mentor anyone. The entrepreneur who waits until market conditions are perfect may never launch their business. The servant who waits until they have all the answers may never begin helping others.

Consider the story of a young teacher who felt called to help struggling students but worried she lacked experience. Instead of waiting until she felt "ready," she started tutoring one child in her neighborhood. That single act of imperfect action grew into a nonprofit organization that has helped thousands of students over two decades. Her impact began not when she felt qualified, but when she chose to act despite her doubts.

The Bible provides a powerful example of this principle in the story of Moses. When God called him to lead the Israelites out of Egypt, Moses offered every excuse: "I'm not eloquent," "I'm not a leader," "What if they don't believe me?" God's response was essentially, "Go anyway. I'll provide what you need along the way." Moses' greatest achievements came not because he felt ready, but because he chose to act in faith despite his inadequacies.

The Compound Power of Small Actions

In our instant-gratification culture, we often underestimate the power of small, consistent actions. We're drawn to dramatic gestures and overnight transformations, but real change—both personal and societal—happens through the accumulation of seemingly insignificant daily choices.

James Clear, in his research on habits, discovered that improving by just 1% every day leads to being 37 times better over the course of a year. This mathematical reality applies powerfully to service and personal growth. The person who makes one encouraging phone call each day touches 365 lives in a year. The leader who reads for 15 minutes daily consumes 24 books annually. The servant who performs one small act of kindness each day creates a ripple effect that touches thousands of lives.

Consider the story of a janitor at a hospital who decided that his work was more than cleaning—it was ministry. Every day, he made small choices: a smile for worried families, a gentle word for stressed nurses, extra attention to making patient rooms welcoming. These small actions accumulated over decades into a legacy of service that touched countless lives. When he retired, the hospital dedicated a garden in his honor, recognizing that his consistent small actions had created an environment of hope and healing.

This is the secret that successful people understand: consistency trumps intensity. The writer who writes 300 words daily will complete more books than the one who writes 3,000 words once a month. The servant who helps one person weekly will impact more lives than the one who volunteers for a massive project once a year. Small actions, repeated consistently, become unstoppable forces.

The Biblical Foundation of Faithful Action

Scripture is filled with examples of ordinary people who achieved extraordinary things through faithful action and persistent service. Noah built the ark one board at a time. David became a king by faithfully tending sheep. Jesus trained his disciples through daily interactions and teachings. In each case, the dramatic outcome was the result of consistent, faithful action over time.

The parable of the talents in Matthew 25 provides profound insight into God's perspective on action and stewardship. The servants who were commended were not those who played it safe, but those who took action with what they were given. They invested, risked, and worked to multiply their master's resources. The servant who was condemned was the one who took no action at all—who buried his talent and waited for his master's return.

This parable reveals a crucial truth: God expects us to act with what we have, not wait until we have what we think we need. The servant with five talents wasn't expected to produce the same results as the one with two talents, but both were expected to act faithfully with their resources. Our responsibility is not to compare our capacity with others, but to act faithfully with what God has entrusted to us.

The concept of stewardship itself demands action. We are not owners of our gifts, opportunities, and resources—we are stewards called to invest them wisely for God's kingdom and the benefit of others. This understanding transforms every action into an act of worship and every service into a sacred responsibility.

The Science of Persistence

Modern psychology has revealed fascinating insights about what separates those who persist from those who quit. Dr. Angela Duckworth's research on "grit" shows that persistence—more than talent, intelligence, or circumstances—is the strongest predictor of success. But persistence isn't just about stubbornly continuing; it's about passionate perseverance toward long-term goals.

Neuroscience tells us that our brains are literally rewired by persistent action. Each time we choose to act despite difficulty, we strengthen neural pathways associated with resilience and determination. Each time we quit when things get hard, we reinforce pathways associated with giving up. This means that persistence is not just a character trait—it's a skill that can be developed through practice.

The key is understanding the difference between productive persistence and stubborn inflexibility. Productive persistence involves adapting methods while maintaining commitment to the goal. Thomas Edison exemplified this when he tried thousands of different materials for the light bulb filament. He wasn't stubbornly repeating the same failed approach; he was persistently pursuing the same goal through varied methods.

This distinction is crucial for servants and leaders. Sometimes persistence means continuing the same helpful actions when progress seems slow. Other times, it means adapting our approach while maintaining our commitment to serve. Wisdom lies in knowing when to stay the course and when to adjust the sails.

Action as Faith in Motion

From a biblical perspective, action is often the tangible expression of faith. James wrote, "Faith without works is dead" (James 2:20), not because works earn salvation, but because gen uine faith naturally produces action. When we truly believe that God has called us to serve, that belief compels us to act.

Consider Abraham, who is called the father of faith. His faith wasn't demonstrated through meditation or declaration, but through action. When God called him to leave his homeland, "he went out, not knowing whither he went" (Hebrews 11:8). His faith was proven through his willingness to act on God's promises, even when he couldn't see the complete plan.

This principle transforms how we approach both challenges and opportunities. When we face a need we feel called to address, faith doesn't wait for certainty—it acts on conviction. When we see an opportunity to serve, faith doesn't demand guarantees—it steps forward in trust. Action becomes not just a practical necessity, but a spiritual discipline.

The result is that our actions develop our faith, and our faith inspires our actions. Each step of obedience increases our capacity for the next step. Each act of service strengthens our confidence in God's provision and guidance. We discover that we serve a God who provides the resources, opens the doors, and supplies the strength as we step forward in faith.

Overcoming the Paralysis of Perfectionism

One of the greatest enemies of action is perfectionism—the belief that we must have everything figured out before we begin. Perfectionism masquerades as high standards, but it's often fear dressed up as excellence. It convinces us that imperfect action is worse than no action at all, which is rarely true.

The perfectionist waits for the perfect business plan before launching their company, the perfect skill level before offering to help, the perfect circumstances before beginning to serve. Meanwhile, the person willing to act imperfectly is gaining experience, building relationships, and making progress toward their goals.

This doesn't mean we should act recklessly or without preparation. It means we should distinguish between responsible preparation and paralyzing perfectionism. Responsible preparation involves reasonable planning and skill development. Paralyzing perfectionism involves endless planning that never leads to action.

The antidote to perfectionism is what we might call "faithful imperfection"—the willingness to act faithfully with our current resources, knowing that we'll learn and improve along the way. This approach honors both the call to excellence and the necessity of progress. We strive to do our best while accepting that our best will improve through practice.

The Multiplication Effect of Persistent Service

When we combine action with persistence in service to others, something remarkable happens: our impact multiplies exponentially. This multiplication occurs through several mechanisms that compound over time.

First, there's the direct impact of accumulated service. Each act of kindness, each moment of help, each investment in another person creates immediate benefit. Over time, these individual acts accumulate into significant impact.

Second, there's the skill development that comes from persistent practice. The person who consistently serves others develops wisdom, compassion, and effectiveness that amplifies their future service. They learn what works, what doesn't, and how to serve more effectively.

Third, there's the network effect. People who consistently serve others build relationships and reputation that create new opportunities for service. They become known as helpers, which attracts more opportunities to help.

Fourth, there's the inspiration effect. When others see persistent, faithful service, they're inspired to serve as well. One person's consistent action creates permission and motivation for others to act.

Finally, there's what we might call the legacy effect. Persistent service creates systems, relationships, and cultures that continue to produce benefit long after the original servant is gone. The teacher whose persistent investment in students creates a generation of leaders. The parent whose faithful service models love and sacrifice for their children. The leader whose consistent service creates a culture of excellence and care.

Action in the Face of Uncertainty

One of the most challenging aspects of action is the need to move forward despite uncertainty. We live in a complex world where outcomes are rarely guaranteed and the path forward is often unclear. Yet action requires us to step into this uncertainty with faith and determination.

The key is understanding that certainty about outcomes is not required for faithful action. What's required is clarity about values, commitment to service, and trust in God's sovereignty. We may not know exactly how our actions will turn out, but we can know that faithful service honors God and benefits others.

This perspective transforms how we approach risk and failure. Instead of avoiding all possibility of failure, we accept that some failures are inevitable parts of growth and service. Instead of demanding guarantees about outcomes, we focus on faithfulness in process. Instead of waiting for perfect information, we act on sufficient information guided by wisdom and prayer.

The result is a kind of courageous persistence that continues to serve even when the way forward is unclear. This is the quality that separates leaders from followers, servants from spectators, and those who make a difference from those who merely wish they could.

PRACTICAL APPLICATIONS
The Action Architecture:
Building Systems for Consistent Progress

Transforming the principles of action and persistence into daily reality requires more than good intentions—it requires practical systems that make consistent action inevitable. The most successful servants and leaders don't rely on motivation alone; they create what we call "action architecture"—structures that support consistent progress even when enthusiasm wanes.

The Daily Action Commitment. Begin each day by identifying your "One Action Forward"—a single, specific action you can take today that moves you toward your service goals. This isn't about massive undertakings; it's about maintaining momentum through consistent forward motion. Examples might include:

- Making one encouraging phone call to someone who needs support
- Reading one chapter of a book that develops your service capacity
- Taking one step toward launching a community initiative
- Writing one paragraph of a project that will help others

- Having one meaningful conversation with a team member

Write this commitment down each morning and check it off each evening. This simple practice creates accountability and builds the neural pathways of consistent action.

The Two-Minute Rule for Service. Borrowed from productivity expert David Allen, the two-minute rule states: if something takes less than two minutes, do it immediately. Apply this to service opportunities throughout your day. When you notice someone needs encouragement, give it now if it takes less than two minutes. When you see a small way to help, act immediately rather than adding it to your mental to-do list.

This practice develops what we call "service reflexes"—the automatic tendency to act on opportunities to help others. Over time, these small, immediate actions accumulate into significant impact and establish you as someone who consistently follows through.

The Weekly Action Review. Every Sunday evening, conduct a brief review of your week's actions. Ask yourself:

- What actions did I take this week that moved me toward my service goals?
- What opportunities for action did I miss, and why?
- What obstacles prevented action, and how can I address them next week?
- What one action commitment will I make for the coming week?

This review process helps you learn from both your successes and your hesitations, gradually improving your action-taking capacity.

Persistence Practices: Building Your Endurance for Long-Term Service

The Milestone Method. Break large service goals into smaller milestones with specific deadlines. Instead of saying "I want to help at-risk youth," create milestones like:

- Week 1: Research three organizations serving at-risk youth
- Week 2: Contact and visit one organization
- Week 3: Complete volunteer application process
- Week 4: Attend first volunteer orientation
- Month 2: Complete first month of regular service

Each milestone reached builds momentum and confidence for the next step. Celebrate these small victories—they're the building blocks of persistent service.

The Persistence Partner System. Find someone who shares your commitment to action and service. Meet weekly or bi-weekly to:

- Share your action commitments and progress
- Discuss obstacles and brainstorm solutions
- Celebrate successes and learn from setbacks
- Hold each other accountable for follow-through

This partnership provides external motivation when internal motivation flags and creates a support system for long-term persistence.

The Failure Reframe Technique. When actions don't produce expected results, practice reframing failure as feedback. Ask:

- What did this outcome teach me about my approach?
- How can I adjust my methods while maintaining my commitment to the goal?
- What unexpected opportunities or insights emerged from this experience?
- How can this experience better prepare me for future service?

Document these insights in a "Learning Journal" that becomes a resource for future decision-making and a reminder of how setbacks contribute to growth.

Overcoming Action Barriers: Practical Solutions for Common Obstacles

The Energy Management Strategy. Recognize that different types of actions require different types of energy. Schedule high-energy actions (like difficult conversations or creative projects) during your peak energy times. Use lower-energy periods for routine actions that still move you forward.

Create an "action menu" categorized by energy level:

- High Energy: Launching new initiatives, having challenging conversations, creative problem-solving
- Medium Energy: Planning, organizing, routine communication, skill development
- Low Energy: Administrative tasks, simple encouragement, reading, reflection

This ensures you can always take some action, regardless of your current energy level.

The Fear-to-Action Bridge. When fear prevents action, use this four-step bridge:

1. Name the fear specifically (not "I'm scared" but "I'm afraid they'll reject my offer to help")
2. Identify the smallest possible action (not "volunteer at the homeless shelter" but "research one homeless shelter online")
3. Set a specific deadline (not "someday" but "by Friday at 5 PM")
4. Create accountability (tell someone about your commitment or schedule it in your calendar)

This process transforms paralyzing fear into manageable action steps.

The Resource Reality Check. When you feel you lack resources to act, conduct a reality check:

- What resources do I actually need versus what I think I need?
- What resources do I already have that I'm not utilizing?
- Who in my network might have the resources I'm missing?

- What's the smallest version of this action I could take with current resources?
- How might starting small create access to additional resources?

Often, we discover that we have more resources than we realized and need fewer resources than we assumed.

Building Your Action Muscle: Progressive Development

Week 1-2: Foundation Building

- Establish the daily "One Action Forward" practice
- Begin weekly action reviews
- Identify your peak energy times for action
- Start documenting your service activities

Week 3-4: Expanding Capacity

- Add the two-minute rule for service opportunities
- Implement the milestone method for one significant goal
- Find and establish contact with a potential persistence partner
- Create your energy-based action menu

Month 2: Deepening Practice

- Expand daily actions to include both personal growth and service to others
- Practice the failure reframe technique with any setbacks
- Regularly use the fear-to-action bridge when hesitation arises
- Begin building your network of service-oriented relationships

Month 3: Integration and Multiplication

- Help someone else develop their action-taking capacity
- Take on a service project that requires sustained persistence
- Share your learning with others who might benefit
- Evaluate and refine your action systems based on experience

Creating Accountability Systems

The Public Commitment. Share your service goals with trusted friends, family, or colleagues. Public commitment creates external motivation and provides opportunities for others to support your efforts. Be specific about what you're committing to do and by when.

The Progress Documentation. Keep a simple record of your daily actions and weekly progress. This serves multiple purposes:

- Provides motivation by showing accumulated progress
- Identifies patterns in your action-taking behavior
- Creates material for encouraging others
- Builds confidence in your ability to follow through

The Celebration Ritual. Establish specific ways to celebrate action milestones:

- Weekly: Acknowledge completion of daily action commitments
- Monthly: Celebrate completion of significant service projects
- Quarterly: Reflect on growth in action-taking capacity and service impact
- Annually: Evaluate the cumulative impact of consistent action over time

Emergency Action Protocols

When Motivation Disappears

- Return to your "why"—remember who you're serving and why it matters
- Take the smallest possible action rather than no action
- Reach out to your persistence partner or accountability system
- Review past successes to rebuild confidence
- Pray for renewed energy and commitment

When Obstacles Seem Insurmountable

- Break the obstacle into smaller, manageable pieces
- Seek advice from someone who has overcome similar challenges
- Look for alternative approaches to the same goal
- Remember that obstacles often become testimonies of persistence
- Trust that God provides solutions as we step forward in faith

When Results Are Disappointing

- Evaluate whether your expectations were realistic
- Look for unexpected benefits or learning opportunities
- Adjust methods while maintaining commitment to the mission
- Seek feedback from those you're serving
- Remember that many seeds grow slowly and invisibly before bearing fruit

CHAPTER CONCLUSION
The Bridge Between Dreams and Reality

As we reach the end of this exploration of action and persistence, it's important to recognize what you've just encountered: the bridge between dreams and reality. Every aspiration you hold for serving others, every vision you have for making a difference, every goal that stirs your heart—they all depend on your willingness to cross this bridge through consistent action and unwavering persistence.

The world is filled with dreamers who never became doers, with planners who never became practitioners, with wishers who never became workers. What separates those who make a lasting impact from those who simply make good intentions is this: they understand that action is not just something you do—it's who you become. Every time you choose to act despite uncertainty, every time you persist through difficulty, every time you serve when it's inconvenient, you're not just accomplishing a task—you're becoming the kind of person who changes the world.

Your Actions Echo in Eternity

The beautiful truth about persistent action in service to others is that its impact extends far beyond what you can see or measure. When you consistently show up, serve faithfully, and refuse to quit, you create ripples that touch lives you may never know about. The encouraging word you speak today may change someone's entire trajectory. The small act of service you perform may inspire someone else to begin their own journey of giving. The persistence you model may give someone else permission to continue when they want to quit.

Remember, you are not just building your own character through action and persistence—you're contributing to the character of your community, your organization, your family, and your generation. Every faithful action is a vote for the kind of world you want to live in. Every persistent effort is a declaration that love is stronger than difficulty, that hope is more powerful than discouragement, and that service is the pathway to significance.

The Divine Partnership

As believers, we have the profound privilege of understanding that our actions and persistence are not solo efforts—they're partnerships with the Divine. Scripture assures us that "it is God which worketh in you both to will and to do of his good pleasure" (Philippians 2:13). This means that every faithful action is empowered by God's strength, every persistent effort is supported by His grace, and every act of service is part of His larger plan for blessing the world.

This understanding transforms how we approach action and persistence. We're not striving in our own strength, hoping our limited efforts will somehow make a difference. We're cooperating with the Creator of the universe, allowing Him to work through our faithful availability. Our responsibility is to show up and act; His promise is to provide the power and multiply the impact.

Your Legacy of Faithfulness

Years from now, when you look back on your life, you won't remember the days you spent thinking about serving others—you'll remember the days you actually served. You won't recall the times you planned to make a difference—you'll recall the times you took action. Your legacy will not be written in your intentions but in your implementations, not in your aspirations but in your applications.

The persistent servant understands that significance is not achieved through spectacular moments but through faithful moments, repeated consistently over time. It's built one action at a time, one day at a time, one choice at a time. Each faithful action becomes part of a mosaic of service that creates lasting beauty and impact.

Your Next Steps

As you move forward from this chapter, carry with you this truth: you already have everything you need to begin. You don't need perfect circumstances, complete knowledge, or unlimited resources. You need only the willingness to take the next faithful step, to serve where you are with what you have, to persist when the way forward seems unclear.

Choose one practice from this chapter and implement it starting today. Whether it's the daily "One Action Forward" commitment, the two-minute rule for service, or the weekly action review—begin building your action muscle now. Remember, the longest journey begins with a single step, and the greatest impact starts with a single act of faithful service.

Looking Ahead

In our next chapter, we'll explore how to set clear goals and develop compelling vision that gives direction to your action and purpose to your persistence. You'll discover how to align your daily actions with your deepest values and highest calling, ensuring that your persistent efforts are focused on what matters most.

But for now, your assignment is simple yet profound: act. Take one step forward in service to someone else. Make one small but meaningful difference in someone's life. Begin the journey from intention to implementation, from dreaming to doing, from wishing to working.

The world is waiting for your faithful action. Your community needs your persistent service. Your calling demands your consistent response. The time for action is not someday—it's today. The place for service is not somewhere else—it's right where you are. The person to begin this journey is not someone else—it's you.

Action and persistence: these are the tools that transform hearts, change communities, and create legacies that echo through eternity. Use them well, use them faithfully, and watch as God multiplies your efforts beyond anything you could ask or imagine.

3
Goal Setting & Vision

Every remarkable journey begins with a destination in mind.

VISION IS THE COMPASS THAT POINTS US toward a future worth striving for, while goals are the stepping stones that mark our path along the way. In business, in service, and in life, those who shape their days with purpose are those who build legacies that endure. Yet, true vision is never just about personal achievement—it is about seeing beyond ourselves, about imagining a world made richer through our service and growth.

Goal setting is more than a productivity hack; it is an act of hope and intention. It is a declaration that our lives matter, that our work can make a difference, and that our time is worth investing wisely. The most effective goals are not just about what we want to accomplish, but about who we want to become and how we want to serve others along the way. As Simon Sinek reminds us, "People don't buy what you do; they buy why you do it." When our vision is anchored in service, our goals become a means of multiplying value, not just for ourselves, but for everyone we touch.

Faith traditions have long recognized the power of vision. "Where there is no vision, the people perish," says Proverbs 29:18. Setting goals, especially those rooted in faith and service, is a way of honoring the gifts and opportunities entrusted to us. It is not about striving in our own strength alone, but about seeking guidance, aligning our plans with higher purposes, and trusting that each step forward is part of a greater story. As one faith-based goal-setting principle puts it, "Start with prayer and reflection; seek God's guidance for the direction He desires for your life". When we set our sights on goals that stretch us, inspire us, and require us to rely on something greater than ourselves, we invite both growth and grace into our journey.

But vision without action is merely a dream. Goals must be clear, specific, and written down. They must be revisited, refined, and pursued with both humility and determination. The process is not always linear—sometimes we must adjust our course, learn from failure, and celebrate small wins along the way. "Commit thy works unto the Lord, and thy thoughts shall be established" (Proverbs 16:3). The act of setting goals, especially those that serve others, is itself a step of faith—a way of saying, "I am willing to grow, to serve, and to be led toward something greater."

The Anatomy of God-Honoring Vision

True vision is not just a mental picture of what we want to achieve—it's a divine download of what could be if we align our efforts with God's purposes. The most compelling visions share certain characteristics that distinguish them from mere wishful thinking or selfish ambition.

First, God-honoring vision always extends beyond personal benefit. While it's natural and healthy to include personal growth and blessing in our vision, the primary focus must be on how our success will serve others and advance God's kingdom. The entrepreneur who envisions building a company sees not just personal wealth, but jobs created, problems solved, and communities strengthened. The teacher who envisions educational impact sees not just career advancement, but lives transformed and potential unlocked.

Second, authentic vision is both inspiring and intimidating. It should be large enough to require faith, yet specific enough to provide direction. As Mark Batterson writes, "The size of your prayers determines the size of your God." If your vision doesn't require divine intervention, it may not be big enough. If it doesn't give you specific steps to take, it may not be clear enough.

Third, powerful vision is rooted in calling, not just ambition. Ambition asks, "What do I want to achieve?" Calling asks, "What has God equipped me to accomplish for His glory and others' good?" This distinction transforms goal-setting from a self-improvement exercise into a spiritual discipline of discovering and pursuing God's design for your life.

Consider the example of George Washington Carver, whose vision extended far beyond personal scientific achievement. He saw his agricultural research as a way to help poor farmers, particularly in the South, become self-sufficient and prosperous. His vision of "helping the man farthest down" drove innovations that revolutionized farming and created new economic opportunities for thousands of families. His goals were specific and measurable, but they were anchored in a vision that served both God and humanity.

The Science of Effective Goal Setting

Modern research has validated many biblical principles about goal setting, revealing why some goals inspire persistent action while others fade into forgotten resolutions. Dr. Edwin Locke's groundbreaking research identified five key characteristics of effective goals, which align remarkably with biblical wisdom about planning and purpose.

Specific goals outperform vague intentions. Instead of "I want to help people," effective goal-setters say, "I will mentor three at-risk youth through the local community center, meeting with each for one hour weekly for six months." Specificity creates clarity, which enables both planning and accountability.

Challenging goals inspire greater effort than easy ones. Goals that require stretch and growth tap into our God-given desire for significance and impact. However, there's a crucial balance: goals must be challenging enough to inspire excellence but achievable enough to maintain hope. This is where faith comes in—we set goals that require us to trust God for resources, wisdom, and favor beyond our natural ability.

Committed goals produce better results than tentative ones. The difference between "I'd like to" and "I will" is often the difference between dreaming and achieving. Biblical goal-setting involves making covenants with God—sacred commitments that we pursue with integrity and persistence.

Feedback-rich goals enable course correction. The most effective goals include built-in mechanisms for measuring progress and adjusting strategy. This isn't about perfectionism, but about stewardship—using information to serve more effectively and achieve greater impact.

Complex goals benefit from action planning. Big visions require broken-down steps, allocated resources, and realistic timelines. The Bible speaks of "counting the cost" before beginning construction (Luke 14:28)—a principle that applies to any significant undertaking.

Vision as Spiritual Warfare

One aspect of vision that's often overlooked is its role in spiritual warfare. When we envision God's kingdom advancing through our service, we're not just daydreaming—we're declaring war on the status quo. We're asserting that things don't have to stay as they are, that problems can be solved, that lives can be transformed, that communities can be healed.

This is why vision is so often met with resistance, both external and internal. The enemy of our souls knows that nothing threatens his territory like people who combine clear vision with persistent action. Discouragement, distraction, and doubt are common weapons used against those who dare to envision significant change.

The antidote to this resistance is what we might call "prophetic stubbornness"—a holy determination to keep believing and working toward God's preferred future despite evidence to the contrary. This stubbornness is not based on human optimism but on divine promises. It's the quality that enabled Noah to keep building when there were no clouds in the sky, Abraham to keep believing when Sarah was barren, and Moses to keep leading when the people complained.

Understanding vision as spiritual warfare also means we approach goal-setting with prayer, fasting, and dependence on God's Spirit. We don't just brainstorm what we'd like to accomplish; we seek revelation about what God wants to accomplish through us. We don't just set personal objectives; we join God's mission and ask how our unique gifts and circumstances can advance His purposes.

The Power of Written Vision

There's something almost mystical about the act of writing down our vision and goals. The prophet Habakkuk received this instruction: "Write the vision, and make it plain upon tables, that he may run that readeth it" (Habakkuk 2:2). This ancient wisdom has been validated by modern research showing that people who write down their goals are 42% more likely to achieve them.

Writing forces clarity. When we're required to put our vision into words, vague feelings and impressions must be refined into specific language. This process often reveals gaps in our thinking and areas that need further development. Writing also creates commitment. There's something powerful about seeing our words on paper—they become more real, more binding, more motivational.

But not all written visions are equally effective. The most powerful written visions share several characteristics:

Present tense language that describes the desired future as if it's already happening. Instead of "I will help homeless families," write "I am serving 20 homeless families each month through our transitional housing program." This creates emotional connection and mental rehearsal that supports achievement.

Sensory details that make the vision vivid and compelling. Don't just describe what you'll accomplish; describe what it will look like, sound like, and feel like when you achieve it. How will you know you've succeeded? What will others say? How will it feel to see lives transformed through your service?

Values integration that connects goals to deeper purposes. Why does this vision matter? How does it align with your understanding of God's character and calling? What biblical principles does it express or advance?

Regular review that keeps the vision fresh and relevant. Written visions are not documents to file away; they're living guides that should be read, reflected upon, and refined regularly.

Balancing Ambition with Surrender

One of the greatest challenges in Christian goal-setting is balancing holy ambition with faithful surrender. How do we pursue significant goals with passion and determination while remaining open to God's redirection? How do we plan diligently while trusting God's sovereignty?

The key is understanding the difference between attachment to outcomes and commitment to process. We can be fully committed to faithful planning, diligent work, and excellent execution while remaining unattached to specific results. We do our part with excellence and trust God for outcomes beyond our control.

This balance is beautifully illustrated in the life of apostle Paul, who could say both "I press toward the mark" (Philippians 3:14) and "Not my will, but thine, be done" (Luke 22:42, speaking of Jesus but exemplifying the same principle). Paul planned extensively, worked diligently, and pursued his goals with remarkable persistence. Yet he remained flexible when God redirected his path, accepting imprisonment, shipwreck, and opposition as part of God's plan.

This perspective transforms goal-setting from a self-improvement exercise into a spiritual discipline. We set goals not because we're trying to force God's hand, but because we're stewarding the gifts and opportunities He's given us. We pursue them with excellence not because our identity depends on achievement, but because our calling demands faithfulness.

The Community Dimension of Vision

While vision often begins with individual revelation, it reaches its full potential through community engagement. God rarely calls us to accomplish significant things alone. Even the most personal goals are enhanced when shared with others who can provide accountability, support, wisdom, and encouragement.

Consider the example of Nehemiah, whose vision to rebuild Jerusalem's walls could only be accomplished through community mobilization. His personal burden became a shared mission that engaged hundreds of workers in coordinated effort. The wall was completed in 52 days not because of Nehemiah's individual effort, but because his vision inspired collective action.

This principle applies to modern goal-setting as well. The entrepreneur who wants to create jobs shares their vision with potential partners and investors. The teacher who wants to improve education connects with other educators and community leaders. The parent who wants to raise godly children builds relationships with other parents who share similar values.

Community also provides essential accountability for goal achievement. When we share our commitments with trusted friends and mentors, we create external motivation that supplements internal drive. We benefit from others' wisdom and experience, avoiding mistakes and accelerating progress.

Most importantly, community ensures that our vision remains other-focused rather than self-serving. When we regularly interact with people whose lives will be affected by our goals, we stay connected to the "why" behind our "what." We remember that our success is not ultimately about us—it's about the difference we make in others' lives.

Overcoming Vision Killers

Every significant vision faces opposition, both external and internal. Learning to recognize and overcome common "vision killers" is essential for maintaining momentum toward meaningful goals.

Perfectionism convinces us that we can't begin until we have everything figured out. It demands complete certainty before any action and perfect execution at every step. The antidote is understanding that vision provides direction, not destination. We can move toward our goals while continuing to refine our understanding and approach.

Comparison measures our progress against others' achievements rather than our own growth and calling. Social media has amplified this challenge, providing constant exposure to others' highlight reels while we live with our behind-the-scenes reality. The antidote is remembering that God has a unique plan for each person, and our responsibility is faithfulness to our calling, not competition with others.

Discouragement focuses attention on obstacles rather than opportunities, on problems rather than possibilities. It's often based on emotional reactions to temporary setbacks rather than objective assessment of long-term progress. The antidote is developing what psychologists call "explanatory style"—the habit of viewing setbacks as temporary, specific, and surmountable rather than permanent, pervasive, and insurmountable.

Distraction offers attractive alternatives that divert energy from primary goals. In our hyperconnected world, new opportunities and urgent demands constantly compete for our attention. The antidote is clarity about priorities and the discipline to say no to good things in order to say yes to great things.

Fear anticipates negative outcomes and catastrophic failures, paralyzing action through anxiety about what might go wrong. The antidote is faith—not the absence of fear, but action in spite of fear, trusting that God's plans for us are good and that He will provide what we need when we need it.

Turning Vision into Strategy

Vision without strategy remains fantasy; strategy without vision becomes drudgery. The bridge between inspiring vision and practical achievement is strategic thinking—the process of breaking down big dreams into manageable steps, allocating resources wisely, and creating systems that support consistent progress.

Effective strategy begins with what we might call "reverse engineering"—starting with the desired outcome and working backward to identify necessary steps. If your vision is to establish a nonprofit that serves 1,000 families annually, you work backward to determine required staff, funding, facilities, programs, and partnerships. Then you work backward further to identify first steps, early milestones, and resource acquisition strategies.

Strategic thinking also involves scenario planning—anticipating potential obstacles and preparing alternative approaches. This isn't pessimism; it's prudent preparation that increases the likelihood of success. What if funding is delayed? What if key partners aren't available? What if the need is greater than anticipated? Having contingency plans reduces anxiety and maintains momentum when challenges arise.

Finally, effective strategy includes regular review and adjustment cycles. Vision may remain constant, but strategy should be flexible, adapting to new information, changing circumstances, and lessons learned through experience. The goal is not to follow the plan perfectly, but to achieve the vision effectively.

PRACTICAL APPLICATIONS
The Vision Clarification Process:
From Impression to Implementation

Transforming vague impressions and general desires into clear, actionable vision requires a systematic approach. The following process has helped thousands of individuals and organizations move from confusion to clarity about their God-given purpose and goals.

The Sacred Space Session. Set aside a half-day for what we call a "Sacred Space Session"—uninterrupted time dedicated to seeking God's direction for your life and service. Begin with prayer, asking God to reveal His heart for your future and your role in His kingdom purposes. Then work through these reflection questions:

- What needs in the world break your heart or stir your passion?
- What unique combination of gifts, experiences, and resources has God given you?
- What would you attempt if you knew you couldn't fail and had unlimited resources?
- What impact do you want to have made when you look back on your life?
- How do you sense God calling you to serve others in this season?

Write your responses without editing or self-censoring. The goal is to capture your heart's true desires and God's whispered invitations, not to create perfect prose.

The Vision Statement Workshop. Using your Sacred Space Session notes, craft a personal vision statement that captures your God-given purpose in 2-3 sentences. A powerful vision statement includes:

- Who you feel called to serve
- What transformation or benefit you want to create
- How your unique gifts and resources will be used
- Why this matters for God's kingdom and human flourishing

Example: "I am called to serve struggling entrepreneurs by providing business mentorship and financial wisdom that helps them build successful, biblically-based enterprises that create jobs and strengthen communities, because I believe God wants His people to prosper and be generous."

The Goals Cascade Method. Once your vision is clear, use the "cascade method" to break it into actionable goals:

1. 10-Year Goals: What major milestones would indicate you're fulfilling your vision?
2. 3-Year Goals: What significant progress should be evident in three years?
3. 1-Year Goals: What must be accomplished this year to stay on track?
4. Quarterly Goals: What specific outcomes will you achieve each quarter?
5. Monthly Goals: What monthly progress will build toward quarterly outcomes?
6. Weekly Actions: What consistent weekly activities support monthly goals?

Each level should clearly support the level above it, creating a coherent pathway from daily actions to ultimate vision.

The SMART-ER Goal Framework for Service-Oriented Achievement

Traditional SMART goals (Specific, Measurable, Achievable, Relevant, Time-bound) provide a solid foundation, but service-oriented goals benefit from two additional dimensions that create the SMART-ER framework.

Specific and Service-Focused. Instead of "improve my leadership skills," write "complete a 6-month leadership development program and apply the principles by mentoring 3 emerging leaders in my organization." Specificity includes not just what you'll do, but how it will serve others.

Measurable and Meaningful. Identify both quantitative measures (numbers, dates, percentages) and qualitative indicators (feedback, testimonials, life changes). Ask: "How will I know I've succeeded, and how will I know I've made a meaningful difference?"

Achievable and Aligned. Goals should stretch your faith and capacity while remaining within the realm of possibility. Test alignment by asking: "Does this goal align with my values, calling, and current season of life?"

Relevant and Relational. Ensure goals connect to your larger vision and consider their impact on relationships. Ask: "How will achieving this goal strengthen my ability to serve others and advance God's kingdom?"

Time-bound and Trustworthy. Set specific deadlines and create accountability systems. Make commitments you can keep, because integrity in small goals builds credibility for larger ones.

Encouraging and Eternal. Add the "ER" dimensions: goals should encourage both you and others, and they should have eternal significance—impact that outlasts your lifetime.

Reviewed and Refined. Establish regular review cycles to assess progress, celebrate achievements, and adjust strategies based on new information or changed circumstances.

Weekly and Monthly Goal Management Systems

The Sunday Planning Ritual. Every Sunday evening, spend 30 minutes reviewing the past week and planning the coming week:

- Review: What progress did I make toward my goals? What obstacles did I encounter? What did I learn?

- Celebrate: What achievements or progress deserve acknowledgment and gratitude?
- Plan: What are my top 3 priorities for the coming week? What specific actions will I take?
- Pray: How can I seek God's guidance and strength for the challenges ahead?

Document your insights in a planning journal that becomes a record of your growth and God's faithfulness.

The Monthly Vision Check. On the last day of each month, conduct a more comprehensive review:

- Vision Alignment: Are my daily actions moving me toward my larger vision?
- Goal Progress: What percentage of my monthly goals did I achieve? What factors supported or hindered progress?
- Relationship Impact: How has my pursuit of goals affected my relationships with family, friends, and those I serve?
- Course Correction: What adjustments do I need to make in strategy, timeline, or approach?
- Resource Assessment: What additional resources, skills, or support do I need to maintain progress?

The Quarterly Strategy Session. Every three months, take a half-day to conduct a comprehensive strategy review:

- Assess progress toward annual goals
- Identify lessons learned and best practices developed
- Adjust strategies based on changed circumstances or new opportunities
- Celebrate milestones achieved and lives impacted
- Seek God's continued guidance for the next quarter

Accountability and Support Systems

The Vision Partner. Find someone who shares your commitment to purposeful goal achievement. This should be someone who:

- Understands and supports your vision
- Has permission to ask hard questions
- Celebrates your successes and encourages you through setbacks
- Meets with you regularly (weekly or bi-weekly) for accountability

The Advisory Circle. Identify 3-5 people who can provide wisdom, perspective, and support for your vision and goals. This might include:

- A mentor who has achieved similar goals
- A peer who is pursuing complementary objectives

- A younger person you're investing in who keeps you grounded
- A family member who understands your personal context
- A spiritual advisor who helps you maintain eternal perspective

Meet with your advisory circle quarterly to share progress, seek advice, and gain perspective on challenges and opportunities.

The Progress Documentation System. Create a simple system for tracking both quantitative progress and qualitative insights:

- Weekly Metrics: Numbers that indicate progress toward specific goals
- Monthly Reflections: Lessons learned, obstacles overcome, relationships strengthened
- Quarterly Reviews: Major milestones achieved, strategies adjusted, vision refined
- Annual Assessment: Overall progress, character development, kingdom impact

This documentation serves multiple purposes: motivation through visible progress, learning through reflection, and testimony of God's faithfulness over time.

Overcoming Common Goal-Setting Obstacles

When Goals Feel Overwhelming

- Break large goals into smaller, daily actions
- Focus on process goals (what you do) rather than outcome goals (what you achieve)
- Celebrate small wins and incremental progress
- Remember that faithful stewardship matters more than spectacular achievement
- Seek support from your accountability partners

When Motivation Wanes

- Reconnect with your "why"—the vision and values behind your goals
- Review past progress and celebrate how far you've come
- Adjust goals if they're no longer relevant or achievable
- Seek fresh perspective from mentors or peers
- Spend time in prayer and Scripture, asking for renewed passion

When Circumstances Change

- Distinguish between core vision (which rarely changes) and specific goals (which may need adjustment)
- Look for opportunities within obstacles
- Consult with advisors before making major changes
- Maintain focus on faithfulness rather than outcomes

- Trust that God can use unexpected detours for good purposes

When Others Don't Understand
- Remember that your calling is from God, not from people
- Share your vision with those who are likely to be supportive
- Stay humble and open to constructive feedback
- Let your results speak louder than your words
- Pray for patience and wisdom in relationships

Technology Tools for Goal Management

Digital Planning Apps
- Use apps like Todoist, Asana, or Notion to organize goals hierarchically
- Set up automated reminders for weekly reviews and monthly assessments
- Create dashboards that show progress across multiple goal areas
- Share appropriate goals with accountability partners through collaborative features

Progress Tracking Systems
- Use spreadsheets or apps to track quantitative metrics
- Take weekly photos or videos documenting progress on visual goals
- Maintain a digital journal for qualitative reflections and insights
- Create annual reports summarizing progress and lessons learned

Communication Tools
- Schedule regular check-ins with accountability partners using calendar apps
- Use messaging apps to share daily or weekly progress updates
- Create shared documents for collaborative goal planning and review
- Set up automated reminders for important deadlines and milestones

Creating Your Personal Goal Management Rhythm

Daily (5 minutes)
- Review today's priorities and align them with weekly goals
- Identify one action that moves you toward your larger vision
- Pray for wisdom, energy, and faithfulness in small things

Weekly (30 minutes)
- Conduct Sunday planning ritual

- Update progress tracking systems
- Connect with accountability partner if scheduled
- Celebrate progress and adjust upcoming week's priorities

Monthly (2 hours)
- Complete comprehensive monthly review
- Adjust quarterly goals based on progress and new information
- Plan major activities and commitments for upcoming month
- Seek God's guidance through prayer and Scripture reflection

Quarterly (half-day)
- Conduct strategic review and planning session
- Meet with advisory circle for input and perspective
- Celebrate major milestones and evaluate lessons learned
- Refresh vision statement if needed and set goals for next quarter

CHAPTER CONCLUSION
The Sacred Art of Divine Partnership

As we conclude this exploration of goal setting and vision, it's crucial to understand what you've just encountered: the sacred art of partnering with God to transform dreams into reality and vision into impact. This is not merely a self-improvement technique or a productivity system—it's a spiritual discipline that aligns your finite efforts with infinite purposes, your temporary existence with eternal significance.

The most profound truth about God-honoring goal setting is this: when you "Commit thy works unto the Lord, and thy thoughts shall be established." (Proverbs 16:3). This means that the very act of seeking His direction, setting goals aligned with His purposes, and pursuing them with faithful persistence invites divine intervention into your plans. You become a co-laborer with the Creator of the universe, participating in His ongoing work of redemption and restoration in the world.

Your Vision as Ministry

Remember that your vision is not just about what you want to accomplish—it's about how God wants to use your unique combination of gifts, experiences, and opportunities to advance His kingdom. Every goal you set with service to others in mind becomes a form of ministry. Every step you take toward meaningful objectives becomes an act of worship. Every obstacle you overcome through persistent faith becomes a testimony to God's faithfulness.

This perspective transforms goal setting from a self-centered exercise into an others-focused mission. When you envision tutoring struggling students, you're not just planning educational activities—you're participating in God's desire to unlock human potential. When you set goals for building a business, you're not just pursuing financial success—you're creating opportunities for others to use their gifts and provide for their families. When you plan to strengthen your marriage or family relationships, you're not just working on personal happiness—you're building a foundation for the next generation.

The Multiplication Effect of Faithful Planning

One of the most encouraging aspects of biblical goal setting is how God multiplies our faithful efforts. When we plan with His guidance, work with His strength, and serve with His love, the impact extends far beyond what we could achieve through human effort alone. The goals you set today may influence lives you never meet, create opportunities you never anticipated, and solve problems you never imagined.

Consider how this chapter's principles might ripple through your community: as you become more intentional about your vision and goals, you'll inspire others to clarify their own sense of purpose. As you serve others through pursuing meaningful objectives, you'll model what it looks like to live with intention and impact. As you persist through challenges while maintaining faith and integrity, you'll become a source of hope for those facing their own obstacles.

The Faithfulness Factor

Success in goal achievement, from God's perspective, is not ultimately measured by the size of our accomplishments but by the faithfulness of our efforts. The servant who is faithful with little will be entrusted with much (Luke 16:10). This means that how you pursue your current goals—with integrity, persistence, and service to others—is more important than the specific outcomes you achieve.

This understanding frees you from the pressure of guaranteed success while maintaining the motivation for excellent effort. You can plan boldly, work diligently, and trust completely because your identity and worth are not tied to your achievements. Your calling is to be faithful; God's promise is to be productive through your faithfulness.

Your Goals as Prayer

Perhaps the most transformative way to view your goals is as prayers made manifest—specific requests to God about how you want to serve His purposes and contribute to His kingdom. When you write down a goal to mentor young entrepreneurs, you're essentially praying, "God, use me to help the next generation succeed." When you set objectives for strengthening your community, you're asking, "Father, work through me to bring healing and hope to my neighbors."

This perspective invites you to approach goal setting with the same reverence and dependence you bring to prayer. You seek God's guidance before setting goals, ask for His strength to pursue them, and trust His sovereignty over the outcomes. Your planning becomes worship, your work becomes service, and your achievements become testimonies to His goodness.

Your Next Steps

As you move forward from this chapter, carry with you the vision clarification exercise from our practical applications. If you haven't already done so, schedule your Sacred Space Session within the next week. Set aside uninterrupted time to seek God's direction for your life and service. Let Him speak to your heart about the unique ways He wants to use your gifts, experiences, and opportunities.

Remember, you don't need to have everything figured out before you begin. Vision often comes in stages, and goals evolve as you gain experience and wisdom. What matters is that you start where you are with what you have, trusting that God will provide clarity and resources as you step forward in faith.

Looking Ahead

In our next chapter, we'll explore how to overcome fear and adversity as you pursue your God-given vision and goals. You'll discover that obstacles are not roadblocks to your dreams but building blocks for your character, and that the very challenges that seem to threaten your progress often become the catalysts for your greatest growth.

But for now, your assignment is both simple and profound: dream God-sized dreams, plan with wisdom and prayer, and take the first step toward the vision He's placed in your heart. Write down your goals, share them with trusted advisors, and begin the journey from where you are to where God is calling you to be.

4

Overcoming Fear & Adversity

Fear is a universal companion on any journey of growth and service.

WHETHER YOU ARE LAUNCHING A NEW VENTURE, leading a team through uncertainty, or simply stepping into unfamiliar territory, fear inevitably whispers doubts and conjures worst-case scenarios. Yet, what if fear is not an enemy to be vanquished, but a messenger inviting us to deeper self-understanding and trust? When we face adversity, it is not just our circumstances that are tested, but our willingness to grow beyond our comfort zones.

The most resilient leaders and fulfilled individuals are not those who never feel fear, but those who learn to move forward in spite of it. They recognize that adversity is not a sign of failure, but a classroom for courage and character. As one coach writes, "Adversity reminds us of past failures and pain," but it also "triggers feelings that we do not want to revisit". The key is not to avoid these feelings, but to acknowledge them, challenge the limiting beliefs they bring, and take small, consistent steps forward.

Practical strategies—like breaking big fears into smaller, manageable steps, visualizing positive outcomes, and surrounding yourself with supportive people—can transform anxiety into action. Each micro-move, no matter how small, is a vote for your future self. Reflection and celebration of progress are just as important as the steps themselves; they remind you that you are more capable than fear would have you believe.

Faith traditions offer a powerful lens for reframing fear. Scripture reminds us, "Be strong and of a good courage; be not afraid, neither be thou dismayed: for the Lord thy God is with thee whithersoever thou goest" (Joshua 1:9). Overcoming fear with faith is not about denying its presence, but about choosing to trust in something greater than your circumstances. As you pray, breathe, and meditate on words of hope, you cultivate a posture of surrender and optimism—one that allows you to see adversity as a stepping stone rather than a stumbling block. "In the world ye shall have tribulation: but be of good cheer; I have overcome the world" (John 16:33).

Fear, when faced with self-compassion and faith, becomes a catalyst for growth. It is only when we step outside our comfort zone that we discover what we are truly capable of—and how deeply we can serve. Each act of courage, no matter how small, is a declaration that you will not let fear define your story.

The Anatomy of Fear: Understanding Your Internal Alarm System

To overcome fear effectively, we must first understand what it is and why it exists. Fear is not inherently evil or destructive—it's a God-given protection system designed to keep us safe from genuine danger. The problem arises when this ancient alarm system, perfectly calibrated for physical threats, begins responding to psychological and spiritual challenges as if they were life-threatening emergencies.

Modern neuroscience reveals that fear originates in the amygdala, an almond-shaped structure in our brain that can trigger fight-or-flight responses in milliseconds. This system served our ancestors well when facing predators or natural disasters, but it struggles to distinguish between a charging lion and a challenging conversation with our boss. Both can trigger the same physiological responses: increased heart rate, shallow breathing, muscle tension, and a flood of stress hormones.

Understanding this process is liberating because it reveals that fear is often a false alarm rather than accurate information about actual danger. When you feel fear about starting a new ministry, launching a business, or having a difficult conversation, your brain is not necessarily warning you about real threats—it's simply responding to uncertainty and change with its default protection program.

The key insight is this: we can acknowledge fear's message without being controlled by its demands. We can say, "Thank you, fear, for trying to protect me, but I choose to move forward anyway because I trust that God has equipped me for this challenge." This doesn't eliminate fear, but it puts it in proper perspective as one input among many rather than the controlling voice in our decision-making.

Consider the story of Gideon, who experienced profound fear when God called him to lead Israel against the Midianites. He asked for multiple confirmations, expressed doubt about his qualifications, and even hid while threshing wheat. Yet God didn't rebuke Gideon for his fear—He provided reassurance, confirmation, and progressive steps that allowed Gideon to move forward despite his anxiety. The victory came not because Gideon conquered his fear, but because he acted faithfully in spite of it.

The Biblical Perspective on Fear and Courage

Scripture has much to say about fear, and its message is both realistic and hopeful. The Bible acknowledges that fear is a common human experience—even the phrase "fear not" appears several hundred times in Scripture. This repetition suggests that fear is so prevalent that we need daily reminders to choose courage over anxiety.

But biblical courage is not the absence of fear; it's faith in action despite fear. Moses experienced anxiety about his speaking ability and leadership qualifications, but he stepped forward in obedience to God's call. Esther might have felt terror about approaching the king uninvited, but she chose to risk her life for her people's sake.

In each case, courage was not a feeling but a choice—the decision to trust God's character and promises more than circumstances and emotions. This understanding transforms our relationship with fear from a battle to be won to a tension to be navigated with wisdom and faith.

The Bible also reveals that some fears are actually appropriate and beneficial. The "fear of the Lord" is described as the beginning of wisdom (Proverbs 9:10). This reverential awe and respect for God's holiness and power provides proper perspective on earthly fears. When we truly grasp God's sovereignty, love, and faithfulness, other fears begin to lose their grip on our hearts and minds.

This divine perspective doesn't promise a life without challenges, but it does promise that we never face those challenges alone. "Yea, though I walk through the valley of the shadow of death, I will fear no evil: for thou art with me; thy rod and thy staff they comfort me" (Psalm 23:4). Notice that the promise is not to avoid the valley, but to be accompanied through it.

The Neurobiology of Courage: Rewiring Your Response System

Recent advances in neuroscience reveal that courage, like fear, has a biological basis—and that we can actually strengthen our capacity for brave action through specific practices. The same brain plasticity that allows fear responses to become habitual also enables us to develop courage patterns that become our default response to challenge.

When we repeatedly choose courage despite fear, we strengthen neural pathways associated with resilience, problem-solving, and emotional regulation. Each brave action makes the next one easier, creating what researchers call "positive spirals" of increasing confidence and capability. This is why people who regularly step outside their comfort zones tend to become more comfortable with discomfort over time.

The process works through several mechanisms. First, successful navigation of feared situations provides evidence that contradicts catastrophic predictions, reducing the brain's assessment of threat level. Second, repeated exposure to manageable challenges builds what psychologists call "self-efficacy"—confidence in your ability to handle difficulties. Third, the neurochemical rewards of accomplishment (dopamine, serotonin, endorphins) create positive associations with brave action.

From a biblical perspective, this scientific understanding confirms what Scripture has always taught: that character is developed through practice, that faith grows through testing, and that God has designed us with the capacity to "be ye transformed by the renewing of your mind" (Romans 12:2). We are not victims of our fears but stewards of our responses, capable of choosing courage even when we don't feel brave.

This knowledge empowers us to approach fear strategically rather than emotionally. Instead of waiting to feel courageous before acting, we can act courageously and allow the feelings to follow. Instead of viewing fear as evidence that we're not ready, we can see it as a normal part of growth that signals we're moving in the right direction.

The Service Antidote: How Focusing on Others Transforms Fear

One of the most powerful antidotes to paralyzing fear is shifting focus from self-protection to service of others. When we're consumed with our own anxiety, uncertainty, and potential embarrassment, fear grows larger and more intimidating. But when we focus on how our courage can benefit others, fear often shrinks to manageable proportions.

This principle works because service naturally redirects our attention from internal anxiety to external opportunity. The speaker who focuses on stage fright experiences more anxiety than the speaker who focuses on how their message might help audience members. The entrepreneur who obsesses over potential failure feels more fear than the entrepreneur who concentrates on problems their business could solve for customers.

Consider the transformation that occurs when parents face danger to protect their children. Suddenly, personal fear becomes secondary to protective instinct. The same psychological shift can occur when we view our challenges through the lens of service. The person terrified of public speaking might find courage when they consider how their story could encourage someone struggling with similar issues.

This shift is not just psychological—it's theological. When we understand that our lives are not our own, that we've been called to serve God's purposes and love our neighbors, courage becomes not just a personal virtue but a spiritual responsibility. Allowing fear to prevent us from serving others becomes a form of disobedience, not just to our calling but to the people who need what we have to offer.

The apostle Paul exemplified this principle when he wrote, "I can do all things through Christ which strengtheneth me" (Philippians 4:13). This famous verse was written not in a context of personal ambition but of service to others. Paul's courage to face imprisonment, persecution, and hardship was fueled by his commitment to spreading the gospel and building up the church. His focus on mission overcame his natural human tendency toward self-preservation.

The Growth Mindset Approach to Adversity

Dr. Carol Dweck's research on growth mindset provides crucial insights for overcoming fear and adversity. People with a fixed mindset believe their abilities are static and unchangeable, leading them to avoid challenges that might reveal inadequacy. People with a growth mindset believe abilities can be developed through effort and learning, leading them to embrace challenges as opportunities for development.

This distinction profoundly affects how we respond to fear and adversity. The fixed mindset interprets fear as evidence of limitation: "I'm afraid of public speaking because I'm not a good speaker." The growth mindset interprets fear as invitation to development: "I'm afraid of public speaking because I haven't developed that skill yet, but I can learn."

From a biblical perspective, growth mindset aligns perfectly with Scripture's teaching about spiritual development. We are called to "grow in grace, and in the knowledge of our Lord and Saviour Jesus Christ" (2 Peter 3:18). The parable of the talents rewards those who develop and multiply their gifts rather than those who play it safe. Jesus himself "increased in wisdom and stature" (Luke 2:52), modeling lifelong growth and development.

Applying growth mindset to fear means viewing every challenge as a classroom, every setback as curriculum, and every fear as a faculty member teaching us something important about ourselves and our capacity. This doesn't make challenges less difficult, but it makes them more meaningful and less threatening.

The growth mindset also recognizes that struggle is not a sign of failure but a requirement for development. Just as physical muscles grow stronger through resistance training, character muscles grow stronger through resistance experiences. The person who has never faced fear has never had the opportunity to develop courage. The person who has never experienced adversity has never had the chance to build resilience.

Faith as the Ultimate Fear Fighter

While practical strategies and psychological insights are valuable, the ultimate antidote to paralyzing fear is faith—not generic optimism or positive thinking, but specific trust in God's character, promises, and presence. This kind of faith doesn't eliminate fear, but it provides a stronger foundation than fear for making decisions and taking action.

Biblical faith is based on evidence—the evidence of God's past faithfulness, revealed character, and specific promises. When Joshua was called to lead Israel into the Promised Land, God didn't tell him to stop being afraid. Instead, He provided reasons for courage: "Have not I commanded thee? Be strong and of a good courage; be not afraid, neither be thou dismayed: for the Lord thy God is with thee whithersoever thou goest" (Joshua 1:9).

Notice the logic: be courageous because I have commanded you (divine authority), because I am with you (divine presence), and because I go wherever you go (divine partnership). Fear says, "What if you fail?" Faith responds, "God has commanded this, promised His presence, and committed to partnership."

This kind of faith transforms our relationship with uncertainty. Instead of needing to know all outcomes before acting, we can act on the basis of knowing the One who controls all outcomes. Instead of requiring guarantees about success, we can proceed on the guarantee of God's faithfulness regardless of visible results.

Faith also provides what psychologists call "meaning-making"—the ability to find purpose and significance even in difficult experiences. The person of faith can face adversity not just with the hope of overcoming it, but with the confidence that God will use it for good purposes: "And we know that all things work together for good to them that love God, to them who are the called according to his purpose" (Romans 8:28).

The Community Factor in Courage Building

One of the most overlooked aspects of overcoming fear is the role of community. Courage is often easier to access when we're surrounded by people who believe in us, support our growth, and share our commitment to serving others. Conversely, isolation and negative relationships can amplify fear and make challenges seem insurmountable.

Scripture consistently emphasizes the importance of community in spiritual growth and courage development. The early church faced tremendous persecution and challenges, but they faced them together: "And let us consider one another to provoke unto love and to good works: Not forsaking the assembling of ourselves together" (Hebrews 10:24-25).

Community provides several essential elements for courage building. First, perspective—others can often see our capabilities and potential more clearly than we can. Second, encouragement—hearing others express faith in our abilities strengthens our own confidence. Third, accountability—public commitments create external motivation to follow through despite fear. Fourth, practical support—others can provide resources, connections, and assistance that make challenges more manageable.

The key is choosing community wisely. Surround yourself with people who share your values, support your growth, and challenge you to become your best self. Limit time with people who are consistently negative, fearful, or discouraging. This isn't about avoiding all criticism or challenge, but about ensuring that the primary voices in your life are those that call you toward courage rather than comfort.

Consider forming or joining what we might call a "courage community"—a group of people committed to supporting each other's growth and service. This could be a formal mastermind group, an informal accountability partnership, or a faith-based support group. The format matters less than the commitment to mutual encouragement and challenge.

Adversity as Curriculum: Learning from Every Challenge

One of the most transformative ways to approach adversity is to view it as curriculum rather than punishment—purposeful training designed to develop specific capacities needed for future service and impact. This perspective doesn't minimize the reality of pain or difficulty, but it provides a framework for finding meaning and benefit even in unwanted experiences.

From a biblical perspective, this approach aligns with Scripture's teaching about the purposeful nature of trials: "My brethren, count it all joy when ye fall into divers temptations; Knowing this, that the trying of your faith worketh patience. But let patience have her perfect work, that ye may be perfect and entire, wanting nothing" (James 1:2-4).

Notice the progression: trials test faith, tested faith develops patience, and developed patience creates maturity and completeness. The adversity is not random suffering but purposeful development. This doesn't mean we should seek out difficulty, but it does mean we can find purpose and benefit in the difficulties that inevitably come.

This curricular view of adversity helps us ask better questions when facing challenges. Instead of "Why is this happening to me?" we can ask "What is this meant to teach me?" Instead of "How can I escape this?" we can ask "How can I grow through this?" Instead of "What did I do wrong?" we can ask "What am I meant to do right?"

The answers to these questions often become clear only in retrospect, but asking them in the moment helps maintain a posture of learning rather than merely enduring. It also helps us recognize patterns in our challenges that might reveal areas where God is particularly focused on our development.

The Testimony Factor: How Your Courage Encourages Others

One of the most motivating aspects of choosing courage despite fear is understanding how your example impacts others. Every time you act bravely in spite of anxiety, every time you serve others despite uncertainty, every time you step forward in faith despite doubt, you create permission and inspiration for others to do the same.

This principle is especially powerful for leaders, parents, and mentors, but it applies to everyone. People are watching how you handle challenges, even when you don't realize it. Your courage in small situations can inspire others to find courage for larger ones. Your willingness to risk failure for the sake of service can motivate others to take their own faith-filled risks.

Consider how your current challenges might become future testimonies. The business owner struggling with financial uncertainty today might become the mentor who helps other entrepreneurs navigate similar difficulties tomorrow. The parent dealing with a challenging child today might become the resource who helps other families facing comparable situations in the future.

This long-term perspective transforms current struggles from meaningless suffering into meaningful preparation. It doesn't make the difficulties less real, but it makes them more purposeful. You're not just surviving your challenges—you're developing wisdom, compassion, and credibility that will enable you to serve others more effectively.

The apostle Paul understood this principle when he wrote, "Blessed be God, even the Father of our Lord Jesus Christ, the Father of mercies, and the God of all comfort; Who comforteth us in all our tribulation, that we may be able to comfort them which are in any trouble, by the comfort wherewith we ourselves are comforted of God" (2 Corinthians 1:3-4). Our comfort becomes others' comfort; our courage becomes others' courage; our testimony becomes others' hope.

PRACTICAL APPLICATIONS
The Fear Assessment and Response Toolkit

Before you can effectively overcome fear, you must first understand its specific nature and triggers in your life. The following assessment tools will help you identify patterns, develop targeted strategies, and track progress as you build courage and resilience.

The Fear Inventory Exercise. Take 30 minutes to complete this comprehensive fear assessment:

1. Current Fears: List your top 5 fears that are currently limiting your service or growth
2. Fear Categories: Classify each fear as:
    - Performance fears (speaking, leading, failing publicly)
    - Relationship fears (rejection, conflict, abandonment)
    - Security fears (financial, physical, emotional safety)
    - Spiritual fears (inadequacy, unworthiness, divine disappoint-ment)
3. Fear Triggers: Identify what specific situations, people, or thoughts activate each fear
4. Fear Responses: Note how you typically respond (avoidance, procrastination, overcompensation, etc.)
5. Fear Costs: Calculate what each fear has cost you in terms of opportunities, relationships, and service potential

The Truth vs. Fear Analysis. For each identified fear, create a two-column comparison:

Fear Says | Truth Says

- "You'll be rejected" | "God accepts you; others' opinions don't define your worth"
- "You'll fail and embarrass yourself" | "Failure is feedback; embarrassment is tempo-

rary"

- "You're not qualified" | "God equips the called; qualifications grow through action"

Use Scripture, past evidence of God's faithfulness, and objective facts to counter fear's distorted messages.

The Courage Inventory. Balance your fear assessment by identifying your courage assets:

- Past situations where you acted bravely despite fear
- People who believe in your capabilities
- Skills and experiences that support your confidence
- Spiritual resources available to you (prayer, Scripture, community)
- Previous evidence of God's faithfulness in your life

Progressive Courage-Building Exercises

The Graduated Exposure Method. Break overwhelming fears into manageable steps using this systematic approach:

1. Identify the Ultimate Goal: What would you do if fear weren't a factor?
2. Create a Fear Ladder: List 10 steps from least to most frightening, all leading toward your goal
3. Start Small: Begin with step 1 and complete it successfully before moving to step 2
4. Celebrate Progress: Acknowledge each completed step as evidence of growing courage
5. Build Momentum: Use success at each level to fuel confidence for the next

Example Fear Ladder for Public Speaking:

1. Read aloud alone in your room
2. Record yourself speaking and watch it back
3. Speak in front of a mirror
4. Share a story with one trusted friend
5. Speak up in a small group discussion
6. Give a short testimony in church
7. Present to a small work team
8. Speak at a community meeting
9. Give a longer presentation to colleagues
10. Deliver a keynote speech

The Daily Courage Challenge. Commit to one small act of courage each day for 30 days:

- Week 1: Speak up in meetings, ask questions, share opinions

- Week 2: Initiate conversations with strangers, offer help to neighbors
- Week 3: Take on new responsibilities, volunteer for challenging projects
- Week 4: Share your faith, mentor someone, start a new initiative

Document each daily challenge and reflect on what you learned about yourself and your capabilities.

The Service-Focused Fear Facing. Transform personal fears into service opportunities:

- If you fear public speaking, volunteer to read Scripture in church
- If you fear financial insecurity, mentor someone with budgeting skills
- If you fear rejection, reach out to encourage someone who seems lonely
- If you fear failure, share your story with someone facing similar challenges

This approach redirects focus from self-protection to other-service, naturally reducing fear's power while increasing your positive impact.

Emergency Fear Response Protocols

The STOP Method for Acute Fear. When fear threatens to overwhelm you in the moment, use this 4-step protocol:

S - Stop: Pause whatever you're doing and take three deep breaths
T - Truth: Remind yourself of one relevant Bible verse or truth about God's character
O - Options: Identify three possible responses to the situation (including the courageous choice)
P - Proceed: Choose the option that aligns with your values and calling, then take action

The 5-4-3-2-1 Grounding Technique. When anxiety creates physical symptoms, use this sensory grounding exercise:

- Name 5 things you can see
- Name 4 things you can touch
- Name 3 things you can hear
- Name 2 things you can smell
- Name 1 thing you can taste

This technique helps calm your nervous system by redirecting attention from internal anxiety to external reality.

The Faith Declaration Method. Create a personalized set of faith declarations to speak over yourself during fearful moments:

- "I can do all things through Christ which strengtheneth me" (Philippians 4:13)
- "For God hath not given me a spirit of fear; but of power, and of love, and of a sound mind" (2 Timothy 1:7)
- "The Lord is my helper, and I will not fear what man shall do unto me" (Hebrews 13:6)
- "I am fearfully and wonderfully made" (Psalm 139:14)

Speak these aloud with conviction, allowing God's truth to override fear's lies.

Building Your Courage Support System

The Courage Accountability Partner. Find someone who will help you move beyond fear into faithful action:

- Selection Criteria: Choose someone who shares your values, has demonstrated courage in their own life, and will lovingly challenge you to grow
- Meeting Frequency: Connect weekly for 30 minutes to share current challenges and progress
- Accountability Structure:
    - Share your weekly courage goals
    - Report on previous week's challenges and victories
    - Pray together for wisdom and strength
    - Receive gentle challenge when fear is limiting your service potential

The Encouragement Network. Identify 3-5 people who can provide different types of support:

- The Cheerleader: Someone who believes in you unconditionally and celebrates your progress
- The Challenger: Someone who will lovingly push you beyond your comfort zone
- The Wise Counselor: Someone with experience who can provide practical guidance
- The Fellow Traveler: Someone facing similar challenges who can provide mutual support

The Testimony Archive. Create a collection of courage-building resources:

- Personal Victory Stories: Document times when you acted courageously and saw positive results
- Biblical Examples: Collect stories of biblical figures who overcame fear through faith
- Contemporary Testimonies: Gather stories of modern believers who have faced similar fears successfully
- Encouraging Quotes: Compile quotes about courage, faith, and service that inspire you
- Photographic Reminders: Take pictures of yourself engaging in courageous activities

Review this archive regularly, especially before facing new challenges.

The Weekly and Monthly Courage Development Plan

Weekly Courage Planning Session (30 minutes every Sunday)

- Review: What fears did I face this week? How did I respond?

- Assess: What courage muscles am I developing? Where do I need more work?
- Plan: What specific courage challenges will I take on this week?
- Prepare: What resources, support, or strategies do I need for upcoming challenges?
- Pray: Ask God for wisdom, strength, and opportunities to serve despite fear

Monthly Courage Evaluation (2 hours monthly)
- Progress Analysis: Compare your current courage level to where you were 30 days ago
- Pattern Recognition: What types of fears are you overcoming? Which ones persist?
- Strategy Adjustment: What techniques are working? What needs modification?
- Goal Recalibration: Are your courage goals still relevant and appropriately challenging?
- Celebration Planning: How will you acknowledge your growth and progress?

Quarterly Courage Intensive (Half-day quarterly)
- Deep Reflection: How has increased courage enhanced your ability to serve others?
- Vision Alignment: How do your courage goals support your larger vision and calling?
- Skill Development: What new courage-building skills do you need to develop?
- Relationship Impact: How has your growing courage affected your relationships and influence?
- Legacy Consideration: What courage legacy are you building for those who observe your life?

Creating Your Personal Courage Manifesto

Write Your Courage Statement. Develop a personal manifesto that captures your commitment to choosing courage despite fear. Include:
- Your understanding of courage as a spiritual discipline
- Your commitment to serving others despite personal anxiety
- Specific fears you're choosing to face for the sake of your calling
- Bible verses that anchor your courage in God's character
- Your vision for how increased courage will enhance your service impact

Example opening: "I choose courage not because I am fearless, but because I am faithful. I will face my fears not for my own comfort, but for the sake of those God has called me to serve..."

Daily Courage Rituals. Establish daily practices that reinforce your courage commitment:
- Morning Declaration: Read your courage manifesto aloud each morning
- Courage Prayer: Ask God for specific opportunities to practice courage each day
- Evening Reflection: Journal about moments when you chose courage or when fear

held you back

- Gratitude Practice: Thank God for His faithfulness in past situations that required courage
- Scripture Meditation: Memorize and meditate on verses that strengthen your faith and courage

Fear-to-Service Transformation Exercises

The Fear Flip Method. Transform each personal fear into a service opportunity:

1. Identify the Fear: "I'm afraid of being judged for my past mistakes"
2. Find the Service Connection: "Others who've made similar mistakes need encouragement"
3. Create the Action: "I'll share my story of redemption with someone struggling with shame"
4. Focus on Impact: "My vulnerability could help someone find hope and healing"

The Empathy Bridge. Use your fear experiences to build bridges of understanding with others:

- If you fear financial insecurity, volunteer with financial counseling ministries
- If you fear loneliness, reach out to elderly or isolated community members
- If you fear health issues, support families dealing with medical challenges
- If you fear professional failure, mentor young people starting their careers

This approach transforms your fear from a liability into an asset for serving others who face similar challenges.

The Legacy Question. When facing fear, ask yourself: "How do I want to be remembered? As someone who let fear limit their service, or as someone who served faithfully despite their fears?"

This question helps shift focus from temporary discomfort to eternal impact, providing motivation to choose courage when fear feels overwhelming.

CHAPTER CONCLUSION
The Sacred Transformation from Fear to Faith

As we reach the end of this exploration of fear and adversity, it's important to recognize the profound transformation that occurs when you choose faith over fear, courage over comfort, and service over self-protection. You've not just learned techniques for managing anxiety—you've discovered the pathway to becoming the person God created you to be, someone who serves boldly despite uncertainty and loves deeply despite risk.

The beautiful paradox of courage is this: it's not about becoming fearless, but about becoming faithful. Every time you acknowledge fear and choose to act anyway, every time you feel inadequate but serve anyway, every time you face uncertainty but trust anyway, you're participating in the kind of faith that moves mountains and changes lives. Your courage doesn't just overcome your own limitations—it creates permission for others to overcome theirs.

Your Fear as a Compass

One of the most liberating truths you can embrace is that your fears often point toward your greatest opportunities for growth and service. The very things that frighten you most may be precisely where God wants to use you most powerfully. Your fear of rejection might indicate you're called to love the unloved. Your fear of failure might signal you're meant to help others overcome their own setbacks. Your fear of inadequacy might reveal you're positioned to serve those who feel similarly unprepared.

This reframe transforms fear from an enemy to be avoided into a compass pointing toward purpose. Instead of running from what scares you, you can walk toward it with curiosity and faith, asking, "How might God want to use this challenge to develop my character and expand my service?" The areas where you feel most vulnerable often become the areas where you can offer the most authentic help to others.

The Multiplication Effect of Courage

Remember that your journey from fear to faith creates ripple effects far beyond your personal experience. When you choose courage, you don't just change your own story—you change the stories of everyone watching. Your children learn that challenges can be faced with faith. Your colleagues discover that risks can be taken with wisdom. Your community sees that problems can be addressed with hope and action.

The courage you develop today becomes the foundation for the influence you'll have tomorrow. The fears you face now prepare you to help others face similar fears later. The adversity you navigate with faith becomes the testimony that encourages others during their own dark moments. You're not just building your own character—you're contributing to a legacy of faithfulness that will inspire generations.

The Divine Partnership in Courage

Perhaps the most encouraging aspect of choosing courage despite fear is understanding that you never do it alone. The same God who called you to serve is the God who promises to equip you for that service. "Fear thou not; for I am with thee: be not dismayed; for I am thy God: I will strengthen thee; yea, I will help thee; yea, I will uphold thee with the right hand of my righteousness" (Isaiah 41:10).

This divine partnership means that your courage is not just human willpower overcoming natural anxiety—it's divine strength flowing through willing vessels. When you choose to trust despite fear, you're not just exhibiting personal bravery; you're demonstrating the reality of God's presence and power in your life. Your faith becomes a testimony to His faithfulness.

The Eternal Perspective on Temporary Fears

As you continue your journey, remember that every fear you face is temporary, but every act of courage has eternal significance. The anxiety you feel about tomorrow's challenge will pass, but the character you build by facing it will last forever. The uncertainty you experience about next steps will resolve, but the faith you develop by trusting God will strengthen you for future challenges.

This eternal perspective doesn't minimize current struggles, but it provides hope that transcends immediate circumstances. You can endure temporary discomfort because you're building permanent character. You can risk temporary embarrassment because you're creating eternal impact. You can accept temporary uncertainty because you're partnering with an eternal God whose plans never fail.

Your Courage Assignment

As you move forward from this chapter, carry with you the fear assessment and graduated exposure exercises from our practical applications. Choose one fear that has been limiting your service potential and begin the process of facing it systematically, with prayer, support, and faith in God's faithfulness.

Remember, you don't need to conquer all your fears at once. Courage is built one choice at a time, one step at a time, one act of faith at a time. Start where you are, use what you have, and trust God for what you need. Every small act of courage makes the next one easier, and every faithful step creates momentum for greater service and impact.

Looking Ahead

In our next chapter, we'll explore how to build daily habits and practices that support your continued growth and service. You'll discover that the courage you're developing now becomes the foundation for the consistent, faithful living that creates lasting change in your life and the lives of others.

But for now, your task is both simple and challenging: face one fear this week for the sake of someone else. Take one step that scares you because it serves someone who needs what you have to offer. Choose faith over fear in one specific situation, trusting that God will provide the strength, wisdom, and resources you need as you step forward.

5

Habits & Daily Practice

The richest lives are not built in a moment but shaped by the quiet power of daily habits.

WHILE INSPIRATION CAN IGNITE CHANGE, it is routine that sustains it. The world's most successful leaders, entrepreneurs, and servant-hearted individuals all share a secret: they have learned to harness the power of small, consistent actions. Habits are the invisible architecture of our days, quietly guiding us toward—or away from—the life we desire.

In business and in service, it's not the grand gestures that create lasting impact, but the steady rhythm of showing up, doing the work, and refining our craft. Whether it's a morning meditation, a gratitude journal, or a daily commitment to listen deeply to others, these small practices compound over time, shaping not only what we do, but who we become. As one productivity expert notes, "Success is the sum of small efforts, repeated day in and day out." Even the most ambitious goals are achieved not in leaps, but in a series of tiny, faithful steps.

Modern research and timeless wisdom agree: routines matter. Simple habits like waking up early, reading, exercising, or setting daily intentions can transform your energy, focus, and resilience. Faith traditions echo this truth, encouraging us to "meditate day and night" (Psalm 1:2) and to be "faithful in that which is least" (Luke 16:10). When we anchor our routines in purpose—pairing daily actions with our deepest values—we invite growth not just in our productivity, but in our character and spirit.

Building new habits doesn't require perfection. In fact, the most effective routines are often the simplest: a prayer whispered while making coffee, a word of encouragement to a colleague, or a moment of reflection at day's end. When we stumble, we start again, remembering that consistency matters more than intensity. Over time, these daily practices become the foundation from which we serve others and grow richly ourselves.

The Neuroscience of Transformation: How Habits Rewire Your Brain

Understanding the science behind habit formation reveals why small, consistent actions have such profound power to transform our lives and enhance our capacity to serve others. Modern neuroscience shows us that our brains are remarkably plastic—constantly forming new neural pathways and strengthening existing ones based on repeated behaviors. This means that every habit we cultivate literally rewires our brain for success or failure, service or selfishness, growth or stagnation.

When we repeat an action consistently, our brain creates what scientists call "neural highways"—efficient pathways that make the behavior increasingly automatic. The first time you attempt a new habit, such as spending time in prayer each morning, your brain must work hard to remember and execute the behavior. But with repetition, the neural pathway becomes smoother and stronger, requiring less conscious effort and willpower. Eventually, the habit becomes so automatic that not doing it feels strange and uncomfortable.

This process explains why initial habit formation can feel difficult while maintaining established habits feels effortless. The entrepreneur who has developed a habit of reading industry publications every morning doesn't struggle with motivation—the behavior has become as automatic as brushing teeth. The servant who has cultivated a practice of daily encouragement doesn't debate whether to reach out to someone—the impulse to serve has become their default response.

From a biblical perspective, this neuroplasticity reveals the wisdom behind Scripture's emphasis on daily practices and consistent faithfulness. When God instructs us to meditate on His word "day and night" (Joshua 1:8), He's not just giving us a spiritual discipline—He's prescribing the neurological path to transformation. When Jesus speaks of taking up our cross "daily" (Luke 9:23), He's describing the habit formation process that creates character transformation.

The implications are profound: we have the power to literally reshape our brains for better service, deeper faith, and richer relationships through intentional habit development. The person who consistently practices gratitude develops neural pathways that automatically notice blessings. The leader who regularly serves others builds mental patterns that default to other-centered thinking. The believer who maintains daily spiritual disciplines creates brain pathways that naturally turn toward God throughout the day.

The Biblical Foundation of Daily Faithfulness

Scripture consistently emphasizes the power of daily practices and regular rhythms in developing character and deepening relationship with God. The concept of daily faithfulness runs throughout the Bible, from the daily manna provided to the Israelites in the wilderness to Jesus' instruction to pray for "daily bread" in the Lord's Prayer.

The book of Daniel provides a powerful example of how daily habits shape character and influence. Daniel "kneeled upon his knees three times a day, and prayed, and gave thanks before his God, as he did aforetime" (Daniel 6:10). This wasn't a crisis response but a consistent practice that had shaped Daniel's character over years. When faced with the choice between compromising his faith or facing the lion's den, Daniel's daily habit of prayer had so formed his identity that the choice was obvious.

Similarly, David's psalms reveal a life structured around regular spiritual practices. He speaks of meditating on God's word "day and night" (Psalm 1:2), of praising God "seven times a day" (Psalm 119:164), and of seeking God "early" (Psalm 63:1). These weren't occasional bursts of spirituality but daily rhythms that kept David connected to God's heart and purposes.

The principle extends beyond personal devotions to habits of service and character. Proverbs repeatedly emphasizes the importance of daily diligence: "The hand of the diligent shall bear rule" (Proverbs 12:24), and "Seest thou a man diligent in his business? he shall stand before kings" (Proverbs 22:29). The diligence described here is not occasional heroic effort but consistent daily faithfulness in small things.

Jesus himself modeled the power of daily habits. Luke tells us that "he went into the synagogue on the sabbath day, as his custom was" (Luke 4:16). Mark records that "in the morning, rising up a great while before day, he went out, and departed into a solitary place, and there prayed" (Mark 1:35). These weren't one-time events but established patterns that shaped Jesus' ministry and maintained His connection with the Father.

The Compound Effect in Service and Character Development

One of the most overlooked aspects of habit formation is its compound effect—the way small, seemingly insignificant daily actions accumulate into dramatic long-term results. Just as compound interest transforms modest savings into substantial wealth over time, compound habits transform modest daily practices into extraordinary character and influence.

Consider the difference compound habits make in service capacity. The person who reads one book per month accumulates twelve books of wisdom annually—enough to become exceptionally knowledgeable in their field within a few years. The leader who has one meaningful conversation daily touches 365 lives annually, building a network of relationships that exponentially increases their influence. The servant who performs one small act of kindness each day creates 365 moments of blessing, establishing a reputation for care that attracts opportunities for greater service.

The mathematics of marginal gains reveals why this works so powerfully. Improving by just 1% daily doesn't feel significant in the moment, but it compounds to make you 37 times better over the course of a year. Conversely, declining by 1% daily makes you 97% worse by year's end. This explains why successful people often seem to have "sudden" breakthroughs—they're simply experiencing the delayed compound effect of years of consistent daily practices.

From a spiritual perspective, this compound effect aligns with Jesus' teaching about faithfulness in small things leading to responsibility for great things (Luke 16:10). The person faithful in the daily discipline of prayer develops the character to handle larger spiritual responsibilities. The servant faithful in small acts of kindness becomes trustworthy for greater ministry opportunities. The leader faithful in daily preparation becomes capable of handling significant challenges and decisions.

The key insight is that compound habits work both positively and negatively. Daily practices of selfishness, negativity, or spiritual neglect also compound, gradually undermining character and diminishing service capacity. This is why the Bible warns about "a little leaven" that "leaveneth the whole lump" (1 Corinthians 5:6)—small negative habits can eventually corrupt entire areas of life.

The Identity-Based Approach to Habit Formation

Traditional habit formation focuses on outcomes: "I want to lose weight," "I want to read more," "I want to serve others better." While outcome goals provide direction, identity-based habits provide motivation and sustainability. Instead of asking "What do I want to achieve?" identity-based habit formation asks "Who do I want to become?"

This shift is profound because our behavior typically aligns with our self-perception. If you see yourself as someone who serves others, you'll naturally look for opportunities to help. If you identify as a person of prayer, you'll find ways to maintain spiritual disciplines even when schedules become challenging. If you consider yourself a lifelong learner, you'll consistently seek growth opportunities.

The process works by creating positive identity reinforcement cycles. Each time you act in alignment with your desired identity, you cast a vote for that type of person. Each vote strengthens your self-concept and makes future aligned actions more likely. The person who wants to become more generous doesn't just set a giving goal—they begin saying "I am someone who looks for ways to bless others" and then acts in ways that prove this identity to themselves.

Scripture supports this identity-based approach through its emphasis on our new nature in Christ. Paul writes, "Therefore if any man be in Christ, he is a new creature: old things are passed away; behold, all things are become new" (2 Corinthians 5:17). This new identity then shapes behavior: "For we are his workmanship, created in Christ Jesus unto good works, which God hath before ordained that we should walk in them" (Ephesians 2:10).

The practical application involves framing habits around identity rather than outcomes. Instead of "I want to read my Bible more," try "I am someone who starts each day with God's word." Instead of "I want to exercise regularly," think "I am someone who takes care of the body God gave me." Instead of "I want to serve others," declare "I am someone who looks for opportunities to bless people."

The Environmental Design of Success

One of the most overlooked aspects of successful habit formation is environmental design—structuring your physical and social environment to make good habits easier and bad habits harder. Our environment shapes our behavior more than we realize, often overriding even strong motivation and good intentions.

Consider how environmental cues trigger automatic behaviors throughout your day. The coffee maker on your counter triggers your morning routine. Your phone's notification sound triggers the urge to check messages. The running shoes by your bed trigger thoughts about exercise. These environmental cues can either support or sabotage your habit formation efforts.

Successful habit builders become environmental architects, designing their surroundings to support their desired behaviors. The person who wants to read more places books in highly visible locations and removes distracting devices from their reading area. The individual seeking to pray more keeps a Bible and journal by their bed or favorite chair. The servant looking to encourage others more writes note cards and keeps them easily accessible.

The principle extends beyond physical environment to social environment. The people you spend time with significantly influence your habits and behaviors. If you want to develop habits of generosity, surround yourself with generous people. If you're building habits of spiritual growth, cultivate relationships with others pursuing similar goals. If you're developing service habits, connect with communities focused on helping others.

From a biblical perspective, this aligns with the principle of being "equally yoked" (2 Corinthians 6:14) and the recognition that "evil communications corrupt good manners" (1 Corinthians 15:33). The relationships and environments we choose either support or undermine our spiritual growth and service capacity.

Environmental design also involves what psychologists call "friction"—the amount of effort required to perform a behavior. Reducing friction for good habits and increasing friction for bad habits creates what researchers call "choice architecture" that guides behavior in positive directions without restricting freedom.

The Power of Keystone Habits

Some habits are more important than others because they naturally trigger positive changes in other areas of life. These "keystone habits" act like dominoes, creating chain reactions that transform multiple aspects of your character and service capacity simultaneously.

Exercise is a classic keystone habit. People who develop consistent exercise routines often simultaneously improve their diet, sleep patterns, productivity, and emotional regulation—not because they're specifically targeting these areas, but because physical fitness creates momentum for other positive changes. The discipline required for regular exercise builds mental muscles that support other challenging behaviors.

For servants and leaders, certain spiritual disciplines often function as keystone habits. A consistent morning prayer routine frequently leads to improved decision-making throughout the day, greater awareness of service opportunities, increased patience with difficult people, and better stress management. The morning connection with God creates a foundation that supports Christ-like behavior in all subsequent interactions.

Similarly, a daily reading habit often becomes keystone for intellectual and spiritual growth. People who read consistently tend to become better communicators, more creative problem-solvers, more empathetic listeners, and more effective leaders. The cognitive stimulation and expanded perspective from reading compound into multiple areas of effectiveness.

The key to identifying your potential keystone habits is looking for behaviors that require multiple positive qualities (discipline, planning, consistency) and that naturally connect to your values and goals.

Habits as Spiritual Disciplines

From a faith perspective, habit formation is not just about personal productivity or character development—it's about spiritual formation and discipleship. The regular practices we cultivate either draw us closer to God's heart or gradually distance us from His purposes. This makes habit formation a profoundly spiritual endeavor requiring wisdom, prayer, and dependence on God's grace.

Traditional spiritual disciplines—prayer, Scripture reading, fasting, solitude, service—are essentially habit formation practices designed to create regular encounters with God that transform our hearts and minds. These disciplines work not because they earn God's favor, but because they position us to receive His grace and align our lives with His purposes.

The key insight is that spiritual disciplines are means of grace, not ends in themselves. The goal is not perfect performance of religious activities but transformation of character that enhances our ability to love God and serve others. This perspective prevents legalism while maintaining the importance of consistent spiritual practices.

Modern believers can learn from ancient monastic communities that structured entire days around spiritual habits. While few of us can adopt monastic schedules, we can learn from their understanding that character formation requires intentional, regular practices that keep us connected to God's presence and purposes throughout our daily activities.

The challenge is integrating spiritual habits into modern life without them becoming mere religious obligations. This requires what brother Lawrence called "practicing the presence of God"—developing habits that maintain awareness of God's presence in ordinary activities rather than compartmentalizing spirituality into specific times and places.

The Service Habit Loop: Automating Generosity and Love

One of the most powerful applications of habit science is automating acts of service and love so they become natural responses rather than forced obligations. When serving others becomes habitual, we stop debating whether to help and start looking for opportunities to bless people.

The habit loop—cue, routine, reward—can be intentionally designed to create automatic service responses. For example, seeing someone struggling (cue) can trigger an automatic impulse to offer help (routine), which generates the satisfaction of making a difference (reward). Over time, this loop becomes so automatic that you naturally notice and respond to others' needs without conscious decision-making.

This automation is crucial for sustainable service because it removes the friction of motivation and decision fatigue. The person who has developed habits of encouragement doesn't debate whether to compliment a colleague—they automatically notice opportunities to build others up. The servant with habits of generosity doesn't wrestle with whether to give—they look for ways to bless others as naturally as they breathe.

Scripture describes this kind of automatic goodness in passages like "out of the abundance of the heart the mouth speaketh" (Matthew 12:34). When our hearts are trained through consistent habits of love and service, good works flow naturally from our character rather than requiring constant conscious effort.

The practical application involves identifying specific service habits that align with your calling and circumstances. This might include daily practices like sending one encouraging message, performing one act of kindness for a family member, or looking for one way to help a colleague succeed.

Habit Stacking and the Architecture of a Servant's Day

Habit stacking—linking new habits to existing behaviors—provides a powerful method for building comprehensive routines that support service-oriented living. Instead of trying to remember new behaviors in isolation, you connect them to things you already do automatically, creating chains of positive actions that flow naturally from one to another.

A servant-hearted morning routine might stack multiple growth and service habits together: After I pour my coffee (existing habit), I will read one chapter of Scripture (new habit). After I read Scripture, I will pray for God to assist me in serving his purpose (new habit). After I pray, I will write down one way I can serve someone today (new habit). After I plan my service, I will review my daily priorities through the lens of love and service (new habit).

This stacking creates what we might call "the architecture of a servant's day"—a structure that naturally guides thoughts and actions toward serving others and growing in character. The beauty of this approach is that it doesn't require dramatic lifestyle changes but rather strategic enhancement of existing routines.

The key to successful habit stacking is choosing appropriate anchor habits—existing behaviors that are already well-established and occur at consistent times. Morning routines often work well because they're typically more stable and less subject to external interruptions than evening routines.

Biblical examples of habit stacking appear throughout Scripture. Daniel's practice of praying three times daily was likely stacked with natural transition points in his schedule. David's evening reflections on God's goodness were probably connected to natural rest periods. Jesus' early morning prayer time was stacked with the natural quiet before daily activities began.

PRACTICAL APPLICATIONS
The 21-Day Habit Foundation System

Building sustainable habits requires a systematic approach that honors both the science of behavior change and the spiritual dimensions of character formation. The following 21-day system provides a structured pathway for establishing new habits while maintaining flexibility for individual circumstances and calling.

Days 1-7: Foundation Week. Focus on establishing the basic behavior without perfectionism or complex variations:

- Choose One Keystone Habit: Select a single habit that aligns with your service calling and has potential to trigger other positive changes

- Start Ridiculously Small: Commit to the smallest possible version (2 minutes of prayer, one page of reading, one encouraging text)

- Link to Existing Routine: Stack your new habit immediately after something you already do consistently

- Track Simply: Use a basic check-mark system to monitor consistency without complex metrics

- Expect Resistance: Recognize that initial difficulty is normal and temporary

Example Foundation Week Habit: "After I brush my teeth each morning, I will read one verse of Scripture and pray."

Days 8-14: Expansion Week. Gradually increase the habit's scope and impact:

- Slightly Increase Duration: Move from 2 minutes to 5 minutes, one page to two pages

- Add Service Connection: Include one element that directly serves others (text encouragement, plan one helpful action)

- Notice Ripple Effects: Observe how the new habit affects other areas of your life and relationships

- Adjust as Needed: Modify timing, location, or approach based on what you've learned

- Celebrate Progress: Acknowledge completion of the first week and momentum building

Days 15-21: Integration Week. Focus on making the habit feel natural and sustainable:

- Reach Target Duration: Achieve the full version of your intended habit

- Connect to Identity: Begin saying "I am someone who..." in relation to your habit

- Plan for Obstacles: Identify potential disruptions and create contingency plans
- Share with Others: Tell someone about your new habit for accountability and encouragement
- Evaluate and Refine: Assess what's working well and what needs adjustment for long-term sustainability

The Service-Centered Daily Routine Builder

Creating a daily routine that supports both personal growth and service to others requires intentional design that balances self-care with other-care. The following framework helps you build routines that enhance your capacity to serve while maintaining spiritual, emotional, and physical health.

Morning Service Launch Sequence (15-30 minutes). Design your morning routine to prepare your heart and mind for serving others throughout the day:

1. Spiritual Connection (5-10 minutes):
   - Brief prayer thanking God for the new day and asking for opportunities to serve
   - Read one chapter of Scripture or devotional material
   - Meditate on how you want to reflect God's love today
2. Service Planning (5 minutes):
   - Choose one specific way you'll serve someone today
   - Review your schedule with a service mindset: "How can I bless others in each interaction?"
3. Personal Preparation (5-15 minutes):
   - Physical preparation (exercise, healthy breakfast, appropriate dress)
   - Mental preparation (review priorities, visualize successful interactions)
   - Emotional preparation (practice gratitude, set positive intentions)

Midday Service Check-In (5-10 minutes). Create a brief midday pause to refocus on service and growth:

- Reflection: How have I served others so far today? What opportunities have I noticed?
- Gratitude: What am I thankful for in this moment?
- Adjustment: What do I need to do differently in the afternoon to better serve others?
- Prayer: Brief prayer for wisdom and energy for remaining daily activities

Evening Service Review (10-15 minutes). End each day by reflecting on growth and service opportunities:

- Celebration: What acts of service or kindness did I perform today?
- Learning: What did I learn about myself, others, or God through today's interactions?

- Gratitude: Record three specific things I'm grateful for from today
- Tomorrow's Intention: How do I want to serve and grow tomorrow?
- Prayer: Thank God for His faithfulness and ask for rest and renewal

The Weekly Habit Assessment and Adjustment Protocol

Sustainable habit formation requires regular evaluation and adjustment. The following weekly protocol helps you maintain momentum while adapting to changing circumstances and growing understanding of what works best for your personality and calling.

Sunday Evening Habit Review (30 minutes). Conduct a comprehensive assessment of your habit progress and plan improvements for the coming week:

Consistency Analysis:
- Which habits did I maintain consistently this week?
- What factors supported my success in these areas?
- Which habits did I struggle with, and what obstacles interfered?
- What patterns do I notice in my successful versus unsuccessful days?

Impact Assessment:
- How have my habits enhanced my ability to serve others?
- What character qualities are developing through my daily practices?
- Which habits are having the greatest positive ripple effects?
- How are others being blessed by my growth in these areas?

Obstacle Identification:
- What specific challenges prevented consistency this week?
- Which obstacles are within my control versus outside my control?
- What environmental changes could reduce friction for good habits?
- Who could provide support or accountability for challenging areas?

Refinement Planning:
- What small adjustments would improve my success rate next week?
- Are any habits too ambitious and need to be scaled back temporarily?
- What new resources, tools, or strategies might help?
- How can I better integrate my habits with my service calling?

Building Your Personal Habit Ecosystem

Rather than trying to build habits in isolation, create a comprehensive ecosystem where each habit supports and reinforces others. This approach recognizes that sustainable change involves multiple interconnected behaviors that work together to create the life you want to live.

Physical Foundation Habits. Establish habits that maintain the physical energy needed for consistent service:

- Sleep Hygiene: Consistent bedtime and wake time that ensure adequate rest
- Nutrition: Regular, healthy meals that sustain energy throughout the day
- Movement: Daily physical activity appropriate to your fitness level and schedule
- Hydration: Consistent water intake to maintain physical and mental clarity

Spiritual Growth Habits. Develop practices that deepen your relationship with God and align your heart with His purposes:

- Daily Scripture: Regular Bible reading that feeds your soul and renews your mind
- Prayer Practice: Consistent communication with God including praise, confession, requests, and listening
- Worship: Regular participation in corporate worship and personal worship practices
- Service: Daily actions that express love for God through service to others

Mental Development Habits. Cultivate practices that expand your capacity to think clearly, solve problems, and serve effectively:

- Reading: Regular consumption of books, articles, or other materials that stimulate growth
- Learning: Consistent pursuit of new skills or knowledge relevant to your calling
- Reflection: Daily time for processing experiences and extracting wisdom
- Planning: Regular goal-setting and strategic thinking about your life and service

Relational Connection Habits Build practices that strengthen your relationships and expand your capacity to love others well:

- Family Time: Consistent, intentional investment in your closest relationships
- Friend Connection: Regular communication and time with supportive friendships
- Mentoring: Both receiving wisdom from others and sharing wisdom with those you can help
- Community Service: Regular participation in activities that serve your broader community

The Emergency Habit Recovery System

Even well-established habits can be disrupted by illness, travel, crises, or major life changes. Having a recovery system prevents temporary disruptions from becoming permanent derailments.

The Minimum Viable Habit Protocol. For each important habit, identify the smallest possible version you can maintain during difficult periods:

- Full Habit: 30 minutes of morning prayer and Scripture reading
- Reduced Habit: 10 minutes of prayer and one chapter reading
- Minimum Viable Habit: One minute of prayer and one Bible verse
- Crisis Habit: One spoken prayer of gratitude during the day

The 48-Hour Rule. Commit to never going more than 48 hours without performing some version of your most important habits. This prevents temporary lapses from becoming extended breaks that require complete restart.

The Recovery Ritual. When you've missed several days of a habit, use this process to restart without shame or discouragement:

1. Acknowledge Without Judgment: "I missed several days of my morning routine"
2. Identify the Cause: "I was traveling and didn't plan for the disruption"
3. Extract the Learning: "I need to create travel versions of my habits"
4. Start Small Again: "Today I'll do the minimum viable version"
5. Plan for Success: "Tomorrow I'll increase back to the reduced version"

The Support System Activation. When habits become difficult to maintain, reach out to your support network:

- Accountability Partner: Share your struggle and ask for encouragement
- Mentor or Coach: Seek advice about overcoming specific obstacles
- Service Community: Reconnect with others who share your values and goals

Technology Tools for Habit Success

While habits should not depend entirely on technology, strategic use of apps and tools can provide helpful support for tracking, reminding, and encouraging habit development.

Habit Tracking Apps

- Simple Tracking: Use apps like Streaks, Habitica, or Way of Life for basic check-mark tracking
- Detailed Analytics: Try apps like Productive or Strides for more comprehensive data about patterns
- Gamification: Consider apps that add game-like elements to make habit building more engaging
- Integration: Look for apps that connect with your calendar, fitness tracker, or other tools you already use

Reminder Systems

- Calendar Integration: Schedule habit time blocks in your regular calendar
- Smart Device Reminders: Use phone or smart home device reminders for habit cues
- Visual Cues: Place physical reminders (books, workout clothes, note cards) in strate-

gic locations

- Social Reminders: Ask family members or roommates to support your habit development

Progress Documentation

- Photo Journals: Take daily photos to document progress on visual habits (exercise, organization, etc.)
- Written Reflection: Use journaling apps or simple notes to record insights and growth
- Video Updates: Create brief weekly videos reflecting on your habit development journey
- Shared Accountability: Use social media or private groups to share progress and receive encouragement

Creating Your 90-Day Habit Transformation Plan

While individual habits can be established in 21 days, comprehensive life transformation typically requires 90 days of consistent practice. Use this framework to create a quarterly plan that builds multiple habits systematically.

Month 1: Foundation (Days 1-30)

- Establish 1-2 keystone habits that align with your core calling
- Focus on consistency over perfection
- Build basic tracking and accountability systems
- Address any environmental obstacles to success

Month 2: Expansion (Days 31-60)

- Add 1-2 additional habits that complement your foundation habits
- Increase the scope or impact of your original habits
- Develop contingency plans for common obstacles
- Begin sharing your progress with others for additional accountability

Month 3: Integration (Days 61-90)

- Fine-tune all habits for long-term sustainability
- Connect habits more explicitly to your service calling and identity
- Help someone else begin their own habit development journey
- Plan your next 90-day cycle based on what you've learned

This systematic approach recognizes that lasting change happens gradually and that sustainable transformation requires both personal commitment and community support.

CHAPTER CONCLUSION
The Sacred Rhythm of Transformation

As we conclude this exploration of habits and daily practice, it's essential to understand what you've discovered: the sacred rhythm of transformation that turns ordinary moments into extraordinary character development and simple actions into profound service. You haven't just learned about productivity techniques or self-improvement strategies—you've uncovered the spiritual discipline of faithful stewardship over the small, seemingly insignificant choices that ultimately determine the trajectory of your entire life.

The beautiful truth about habit formation is that it mirrors God's own character. He is described as the same "yesterday, and today, and forever" (Hebrews 13:8)—absolutely consistent in His love, faithfulness, and commitment to our good. When we develop habits of consistency in our own lives, we reflect His character and position ourselves to receive His grace more fully. Our daily faithfulness becomes a form of worship, declaring our trust that small acts done with love matter deeply to our Creator.

Your Daily Life as Ministry

Perhaps the most transformative perspective on habits is understanding that your daily routine is your primary ministry platform. The habits you build don't just change you—they create the character foundation from which you serve others. The discipline you develop through consistent spiritual practices becomes the inner strength that enables you to love difficult people. The morning routine that centers your heart becomes the source of peace you offer to anxious friends. The daily acts of service you build into your schedule become the automatic responses that bless everyone around you.

This means that working on your habits is not selfish self-improvement—it's preparation for greater service. When you become the kind of person who consistently chooses love over fear, kindness over irritation, and service over selfishness, you become a walking testimony to the transforming power of God's grace. Your life becomes a demonstration that ordinary people can live extraordinary lives through the power of faithful daily choices.

The Compound Legacy of Faithful Days

Remember that every habit you build creates ripple effects that extend far beyond your personal experience. Your children observe your morning routine and learn about priorities. Your colleagues notice your consistent kindness and experience hope. Your community benefits from your reliable service and discovers what dependability looks like. The habits you build today become the legacy you leave tomorrow.

This understanding elevates habit formation from personal development to generational impact. The parent who consistently shows patience is training future parents in emotional regulation. The leader who maintains daily learning habits is modeling lifelong growth for their team. The servant who builds habits of encouragement is creating a culture of support that others will perpetuate.

Years from now, people may not remember your specific words or individual acts of service, but they will remember how consistently you showed up, how reliably you served, and how faithfully you lived. Your habits become your character, your character becomes your influence, and your influence becomes your legacy.

The Grace Foundation of Habit Building

As you continue building habits that support your growth and service, remember that sustainable change is built on grace, not guilt. When you miss a day, stumble in your routine, or fall short of your ideals, God's love for you doesn't diminish. His calling on your life doesn't change. His commitment to your growth doesn't waver. The foundation of all healthy habit building is the secure knowledge that your worth comes from His love, not your performance.

This grace foundation actually makes habit building easier, not harder. When you're not trying to earn God's approval through perfect consistency, you can focus on faithful progress. When you're not afraid of His disappointment over your failures, you can quickly recover and restart. When you understand that He's more interested in your heart than your track record, you can build habits from love rather than fear.

The goal is not perfect performance but faithful partnership with God's transforming work in your life. He provides the power; you provide the willingness. He supplies the grace; you supply the consistency. He creates the results; you create the routines that position you to receive His blessings.

Your Next Faithful Step

As you move forward from this chapter, carry with you the 21-day habit foundation system from our practical applications. Choose one keystone habit that aligns with your calling to serve and grow richly. Start ridiculously small, link it to an existing routine, and focus on consistency over perfection for the next three weeks.

Remember, you don't need to transform your entire life overnight. Sustainable change happens one habit at a time, one day at a time, one choice at a time. The person who faithfully builds one service-oriented habit over 21 days is infinitely better positioned to serve others than the person who plans elaborate changes but never begins.

Your assignment is both simple and profound: identify one daily practice that would enhance your capacity to serve others, then commit to it for the next 21 days. Whether it's five minutes of prayer, one daily act of encouragement, or a morning routine that centers your heart on service, begin building the habit that will become the foundation for greater impact.

Looking Ahead

In our next chapter, we'll explore how to discover and live out your unique purpose and meaning. You'll learn how the habits you're building now create the character foundation needed to discern God's specific calling for your life and to pursue it with confidence and clarity.

But for now, embrace the power of small beginnings. Trust that God honors faithful consistency in little things. Believe that your daily choices matter more than you can imagine. And begin building the habits that will transform you into the servant-leader God created you to be.

6

Purpose & Meaning

At the heart of every fulfilling life and enduring legacy is a deep sense of purpose—a reason for being that transcends daily routines and fleeting achievements.

PURPOSE IS WHAT FUELS OUR RESILIENCE IN HARD TIMES, gives meaning to our work, and inspires us to serve beyond ourselves. It is the compass that points us toward a life that is not only successful, but significant.

Finding your purpose is not a one-time event, but an unfolding journey. It often begins with curiosity: What brings you joy? What are you passionate about? What needs in the world tug at your heart? As Jack Canfield suggests, "Your purpose is based on the things you care most about." Sometimes, purpose emerges from our greatest joys, and other times from our deepest pain. By reflecting on the themes and turning points of our lives—moments when we felt most alive, or most needed—we begin to see the unique ways we are called to contribute.

Living with purpose means aligning your daily choices with your deepest values. It is about integrity—letting your actions reflect what truly matters to you. As you clarify your purpose, you'll find it becomes a compass for decision-making, helping you say "yes" to what aligns and "no" to what distracts. This process is not about fitting into someone else's mold, but about discovering your own path and embracing the unique gifts you have to offer.

Service is a powerful gateway to meaning. Volunteering, mentoring, or simply helping a neighbor can reveal passions and strengths you never knew you had. Research shows that serving others not only benefits the community, but also increases our own sense of happiness and longevity. When we give our time and talents generously, we find ourselves woven into a larger story—one where our actions ripple outward, touching lives in ways we may never fully see.

Faith traditions remind us that purpose is both discovered and received. The Bible assures us, "For I know the plans I have for you... plans to give you hope and a future" (Jeremiah 29:11). Sometimes, discovering purpose means quieting the noise, seeking God's guidance, and trusting that even small acts of service have eternal significance. Practicing gratitude for where you are and what you have can open your eyes to the blessings and opportunities already present in your life. As you seek purpose, remember that it is often found not in grand gestures, but in daily faithfulness and a willingness to serve where you are planted.

The Architecture of Divine Purpose

Understanding purpose requires recognizing that it operates on multiple interconnected levels, like the floors of a magnificent building. At the foundation level lies your universal human purpose—to love God and love others as yourself (Matthew 22:37-39). This foundational purpose applies to every person and provides the bedrock for all other purposes. Above this foundation, God builds unique individual purposes that reflect your specific gifts, experiences, circumstances, and calling.

Your individual purpose is not arbitrary or accidental—it's carefully architected by a loving Creator who "formed thee in the belly" and knew you before you were born (Jeremiah 1:5). This means that discovering your purpose is not about creating something from nothing, but about uncovering something that already exists. Like an archaeologist carefully brushing away dirt to reveal ancient treasures, finding your purpose involves removing the layers of others' expectations, cultural pressures, and personal fears to uncover the unique calling God has placed within you.

The third level is your seasonal purpose—the specific ways God wants to use you in your current season of life. A parent's seasonal purpose might center on raising godly children, while maintaining their individual purpose as a teacher, artist, or entrepreneur. A retiree's seasonal purpose might involve mentoring younger generations, while expressing their individual purpose through volunteer service. Understanding that purpose has seasons prevents us from feeling guilty when our focus shifts with life circumstances and helps us embrace the unique opportunities available in each phase.

Finally, there's your situational purpose—the specific ways God wants to use you in particular moments and circumstances. This might be comforting a grieving friend, speaking up for justice in a difficult situation, or simply offering a smile to someone having a bad day. These moment-by-moment purposes often seem small, but they're the daily expression of your larger calling and the means by which your broader purpose touches real lives.

The beauty of this multi-level understanding is that it provides both stability and flexibility. Your foundational purpose never changes, giving you a reliable north star for decision-making. Your individual purpose provides long-term direction and meaning. Your seasonal purpose helps you prioritize and focus your energy appropriately. And your situational purpose keeps you alert to immediate opportunities for service and impact.

The Biblical Framework for Calling and Purpose

Scripture reveals that every believer has been given both a general calling shared with all Christians and a specific calling unique to their individual circumstances and gifts. Understanding this dual nature of calling is crucial for discovering and living out your purpose without falling into either legalism or license.

The general calling of every believer is clearly articulated throughout Scripture: to love God with all your heart, soul, mind, and strength, and to love your neighbor as yourself. This calling includes being salt and light in the world, making disciples of all nations, and living as ambassadors of Christ's kingdom. This general calling applies equally to the CEO and the janitor, the pastor and the plumber, the parent and the single person.

Your specific calling, however, is as unique as your fingerprint. It emerges from the intersection of your gifts, passions, experiences, and opportunities. Paul writes, "For we are his workmanship, created in Christ Jesus unto good works, which God hath before ordained that we should walk in them" (Ephesians 2:10). The "good works" mentioned here are not generic religious activities but specific acts of service that God has prepared beforehand for each individual believer.

This understanding liberates us from trying to copy others' calling while challenging us to discover our own. You don't need to be Billy Graham to have a significant purpose—God may have called you to influence your workplace, neighborhood, or family in ways that are just as important but less visible. The key is faithfulness to your unique calling rather than comparison with others' assignments.

Biblical examples illustrate this beautifully. Nehemiah was called to rebuild walls, Esther to influence government, Daniel to serve in a foreign administration, and the woman at the well to evangelize her community. Each calling was perfectly suited to the individual's gifts, circumstances, and the needs of their time. None was more valuable than the others in God's economy.

The process of discovering your specific calling often involves what the Puritans called "particular faith"—seeking God's specific guidance for your unique circumstances through prayer, Scripture study, wise counsel, and careful attention to how He has gifted and positioned you. This isn't about hearing audible voices or receiving dramatic revelations, but about discerning God's leading through ordinary means of grace.

The Intersection Model: Where Passion Meets Service

One of the most practical frameworks for discovering purpose is what we might call the "intersection model"—finding the sweet spot where your deepest passions, greatest strengths, most significant experiences, and the world's greatest needs come together. This intersection often reveals the unique contribution God has designed you to make.

Your passions are the things that energize and motivate you, the issues that capture your heart and hold your attention. These aren't necessarily your hobbies or entertainment preferences, but the causes, problems, or opportunities that stir something deep within you. For some, it might be education and helping people learn. For others, it could be justice and helping the oppressed. Still others might be passionate about creativity, innovation, or bringing beauty into the world.

Your strengths include both your natural talents and your developed skills. Natural talents are the abilities you seem to have been born with—perhaps you've always been good with numbers, naturally compassionate with hurting people, or gifted at seeing solutions to complex problems. Developed skills are capabilities you've cultivated through education, experience, and practice. The combination of your natural talents and developed skills creates your unique capability profile.

Your experiences include both your successes and your struggles, your joys and your pain. Often, God uses our most difficult experiences to prepare us for our most significant service.

The person who has struggled with addiction may be uniquely qualified to help others find freedom. The parent who has navigated a difficult divorce might be perfectly positioned to support other families in crisis. The entrepreneur who has failed and recovered could be exactly what struggling business owners need.

The world's needs are the problems, challenges, and opportunities that exist in your sphere of influence. This might be your family, workplace, community, or larger society. The key is to pay attention to the needs that particularly capture your attention and concern—the problems that make you think, "Someone should do something about that."

When these four elements—passion, strengths, experiences, and recognized needs—begin to align, you've likely discovered an area where God wants to use you significantly. The intersection might reveal itself suddenly through a dramatic realization, or it might emerge gradually as you gain experience and self-understanding.

The Purpose Paradox:
Losing Your Life to Find It

One of the most counterintuitive aspects of finding purpose is Jesus' teaching that we must lose our life to find it (Matthew 16:25). This paradox reveals that true purpose is never found through self-focused seeking but through self-forgetting service. The more we focus on discovering our purpose for our own satisfaction, the more elusive it becomes. But when we focus on serving others and loving God, purpose often emerges naturally.

This principle challenges our culture's emphasis on "finding yourself" and "following your passion" as starting points for purpose discovery. While self-knowledge and passion are important, they become meaningful only when connected to something larger than ourselves. The person who spends years in introspective self-analysis may never find purpose, while the person who begins serving others often discovers their calling in the process of giving themselves away.

The paradox works because purpose is relational rather than individual. We don't have purpose in isolation—we have purpose in connection with God and others. When we serve others, we discover what we're good at, what energizes us, and what makes a difference. We also begin to see how God has uniquely equipped us for specific types of service.

This doesn't mean we should serve randomly or without thought. Rather, it means we should begin serving somewhere—anywhere—and trust that God will use our experiences of service to reveal and refine our understanding of His specific calling for our lives. The person who volunteers at a homeless shelter might discover a calling to social work. The individual who helps with children's ministry might realize they're meant to be an educator. The business professional who mentors young entrepreneurs might find their purpose in developing the next generation of ethical leaders.

The lose-your-life-to-find-it principle also protects us from the subtle idolatry of making our purpose ultimate. When we serve God through our purpose rather than serving our purpose as god, we remain free to adjust, adapt, and even change direction as He leads. Our identity remains secure in Christ rather than dependent on our achievements or significance.

Purpose in the Ordinary:
The Sanctification of Daily Life

One of the greatest misconceptions about purpose is that it must involve dramatic, highly visible service to be meaningful. This misconception causes many people to undervalue their current circumstances and miss opportunities for significant impact in ordinary settings. The truth is that God often accomplishes His greatest purposes through faithful service in seemingly mundane situations.

Consider the biblical account of Joseph, whose purpose was fulfilled not through seeking a grand destiny but through faithful service in whatever circumstances he found himself—whether as a slave in Potiphar's house, a prisoner in Pharaoh's dungeon, or an administrator in Pharaoh's court. In each situation, Joseph served faithfully and excellently, trusting God to use his circumstances for larger purposes. Only in retrospect could he see how each season prepared him for his ultimate role in preserving his family and nation during famine.

This principle applies powerfully to modern believers. The parent changing diapers and wiping noses is participating in the profound purpose of shaping the next generation. The factory worker maintaining quality standards is contributing to products that serve human needs. The accountant ensuring financial accuracy is participating in the stewardship of resources. The teacher grading papers is investing in human potential. Each role, when performed with integrity and service-mindedness, becomes a ministry and an expression of divine purpose.

The key is approaching ordinary tasks with extraordinary love and excellence. Brother Lawrence, a 17th-century monk, discovered that washing dishes could be as much an act of worship and service as leading public prayer. His secret was "practicing the presence of God" in every activity, treating each task as an opportunity to serve Christ through serving others.

This understanding transforms how we view our current circumstances. Instead of waiting for a "better" situation to begin living purposefully, we can begin living purposefully in our current situation. Instead of seeking more impressive platforms for service, we can serve faithfully on the platforms already available to us. Often, faithful service in small things leads to opportunities for larger service, but even if it doesn't, the service itself is meaningful and pleasing to God.

The Community Dimension of Purpose Discovery

While purpose feels deeply personal, it's rarely discovered or lived out in isolation. Community plays crucial roles in purpose discovery, confirmation, and implementation. Others often see our gifts and calling more clearly than we do, provide opportunities for service that reveal our purpose, and offer the support and accountability needed to pursue our calling faithfully.

Scripture emphasizes the body of Christ metaphor precisely because individual purposes are designed to work together. "For as we have many members in one body, and all members have not the same office: So we, being many, are one body in Christ, and every one members one of another" (Romans 12:4-5). Your purpose is not just about your individual fulfillment—it's about your contribution to the larger body and mission of Christ's church.

Community helps with purpose discovery through what we might call "external confirmation." Others can observe patterns in your life, gifts in your service, and impact in your relationships that you might not notice yourself. They can point out themes in your interests, strengths in your abilities, and effectiveness in your efforts that provide clues about your calling.

Wise mentors and counselors can ask probing questions that help you explore potential purposes: "What activities make you lose track of time?" "When do people most often come to you for help?" "What injustices or needs consistently capture your attention?" "What would you do if you knew you couldn't fail?" "What would you regret not attempting if you knew you only had five years to live?"

Community also provides platforms for purpose exploration and expression. Churches, organizations, and informal networks offer opportunities to try different types of service, develop new skills, and discover what energizes versus drains you. The person unsure about their calling might volunteer in multiple areas to see where they feel most effective and fulfilled.

Perhaps most importantly, community provides the support system needed to pursue purpose consistently. Living purposefully often requires courage, persistence, and sacrifice. Having others who understand and support your calling makes the difference between sustainable pursuit and eventual burnout or abandonment.

The Evolution of Purpose Through Life Seasons

Understanding that purpose evolves through different life seasons prevents frustration and provides hope during times of transition. While your core calling may remain consistent, how you express that calling will change as your circumstances, resources, and opportunities shift throughout life.

The young adult's expression of purpose might focus on preparation—developing skills, building character, exploring interests, and gaining experience that will support later service. This preparation period is not purposeless but rather purposeful in a different way. The medical student studying anatomy is expressing their purpose of healing others, even though they're not yet treating patients.

The established adult's expression of purpose often centers on production—using developed skills and accumulated resources to create maximum impact. This might involve building businesses, raising families, developing organizations, or creating artistic works. This is often the season of highest visibility and measurable achievement.

The mature adult's expression of purpose frequently shifts toward multiplication—investing in others who will carry on important work. This might involve mentoring, teaching, funding others' efforts, or passing on wisdom gained through experience. While production may decrease, influence often increases during this season.

The elderly person's expression of purpose often emphasizes legacy—ensuring that important values, wisdom, and causes continue beyond their lifetime. This might involve writing, storytelling, financial stewardship, or simply modeling faithfulness for younger generations.

Understanding these seasonal shifts helps prevent the common mistake of trying to force one season's expression of purpose into another season's circumstances. The young parent shouldn't feel guilty for having less time for outside ministry while raising small children. The retiree shouldn't feel useless because they can't maintain the pace of their middle-aged productivity. Each season has its appropriate expression of purpose.

The key is remaining alert to how God wants to use you in your current season while preparing for the next season's opportunities. This requires both contentment with present circumstances and wisdom about future preparation.

Purpose and Suffering: Finding Meaning in Pain

One of the most challenging aspects of purpose discovery is understanding how suffering and difficulty fit into God's plan for our lives. Many people struggle to find meaning when circumstances seem to contradict their sense of calling or when pain overshadows their ability to serve effectively.

Scripture reveals that suffering often serves multiple purposes in God's economy. It develops character qualities that enhance our ability to serve others: "And not only so, but we glory in tribulations also: knowing that tribulation worketh patience; And patience, experience; and experience, hope" (Romans 5:3-4). The person who has suffered develops empathy, resilience, and wisdom that become tools for helping others navigate similar difficulties.

Suffering also often redirects our purpose in meaningful ways. The athlete whose career-ending injury leads to coaching others. The business executive whose layoff results in starting a nonprofit. The parent whose child's disability awakens a passion for special needs advocacy. What initially appears to derail purpose often refines and redirects it toward more significant impact.

Perhaps most importantly, suffering teaches us that our ultimate purpose transcends our circumstances. When we can maintain faithfulness and even joy despite difficulty, we demonstrate that our purpose is rooted in something deeper than external success or comfort. This testimony often has greater impact than our achievements during easier seasons.

The key is learning to ask different questions during difficult seasons. Instead of "Why is this happening to me?" we can ask "How might God want to use this experience to develop my character or prepare me for future service?" Instead of "How can I escape this situation?" we can ask "How can I serve and trust God within this situation?"

This doesn't mean we should seek suffering or passively accept preventable hardship. Rather, it means we can find purpose and meaning even when circumstances don't align with our preferences or expectations. The person facing illness can find purpose in modeling faith, the individual experiencing job loss can discover calling in helping others navigate career transitions, and the family dealing with tragedy can minister to others facing similar pain.

PRACTICAL APPLICATIONS
The Purpose Discovery Expedition:
A Comprehensive Self-Assessment

Finding your unique purpose requires intentional exploration of your inner landscape—your values, passions, strengths, experiences, and the needs that stir your heart. The following expedition provides a systematic approach to this discovery process.

Phase 1: Values Archaeology (Week 1). Dig deep to uncover your core values—the fundamental beliefs that drive your decisions and define what matters most to you:

Values Identification Exercise:

- List 10-15 values that resonate with you (integrity, family, justice, creativity, etc.)
- Narrow the list to your top 5 by asking: "If I could only live by five principles, which would they be?"
- For each core value, write a paragraph explaining why it matters to you and how it shows up in your daily life
- Identify moments when compromising these values made you feel empty or conflicted

Values-in-Action Assessment:

- Review your calendar and financial records from the past three months
- Ask: "What do my time and money allocation reveal about my actual values versus

my stated values?"

- Identify gaps between your stated values and your lived values
- Create one specific action step to better align your life with each core value

Phase 2: Passion Mapping (Week 2). Explore the issues, activities, and causes that energize and motivate you:

Energy Audit:

- For one week, track your energy levels throughout each day
- Note which activities, conversations, and experiences increase your energy
- Identify which tasks, people, and situations drain your energy
- Look for patterns in what energizes versus depletes you

Issue Exploration:

- List social, cultural, or personal issues that capture your attention or concern
- For each issue, ask: "What would happen if no one addressed this problem?"
- Identify which issues make you think, "Someone should do something about that"
- Research organizations already working on these issues to understand current efforts

Historical Pattern Analysis:

- Reflect on your childhood dreams and interests
- Identify themes in your volunteer activities over the years
- Review compliments you've received—what do people consistently notice about you?
- Consider problems you naturally try to solve in your family, workplace, or community

Phase 3: Strengths Discovery (Week 3). Identify your unique combination of natural talents and developed skills:

Natural Talents Assessment:

- Ask five people who know you well: "What do you see as my natural strengths?"
- Reflect on activities you learned quickly or found easier than others did
- Consider what people often ask for your help with
- Identify areas where you achieve results with less effort than peers

Skills Inventory:

- List all skills you've developed through education, training, and experience
- Categorize skills as: Expert level, Proficient level, or Developing level
- Identify which skills you most enjoy using
- Consider which skills combinations make you unique

Impact Analysis:

- Review times when you've made a significant positive difference
- Ask: "What combination of strengths enabled that impact?"
- Look for patterns in how your strengths create value for others
- Consider how your strengths might address the issues you're passionate about

Phase 4: Experience Integration (Week 4). Examine how your life experiences—both positive and challenging—have shaped you for unique service:

Story Mapping:

- Identify 5-7 major experiences that significantly shaped who you are today
- For each experience, ask: "How did this develop my character, skills, or perspective?"
- Consider how difficult experiences created empathy for others facing similar challenges
- Look for themes across your experiences that might point toward your calling

Wound-to-Wisdom Transformation:

- Identify your most significant struggles or pain points
- Ask: "How might this experience prepare me to help others facing similar challenges?"
- Consider what insights, strength, or compassion you've gained through difficulty
- Explore how your "mess might become your message"

The Purpose Clarification Workshop

After completing your discovery expedition, use this workshop format to synthesize your insights into a clear purpose statement.

The Intersection Analysis. Create a visual diagram with four overlapping circles representing:

1. What You Love (passions and values)
2. What You're Good At (strengths and skills)
3. What You've Experienced (unique background and perspectives)
4. What the World Needs (problems and opportunities you've identified)

In the center intersection, write potential purposes that incorporate all four elements. This intersection often reveals your unique calling.

Purpose Statement Development. Craft a 2-3 sentence purpose statement using this framework: "I am called to serve [WHO] by providing [WHAT] so that [IMPACT] because [WHY IT MATTERS]."

Example: "I am called to serve struggling entrepreneurs by providing business mentoring and financial guidance so that they can build sustainable, ethical businesses because I believe everyone deserves the opportunity to use their gifts to serve others while providing for their families."

Reality Testing Your Purpose. Before finalizing your purpose statement, test it against these criteria:

- Authenticity: Does this feel true to who you are at your core?
- Energy: Does thinking about this purpose energize or drain you?
- Sustainability: Could you pursue this purpose for decades without burning out?
- Impact: Would pursuing this purpose make a meaningful difference in others' lives?
- Growth: Would living this purpose stretch you to become more than you are today?

Purpose Implementation Strategy

Having clarity about your purpose is only the beginning. Implementation requires strategic planning and consistent action.

The 90-Day Purpose Pilot Program. Instead of making dramatic life changes immediately, test your purpose through a 90-day pilot program:

Days 1-30: Exploration Phase

- Volunteer or engage in activities related to your identified purpose
- Connect with people already working in this area
- Read books and resources about your purpose area
- Keep a journal of insights, energy levels, and impact observations

Days 31-60: Experimentation Phase

- Take on a small project or responsibility related to your purpose
- Seek feedback from others about your effectiveness and fit
- Adjust your understanding based on real-world experience
- Begin building skills or knowledge gaps you've identified

Days 61-90: Evaluation Phase

- Assess whether your purpose statement still feels accurate
- Consider what changes or refinements are needed
- Plan your next steps for deeper engagement
- Decide whether to commit more fully or explore alternative directions

Purpose Integration Planning. Create a plan for gradually integrating your purpose into your current life circumstances:

Immediate Integration (Next 30 days):

- Identify one way to express your purpose in your current job

- Find one volunteer opportunity aligned with your purpose
- Begin one learning activity that develops purpose-related skills
- Connect with one person who shares your purpose passion

Short-term Integration (3-6 months):
- Take on additional responsibilities at work that align with your purpose
- Increase your volunteer commitment or leadership role
- Complete a course or certification related to your purpose
- Build relationships with 3-5 people in your purpose area

Medium-term Integration (6-12 months):
- Consider career moves that better align with your purpose
- Launch a side project or ministry related to your purpose
- Become a mentor or teacher in your purpose area
- Evaluate major life decisions through the lens of your purpose

Long-term Integration (1-3 years):
- Make career or life changes necessary for full purpose expression
- Take on leadership roles in organizations aligned with your purpose
- Create new initiatives or organizations if needed
- Measure your life success by purpose fulfillment rather than conventional metrics

Purpose Accountability and Support Systems

Living purposefully requires ongoing support, accountability, and community. Establish systems that help you stay aligned with your calling.

Purpose Accountability Partnership. Find someone who will help you stay true to your purpose:

- Selection Criteria: Choose someone who shares your values, has demonstrated purposeful living, and cares enough to challenge you lovingly
- Meeting Structure: Meet monthly for 90 minutes to discuss purpose-related goals, challenges, and progress
- Accountability Elements:
    - Share specific purpose-related commitments and deadlines
    - Report on progress and obstacles from the previous month
    - Receive feedback and challenge about alignment between stated purpose and actual choices
    - Pray together for wisdom, courage, and faithfulness

Purpose Advisory Board. Assemble 3-5 people who can provide different perspectives on your purpose journey:

- The Wise Counselor: Someone with life experience who can provide perspective on major decisions
- The Industry Expert: Someone working successfully in your purpose area who can provide practical guidance
- The Spiritual Mentor: Someone who can help you discern God's leading and maintain spiritual grounding
- The Honest Friend: Someone who knows you well and will speak truth about your blind spots
- The Cheerleader: Someone who believes in you unconditionally and encourages you during difficult seasons

Meet with your advisory board quarterly to seek input on major purpose-related decisions and receive perspective on your growth and development.

Purpose Progress Tracking. Develop systems for monitoring your purpose alignment and impact:

Monthly Purpose Review:

- Alignment Assessment: How well did my choices this month align with my stated purpose?
- Impact Evaluation: What difference did I make in my purpose area this month?
- Growth Tracking: How did I develop skills, knowledge, or character related to my purpose?
- Course Correction: What adjustments do I need to make for better purpose alignment?

Annual Purpose Retreat:

- Spend a day or weekend in reflective planning
- Review your purpose statement for continued accuracy and relevance
- Assess progress toward purpose-related goals
- Plan major initiatives or changes for the coming year
- Seek God's guidance for the next season of purpose expression

Overcoming Purpose Implementation Obstacles

Common obstacles can derail purpose pursuit. Develop strategies for overcoming these challenges before they arise.

When Purpose Conflicts with Current Responsibilities

- Look for ways to express your purpose within current roles before assuming you need to leave

- Make gradual transitions rather than sudden dramatic changes
- Seek creative solutions that honor both your purpose and your obligations
- Consider how current responsibilities might be preparing you for future purpose expression

When Others Don't Understand or Support Your Purpose

- Remember that your calling comes from God, not from people's approval
- Share your purpose with those most likely to be supportive
- Let your results speak louder than your explanations
- Maintain humility and openness to legitimate concerns from people who care about you

When Purpose Feels Overwhelming or Impossible

- Break your purpose into smaller, manageable steps
- Focus on faithfulness in small things rather than dramatic impact
- Remember that God equips those He calls
- Seek mentorship from others who have navigated similar callings

When Purpose Seems to Change or Evolve

- Recognize that purpose often becomes clearer through experience
- Distinguish between core calling and specific expressions of that calling
- Allow for seasonal variations in how you express your purpose
- Trust that God can use apparent detours and delays for good purposes

When Purpose Pursuit Feels Selfish

- Remember that pursuing your God-given purpose is an act of stewardship, not selfishness
- Focus on how your purpose serves others rather than just fulfills you
- Maintain balance between purpose pursuit and other responsibilities
- Trust that God created you with specific gifts for specific purposes that benefit His kingdom

CHAPTER CONCLUSION
The Sacred Journey of Becoming

As we reach the end of this exploration of purpose and meaning, it's important to understand the profound transformation that has taken place within you. You haven't simply learned techniques for self-discovery—you've embarked on the sacred journey of becoming who God created you to be. Purpose is not a destination you arrive at, but a path you walk daily, a calling you live out moment by moment, and an identity you grow into through faithful service and surrendered obedience.

The beautiful truth about purpose is that it's both deeply personal and ultimately relational. While your specific calling is uniquely yours, it finds its meaning only in connection with God's larger story and in service to others' needs. You were created not for isolated self-fulfillment but for meaningful contribution to the body of Christ and the broader human community. Your purpose is God's gift to you, but your faithful pursuit of that purpose is your gift back to Him and to those you're called to serve.

Purpose as Daily Worship

Perhaps the most transformative perspective on purpose is understanding that living it out is a form of worship. When you use your God-given gifts to serve others, when you address needs that capture your heart, when you pour your energy into causes that matter eternally, you're not just pursuing personal fulfillment—you're offering your life as a living sacrifice, holy and pleasing to God (Romans 12:1).

This means that your Monday morning work can be as much an act of worship as your Sunday morning praise. The teacher preparing lessons is worshiping through education. The entrepreneur solving problems is worshiping through innovation. The parent raising children is worshiping through nurturing. The artist creating beauty is worshiping through creativity. When our daily activities align with our God-given purpose, ordinary moments become sacred offerings.

This understanding elevates every aspect of purposeful living from duty to devotion. You're not just pursuing goals or fulfilling responsibilities—you're participating in God's ongoing work in the world. You're allowing His love to flow through you to touch others' lives. You're becoming a vessel through which His character and compassion reach a broken world.

The Ripple Effect of Aligned Living

Remember that living aligned with your purpose creates ripple effects far beyond what you can see or measure. When you operate in your sweet spot—using your gifts to address needs you care about—you don't just accomplish tasks, you inspire transformation. Your authenticity gives others permission to be authentic. Your purposefulness challenges others to examine their own calling. Your faithful service models what it looks like to live with meaning and intention.

Years from now, people may not remember all the specific things you accomplished, but they will remember how your purposeful living affected them. They'll recall how your passion inspired their own sense of calling. They'll remember how your authenticity encouraged them to stop pretending and start being real. They'll treasure how your faithful service showed them what love looks like in action.

This ripple effect means that discovering and living your purpose is never just about you. It's about the chain reaction of meaning and inspiration that flows through your faithful obedience to God's calling. You become a link in the great chain of purpose that stretches from generation to generation, connecting God's heart to human need through willing servants who say yes to their calling.

Purpose in Every Season

As you continue forward, remember that purpose is not dependent on perfect circumstances or ideal timing. God wants to use you right where you are, with what you have, in your current season of life. The young adult still discovering their gifts has a purpose. The busy parent juggling multiple responsibilities has a purpose. The professional climbing the career ladder has a purpose. The retiree with newfound freedom has a purpose. The person facing health challenges has a purpose.

Your purpose may be expressed differently in different seasons, but it never disappears. Sometimes it's highly visible and dramatically impactful. Other times it's quiet and seemingly small. Both expressions matter equally to God and to those you're called to serve. The key is remaining alert to how He wants to use you in each season while being faithful with the opportunities currently available.

This seasonal understanding prevents the frustration that comes from trying to force one season's expression of purpose into another season's circumstances. It also provides hope during difficult seasons when purpose feels unclear or impossible to pursue. God hasn't forgotten about you, and He hasn't withdrawn your calling. He's simply asking you to trust Him with the timing and methods of your purpose expression.

Your Purpose Assignment

As you move forward from this chapter, carry with you the Purpose Discovery Expedition from our practical applications. Commit to completing all four phases over the next month, treating this not as an academic exercise but as a spiritual journey of seeking God's heart for your life.

Begin with Phase 1 this week—the Values Archaeology. Set aside time to honestly examine what matters most to you and how those values should shape your choices. Remember, this is not about finding the "right" answers but about discovering your authentic answers. God wants to use the real you, not the version of you that you think He should want.

As you work through this process, remain open to surprises. God often calls us to purposes that don't match our initial expectations or preferences. The person who thought they were meant for business might discover they're called to education. The individual who expected to serve through direct ministry might find their calling in marketplace influence. Trust the process and trust the God who created you with specific purposes in mind.

Looking Ahead

In our next chapter, we'll explore how to discover and embrace your authentic identity as the foundation for purposeful living. You'll learn how understanding who you are in God's eyes empowers you to pursue your calling with confidence and authenticity.

But for now, embrace the adventure of purpose discovery. Trust that the God who called you before you were born has also prepared good works for you to walk in (Ephesians 2:10). Believe that your unique combination of gifts, experiences, and passions is not accidental but intentional. And begin living as if your life has profound meaning and purpose—because it does.

7

Self-Discovery & Identity

*True service and authentic growth begin with
knowing who you are at your core.*

IN A WORLD THAT CONSTANTLY URGES US TO FIT IN, self-discovery is a courageous act—a journey inward to uncover your unique strengths, values, and purpose. This journey is not about constructing a new identity, but about peeling away the layers of expectation, fear, and old stories to reveal the person you were always meant to be.

Self-discovery is deeply personal and transformative. It invites you to explore your true nature, purpose, and innermost desires, and to live in alignment with your deepest values. For many, this process is intertwined with spirituality—a connection to something greater than ourselves, whether that's God, a higher power, or the wisdom of our own hearts. Practices like meditation, prayer, and journaling can help quiet the noise of daily life, allowing you to listen for the still, small voice within. As you cultivate mindfulness and presence, you gain insight into your thoughts, beliefs, and emotional patterns—some of which may be holding you back from your fullest potential.

Faith traditions remind us that our true identity is not found in what we do or what others say about us, but in our relationship with the divine. The Bible encourages us to "examine yourselves, whether ye be in the faith; prove your own selves" (2 Corinthians 13:5). Self-awareness, then, is not only about understanding our strengths and weaknesses, but about recognizing the image of God within us and seeking to align our lives with His purpose. As we draw near to God—through His Word, His Spirit, and His people—we are transformed, becoming more like Christ and more fully ourselves.

The journey of self-discovery is ongoing. It is marked by moments of clarity and periods of uncertainty, by the shedding of old identities and the emergence of something truer and freer. Along the way, you may find that your greatest gifts are often hidden beneath your deepest wounds, and that embracing your authentic self is the key to serving others with compassion and courage. When you know who you are, you can give from a place of abundance rather than striving for approval or validation.

The Architecture of Identity: Understanding Your Multi-Layered Self

Identity is not a single, monolithic concept but rather a complex architecture with multiple interconnected layers. Understanding these layers helps us navigate the sometimes confusing process of self-discovery and provides a framework for authentic living. Like an archaeological dig, we must carefully excavate each layer to understand how they work together to form our complete identity.

The foundational layer is your core identity—who you are in God's eyes. This layer includes your status as His beloved child, created in His image, with inherent worth and dignity that nothing can diminish. This identity transcends your performance, achievements, failures, or circumstances. It's the bedrock truth that "you are a chosen generation, a royal priesthood, an holy nation, a peculiar people" (1 Peter 2:9). This core identity provides security and stability that enables healthy exploration of other identity layers.

The second layer is your designed identity—the unique combination of temperament, gifts, and inclinations that God has woven into your being. This includes your personality type, natural talents, learning style, and emotional patterns. Some people are naturally analytical while others are intuitive. Some thrive in crowds while others prefer solitude. Some are energized by variety while others flourish with routine. Understanding your designed identity helps you work with your nature rather than against it.

The third layer is your developed identity—the skills, knowledge, experiences, and character qualities you've cultivated over time. This includes your education, career expertise, life lessons learned, relationships formed, and wisdom gained through both successes and failures. Your developed identity is malleable and continues evolving throughout your life as you grow and learn.

The fourth layer is your declared identity—the roles, commitments, and values you consciously choose to embrace. This includes your career choices, relationship commitments, lifestyle decisions, and the causes you champion. While influenced by your other identity layers, your declared identity represents the conscious choices you make about how to live and what to prioritize.

The fifth layer is your displayed identity—how others perceive you based on your words, actions, and presence. This may or may not align perfectly with your other identity layers. Sometimes there are gaps between who you are internally and how you're perceived externally, which can provide valuable feedback about areas for growth or better communication.

Understanding these layers prevents the common mistake of trying to find your "one true self." Instead, you recognize that identity is multifaceted and dynamic while still being fundamentally rooted in unchanging truths about your worth and calling in Christ.

The Biblical Foundation of Human Identity

Scripture provides the most reliable foundation for understanding human identity because it reveals both our original design and our ultimate destiny. The biblical account of human creation establishes truths about identity that transcend cultural shifts and personal circumstances.

The foundational truth is that humans are created "in the image of God" (Genesis 1:27). This image-bearing nature means that every person possesses inherent dignity, worth, and significance that cannot be earned or lost. You matter not because of what you do but because of whose you are. This understanding liberates us from the exhausting pursuit of proving our worth through performance and frees us to discover our authentic selves.

The image of God in humanity is reflected in several key capacities: the ability to reason and make moral choices, the capacity for relationship and love, the inclination toward creativity and beauty, and the longing for meaning and purpose. These capacities are not distributed equally among all people, but they exist in some measure in every person, creating the foundation for both self-worth and respect for others.

Scripture also reveals that human identity was damaged but not destroyed by the fall. Sin affects every aspect of human nature, creating internal conflicts, relational breakdowns, and spiritual separation from God. This explains why self-discovery is often difficult and why we sometimes struggle to understand or accept ourselves. We are simultaneously "fearfully and wonderfully made" (Psalm 139:14) and in need of redemption and transformation.

The gospel provides the pathway to restored identity. Through Christ, we become "new creatures" (2 Corinthians 5:17) while remaining the unique individuals God originally created us to be. Salvation doesn't erase our personality or replace our fundamental design—it redeems and redirects them toward their intended purposes. The introverted person doesn't become extroverted through salvation, but their introversion is sanctified and used for God's glory.

This biblical understanding prevents both the pride that comes from thinking we are self-made and the despair that comes from thinking we are worthless. We are valuable because God made us, fallen because we chose rebellion, and redeemable because Christ died for us. This framework provides both realistic assessment of our current condition and hopeful anticipation of our ultimate transformation.

The Enneagram and Other Tools: Maps for the Journey Inward

While Scripture provides the theological foundation for understanding identity, various psychological and personality assessment tools can serve as helpful maps for the journey of self-discovery. These tools are not infallible or comprehensive, but they can provide valuable insights when used within a biblical framework.

The Enneagram, in particular, has gained popularity among Christians because it addresses not just what people do but why they do it—the underlying motivations, fears, and desires that drive behavior. Unlike some personality systems that focus primarily on preferences and tendencies, the Enneagram explores the deeper emotional and spiritual dynamics that shape how we see ourselves, others, and the world.

The nine Enneagram types each represent a different strategy for navigating life's challenges and finding security, significance, and connection. The Reformer seeks perfection and rightness, the Helper seeks love through serving others, the Achiever seeks worth through success, and so on. Understanding your type can illuminate both your strengths and your blind spots, your gifts and your growing edges.

What makes the Enneagram particularly valuable for Christians is its emphasis on transformation and growth. Each type has a direction of movement toward health (integration) and toward stress (disintegration). The healthy version of each type reflects qualities that mirror the character of Christ, while the unhealthy versions reveal how our fundamental motivations can become distorted when not surrendered to God.

Other assessment tools can also provide valuable insights. The Myers-Briggs Type Indicator explores how you prefer to take in information and make decisions. StrengthsFinder identifies your natural talents and how to develop them. The DISC assessment examines your behavioral style and communication preferences. Each tool offers a different lens through which to understand yourself.

The key is to use these tools as starting points for deeper reflection rather than as definitive declarations of who you are. They can highlight patterns you might not have noticed, provide vocabulary for describing your inner experience, and suggest areas for development. But they should never become boxes that limit your growth or excuses for staying stuck in unhealthy patterns.

The Shadow Self: Integrating Your Dark and Light

One of the most challenging aspects of authentic self-discovery is acknowledging and integrating what Carl Jung called the "shadow self"—the parts of ourselves that we've rejected, denied, or hidden because they don't align with our idealized self-image. For Christians, this includes recognizing the ongoing reality of sin in our lives while maintaining confidence in our identity as beloved children of God.

The shadow often contains not only our moral failures and character flaws but also positive qualities that we've suppressed because they didn't fit family expectations, cultural norms, or religious environments. The naturally assertive person raised in a context that valued compliance might have buried their leadership gifts. The creative individual in a highly analytical family might have learned to hide their artistic inclinations. The emotionally sensitive person in a stoic environment might have developed shame around their empathy.

Scripture acknowledges this inner complexity. Paul wrote about the internal conflict between his desires to do good and his tendency toward sin (Romans 7:15-25). These biblical examples normalize the experience of internal contradiction and provide hope that God can use flawed people for His purposes.

Healthy shadow integration involves several key practices. First, developing self-compassion that allows you to acknowledge your flaws without being crushed by shame. Second, practicing honest self-examination that neither minimizes sin nor maximizes condemnation. Third, seeking accountability relationships where you can be known fully and loved completely. Fourth, learning to distinguish between temptation and identity—recognizing that experiencing wrong desires doesn't make you a wrong person.

The goal is not to eliminate your shadow but to transform it through God's grace. The individual who battles pride might find that their drive for excellence can serve others when properly directed. The person dealing with fear might realize that their cautious nature provides valuable wisdom for protecting others.

This integration process often reveals that our greatest strengths and our greatest weaknesses are closely related. The gift and the wound, the strength and the struggle, often spring from the same source. Understanding this connection helps us develop humility about our strengths and hope about our weaknesses.

Identity vs. Role:
Distinguishing Who You Are from What You Do

One of the most common sources of identity confusion in our achievement-oriented culture is the conflation of identity with role. We begin to believe that we are what we do—I am a teacher, I am a parent, I am an entrepreneur—rather than understanding that these are roles we play as expressions of who we are at a deeper level.

This confusion becomes problematic when roles change, as they inevitably do throughout life. The parent whose children leave home, the professional who loses their job, the athlete who suffers a career-ending injury, or the volunteer whose service opportunities disappear can experience profound identity crises if they've built their sense of self primarily on their roles.

Biblical examples illustrate the difference between identity and role beautifully. David was a shepherd, a warrior, a fugitive, and a king, but his core identity remained "a man after God's own heart" regardless of his circumstances. Paul was a Pharisee, a persecutor, an apostle, and a prisoner, but his foundational identity was as one who was "called to be an apostle of Jesus Christ through the will of God" (1 Corinthians 1:1).

Understanding this distinction provides both freedom and responsibility. Freedom because you're not trapped by your current roles or limited by others' expectations of what those roles should look like. You can be an unconventional teacher, an innovative parent, or an entrepreneurial employee because your role expression flows from your unique identity rather than conforming to external templates.

The distinction also provides responsibility because it means you must actively choose how to express your identity through your roles. The person whose core identity includes creativity has the responsibility to find ways to express that creativity whether they're working as an accountant, serving as a parent, or volunteering in their community. The individual whose identity includes a heart for justice must find appropriate ways to advocate for fairness in whatever roles they occupy.

This understanding also helps explain why some people seem to thrive in roles that others find draining. The role aligns with their deeper identity, allowing them to be authentic while serving. When there's misalignment between identity and role, even successful performance often feels hollow and unsustainable.

The key is learning to ask not just "What roles should I play?" but "How can I express my authentic identity through the roles available to me?" This question transforms role selection from external conformity to internal congruence.

The Wounded Healer:
How Pain Becomes Purpose

One of the most profound aspects of authentic self-discovery is recognizing how our deepest wounds often point toward our greatest calling. Henri Nouwen's concept of the "wounded healer" suggests that our pain, when processed and redeemed, becomes the source of our most authentic and effective service to others.

This principle appears throughout Scripture. Joseph's experience of betrayal and imprisonment prepared him to serve Egypt and preserve his family during famine. Moses' experience as an outsider in two cultures positioned him to lead the Israelites from slavery to freedom. David's experience of being hunted and persecuted equipped him to comfort others who felt abandoned and afraid. Paul's experience of religious zealotry and subsequent transformation gave him unique credibility in reaching both Jews and Gentiles.

The wounded healer principle works because shared suffering creates connection and credibility that can't be manufactured. The person who has struggled with addiction has instant rapport with others facing similar battles. The parent who has lost a child can offer comfort to other grieving families in ways that well-meaning but unexperienced people cannot. The individual who has overcome poverty understands the psychological and practical challenges facing the economically disadvantaged.

However, wounds don't automatically become healing tools. Pain must be processed, lessons must be learned, and healing must occur before wounds can serve others constructively. The person still drowning in their own pain is not yet ready to rescue others. The individual consumed by bitterness about their past experiences may hurt rather than help those facing similar challenges.

The transformation process typically involves several stages. First, acknowledging the reality and impact of the wound without minimizing or dramatizing it. Second, seeking healing through prayer, counseling, community support, or other appropriate means. Third, extracting lessons and wisdom from the experience. Fourth, gradually beginning to share insights and support with others facing similar challenges.

This process is not linear or quick. Some wounds require years of processing before they can serve others constructively. Some experiences are so significant that they create lifelong themes in our service calling. The key is remaining open to how God might use our pain for others' good while not rushing the process or forcing premature ministry.

The wounded healer concept also provides comfort during difficult seasons. When we're experiencing pain, confusion, or loss, we can trust that God wastes nothing in His economy. The current struggle that feels meaningless may become the foundation for future ministry. The present confusion that seems pointless may develop wisdom that others desperately need.

Authenticity vs. Perfection: Embracing Your Humanity

In Christian circles, there's often confusion between authenticity and perfection, leading some people to believe that being "real" means accepting sinful patterns or that growing in holiness requires hiding their struggles. True authenticity involves honest acknowledgment of both your beauty and your brokenness, your gifts and your limitations, your progress and your ongoing need for grace.

Jesus modeled this balance perfectly. He was without sin yet openly experienced and expressed the full range of human emotions. He was confident in His identity and mission yet vulnerable about His struggles, asking for support in prayer. His authenticity enhanced rather than undermined His effectiveness in ministry.

Authentic self-discovery requires what Brené Brown calls "vulnerable courage"—the willingness to be seen and known even when you can't control the outcome. This means acknowledging your mistakes without being defined by them, sharing your struggles without being consumed by shame, and celebrating your gifts without falling into pride.

This kind of authenticity is attractive and inspiring to others because it creates permission for them to be real as well. When you stop pretending to have it all together, others feel free to drop their masks. When you share how God is working in your imperfect life, others gain hope that He can work in theirs. When you demonstrate that spiritual maturity includes ongoing growth rather than arrival at perfection, others are encouraged to continue their own journey.

Practical authenticity involves several key practices. First, developing accurate self-awareness that neither inflates your strengths nor ignores your growth areas. Second, practicing appropriate vulnerability that shares honestly without oversharing inappropriately. Third, maintaining accountability relationships where you can be known and loved completely. Fourth, learning to receive feedback and correction as gifts rather than attacks.

The goal is not to become perfect but to become real—the unique person God created you to be, growing increasingly into His likeness while remaining authentically yourself. This kind of authenticity becomes a gift to others and a testimony to God's transforming grace.

The Integration Process: Becoming Whole

True self-discovery culminates not in endless analysis but in integration—bringing together all aspects of yourself into a coherent, authentic way of living. This integration process involves accepting your complexity, aligning your choices with your values, and expressing your authentic self through your daily decisions and relationships.

Integration requires what Richard Rohr calls "both/and" thinking rather than "either/or" thinking. You can be both confident and humble, both strong and gentle, both direct and compassionate. You don't have to choose between being spiritual or practical, creative or analytical, independent or collaborative. Healthy integration embraces the full spectrum of human capacity while maintaining coherence around core values and identity.

The integration process often involves reconciling apparent contradictions within yourself. The person who values both excellence and grace must learn to pursue high standards without becoming perfectionistic. The individual who prizes both independence and community must find ways to maintain autonomy while building meaningful connections. The person who embraces both truth and love must learn to speak honestly while remaining compassionate.

Scripture models this kind of integration through the concept of the fruit of the Spirit (Galatians 5:22-23). Love, joy, peace, patience, kindness, goodness, faithfulness, gentleness, and self-control are not competing virtues but complementary aspects of Christ-like character. A person can be simultaneously joyful and patient, kind and truthful, gentle and strong.

Practical integration involves making choices that honor your authentic self while serving others effectively. This might mean choosing career paths that utilize your gifts while addressing needs you care about. It could involve building relationships that allow you to be fully known while encouraging others' growth. It often requires saying no to opportunities that don't align with your values and yes to challenges that stretch you in healthy directions.

The ultimate goal of integration is becoming what Dallas Willard called a "complete person"—someone whose inner life and outer expression are aligned, whose private character and public persona are consistent, and whose natural gifts and spiritual calling work together harmoniously. This kind of wholeness becomes a blessing to others and a source of deep satisfaction and peace.

PRACTICAL APPLICATIONS
The Identity Excavation Process: Uncovering Your Authentic Self

Self-discovery requires intentional excavation of the layers of identity that have been built up over time. This process involves both removing false constructs and uncovering authentic truths about who you are at your core.

Layer 1: The False Self Inventory. Begin by identifying aspects of your current identity that may be built on external expectations rather than internal authenticity:

Family Messages Audit:

- What spoken and unspoken messages did you receive about who you should be?
- Which family expectations do you still carry that may not align with your authentic self?
- What family roles did you adopt (the responsible one, the peacemaker, the achiever) that may be limiting your full expression?
- How do family dynamics still influence your identity choices today?

Cultural Conformity Assessment:

- What cultural definitions of success have you unconsciously adopted?
- Which societal expectations about your gender, age, or background feel restrictive?
- How has your professional environment shaped your identity in ways that may not be authentic?
- What "shoulds" do you carry that come from external sources rather than internal conviction?

Performance-Based Identity Recognition:

- In what areas do you feel you must perform to maintain others' approval?
- Where do you experience anxiety about not meeting expectations?
- How do you react when you fail or make mistakes in different areas of life?
- What achievements or roles feel most central to your sense of worth?

Layer 2: The Core Values Clarification. Distinguish between adopted values and authentic values through deep reflection:

Values Origin Analysis: For each value you identify as important, ask:

- Did I choose this value or inherit it from others?
- Does living this value energize me or drain me?
- How does this value show up in my daily choices and priorities?
- What happens inside me when this value is violated or honored?

Values Conflict Exploration:

- Which values do I hold that sometimes conflict with each other?
- How do I typically resolve these conflicts?
- What does my resolution pattern reveal about my deepest priorities?
- Are there values I claim to hold but don't actually live by?

Values Integration Exercise:

- Choose your top 5 core values and write a paragraph about why each matters to you
- Identify one specific way you could better express each value in your current circumstances
- Consider how these values could work together rather than compete with each other
- Plan one major life decision using these values as your primary filter

The Personality and Temperament Assessment Journey

Understanding your natural temperament and personality patterns provides crucial insight into how God has uniquely designed you for specific types of service and relationships.

Multi-Tool Assessment Approach. Take several different personality assessments and look for patterns across the results:

Recommended Assessments:

- Enneagram: Focus on motivations and fears that drive behavior
- Myers-Briggs Type Indicator (MBTI): Explore how you prefer to take in information and make decisions
- StrengthsFinder: Identify your top natural talents and how to develop them
- DISC: Understand your behavioral style and communication preferences
- Big Five Personality Traits: Examine openness, conscientiousness, extraversion, agreeableness, and neuroticism

Pattern Recognition Process:

- What themes appear across multiple assessments?
- Which results surprise you, and which confirm what you already suspected?
- How do these insights help explain past successes and struggles?
- What do these patterns suggest about optimal environments and relationships for you?

Integration and Application:

- How can you leverage your natural strengths more effectively?
- What growth areas do the assessments highlight?
- How might your personality type express itself differently in various life seasons?
- What does this understanding suggest about your calling and service opportunities?

The Life Story Analysis Method

Your personal history contains valuable clues about your authentic identity and calling. This analysis helps you identify patterns, themes, and turning points that reveal who you really are.

Timeline Construction. Create a visual timeline of your life including:

- Peak Experiences: Moments when you felt most alive, authentic, and effective
- Valley Experiences: Times of struggle, loss, or significant challenge
- Turning Points: Decisions or events that significantly changed your direction
- Recurring Themes: Patterns that appear repeatedly throughout different life seasons
- Unexpected Discoveries: Times when you surprised yourself or others

Story Pattern Analysis. Look for recurring themes across your life story:

Strengths Patterns:
- When have you been most effective and impactful?
- What kinds of problems do you naturally solve or challenges do you tackle?
- What do people consistently come to you for help with?
- In what situations do you feel confident and capable?

Values Patterns:
- When have you felt most fulfilled and satisfied?
- What injustices or needs consistently capture your attention?
- What causes are you willing to sacrifice for?
- What achievements feel most meaningful versus those that feel empty?

Growth Patterns:
- What kinds of challenges stretch you in healthy ways?
- How do you typically respond to change and uncertainty?
- What feedback do you receive consistently from others?
- Where do you see the most transformation in your character over time?

Calling Clues Discovery:
- What childhood dreams or interests keep resurfacing?
- What would you do if you knew you couldn't fail?
- What problems in the world make you think, "Someone should do something about that"?
- If you had unlimited resources, how would you spend your time serving others?

The Shadow Work Integration Process

Healthy self-discovery requires acknowledging and integrating the parts of yourself that you've rejected or hidden. This process should be approached with prayer, grace, and ideally with professional or pastoral support.

Shadow Recognition Exercises

Projection Identification:

- What qualities in others consistently irritate or trigger you?
- What do you judge most harshly in other people?
- What do you find yourself defending against even when not accused?
- These reactions often point to disowned aspects of yourself

Family Shadow Exploration:

- What qualities were discouraged or criticized in your family of origin?
- What parts of yourself did you learn to hide to gain approval?
- Which family members' traits do you most want to avoid, and how might you have overcorrected?
- What positive qualities were you told to suppress (assertiveness, creativity, sensitivity)?

Perfectionism and Shame Audit:

- What aspects of yourself do you work hardest to hide from others?
- Where do you experience shame versus healthy conviction?
- What would happen if others knew your struggles, fears, or imperfections?
- How does perfectionism limit your authenticity and growth?

Shadow Integration Practices

Compassionate Self-Awareness:

- Practice acknowledging your flaws without condemning yourself
- Distinguish between your behavior and your identity ("I made a mistake" vs. "I am a mistake")
- Develop language for discussing your struggles that includes both responsibility and grace
- Learn to receive feedback as information rather than attack

Redemptive Reframing:

- How might your greatest weakness be related to your greatest strength?
- What positive motivations might underlie negative behaviors?
- How could your struggles prepare you to help others facing similar challenges?
- What character qualities might God be developing through your imperfections?

Accountability and Vulnerability:

- Identify safe relationships where you can practice being fully known

- Share your struggles and growth areas with trusted friends or mentors
- Ask for specific prayer and support in areas where you're working on growth
- Practice receiving love and acceptance despite your imperfections

The Daily Identity Practices: Living from Your True Self

Knowing your authentic identity is only valuable if it translates into daily living. These practices help you gradually align your choices and behaviors with your discovered identity.

Morning Identity Affirmation Routine. Begin each day by reminding yourself of core identity truths:

- "I am God's beloved child, created with intention and purpose"
- "I am uniquely gifted to serve in ways that only I can provide"
- "I am both beautifully made and continually growing"
- "My worth comes from God's love, not my performance"
- Add personal affirmations based on your specific identity discoveries

Decision-Making Identity Filter. Before making significant decisions, ask:

- Does this choice align with my core values and identity?
- Will this opportunity allow me to express my authentic self?
- How does this decision serve my calling to love God and others?
- What would my truest, most integrated self choose in this situation?

Weekly Identity Alignment Review. Every Sunday, spend 30 minutes reflecting on the past week:

- When did I feel most authentic and alive this week?
- What situations or relationships brought out my best self?
- Where did I compromise my values or authentic identity?
- How can I better align my choices with my true self in the coming week?
- What adjustments do I need to make in my schedule, relationships, or commitments?

Monthly Identity Development Planning. Once monthly, assess your growth in authentic living:

- What aspects of my identity am I expressing well?
- What parts of my authentic self need more development or expression?
- Are there areas where I'm still living from others' expectations rather than my own values?
- What opportunities exist for greater integration and authenticity?

- How is my understanding of my identity evolving and deepening?

Building Your Identity Support System

Authentic self-discovery and expression require supportive relationships that encourage your growth and accept your authenticity.

Identity Witnesses. Identify people who see and affirm your authentic self:

- The Mirror: Someone who reflects back what they see in you, helping you recognize your gifts and growth
- The Challenger: Someone who lovingly confronts you when you're not living authentically
- The Cheerleader: Someone who celebrates your growth and encourages you during difficult seasons
- The Wise Counselor: Someone with experience who can provide perspective on your journey
- The Fellow Traveler: Someone on a similar path who can provide mutual support and accountability

Creating Safe Spaces. Develop environments where you can practice authenticity:

- Join or create small groups focused on spiritual growth and authentic community
- Seek counseling or spiritual direction to explore identity issues in a safe setting
- Find mentoring relationships where you can be honest about your struggles and growth
- Participate in support groups related to specific challenges you're facing

Boundary Development. Learn to protect your authentic self while remaining appropriately vulnerable:

- Identify relationships and environments that consistently pressure you to be inauthentic
- Practice saying no to opportunities that conflict with your values or drain your authentic expression
- Develop scripts for handling questions or expectations that feel invasive or inappropriate
- Learn to share appropriately without oversharing or undersharing

Community Integration. Find ways to contribute your authentic gifts to your community:

- Volunteer in areas that utilize your natural strengths and passions
- Offer to teach or mentor others in areas where you have expertise or experience
- Participate in causes that align with your values and calling
- Share your story and insights with others who might benefit from your journey

This comprehensive approach to self-discovery and identity development provides both the introspective work needed for authentic self-knowledge and the practical applications necessary for living from your true self in daily life.

CHAPTER CONCLUSION
The Beautiful Journey Home to Yourself

As we conclude this exploration of self-discovery and identity, it's important to recognize what you've just experienced: not the creation of a new self, but the uncovering of the person God always intended you to be. Self-discovery is not about reinventing yourself or conforming to someone else's template—it's about coming home to your authentic self, the unique individual lovingly crafted by your Creator with specific gifts, purposes, and capacities for service.

The beautiful paradox of Christian self-discovery is that the more you understand who you truly are, the more you reflect who God is. As you embrace your authentic design, develop your unique gifts, and live from your genuine values, you become a clearer reflection of the Creator who made you in His image. Your authenticity becomes a form of worship, declaring that God's creative work in you is "fearfully and wonderfully made" (Psalm 139:14).

Identity as Foundation for Service

Perhaps the most liberating truth about authentic self-discovery is that it enhances rather than hinders your ability to serve others effectively. When you know who you are—your strengths and limitations, your passions and callings, your gifts and growing edges—you can serve from a place of authenticity rather than striving. You can offer your genuine gifts rather than trying to be someone you're not. You can contribute from your overflow rather than your emptiness.

This authentic foundation makes your service more sustainable and impactful. People are drawn to authenticity because it gives them permission to be real themselves. When you stop pretending to be perfect and start being genuine, others feel safe to drop their masks as well. When you serve from your true strengths rather than from obligation or comparison, your impact multiplies because you're operating in your sweet spot.

Your journey of self-discovery also increases your capacity for compassion and understanding. As you learn to accept your own complexity and extend grace to yourself for your imperfections, you naturally become more patient and understanding with others' struggles. The person who has faced their own shadow can sit with others in their darkness without judgment or fear.

The Ongoing Nature of Identity Development

Remember that self-discovery is not a destination but a lifelong journey. Your understanding of yourself will continue to deepen and evolve as you gain new experiences, face fresh challenges, and encounter different seasons of life. The person you are at twenty-five is the same core individual as the person you'll be at sixty-five, but your expression of that identity will mature, develop, and hopefully become more integrated over time.

This understanding provides both comfort and challenge. Comfort because you don't have to figure everything out immediately or achieve perfect self-knowledge before you can begin living authentically. Challenge because growth never stops, and there will always be new layers to discover, new integration to achieve, and new aspects of yourself to develop.

Each season of life offers new opportunities for self-discovery. Young adulthood often focuses on exploring possibilities and testing different expressions of identity. Middle age frequently involves integrating various aspects of yourself and accepting both your strengths and limitations. Later life often brings opportunities for wisdom-sharing and legacy-building that reveal new dimensions of purpose and meaning.

The key is remaining curious about yourself while accepting yourself, staying open to growth while appreciating who you are right now, and continuing to explore new facets of your identity while maintaining confidence in your core worth and calling.

Your Identity as Gift to Others

As you continue your journey of self-discovery, remember that your authentic identity is not just a personal treasure but a gift you offer to the world. When you live from your true self, you give others something they cannot get from anyone else—your unique perspective, your particular gifts, your specific experiences, and your distinctive way of reflecting God's character.

The world needs who you really are, not who you think you should be or who others expect you to be. Your authentic identity fills a space in God's kingdom that no one else can fill. Your genuine gifts meet needs that others cannot meet in quite the same way. Your real story encourages and inspires people that polished presentations cannot reach.

This understanding transforms self-discovery from self-indulgence into service preparation. You're not exploring your identity for your own satisfaction but to better understand how God wants to use your unique design for His purposes and others' good. You're not developing authenticity for personal fulfillment but to become a more effective instrument of His love and grace in the world.

Your Next Step in Becoming

As you move forward from this chapter, carry with you the Identity Excavation Process from our practical applications. Begin with the False Self Inventory this week, honestly examining which aspects of your current identity may be built on external expectations rather than internal authenticity. Approach this not as harsh self-criticism but as loving archaeological work, gently brushing away what doesn't belong to reveal the authentic treasures beneath.

Remember that this process requires both courage and grace—courage to face what you discover about yourself and grace to accept your humanity while continuing to grow. You don't need to condemn yourself for the masks you've worn or the expectations you've accepted. Simply acknowledge them and begin the gentle work of aligning your life more closely with your authentic self.

Looking Ahead

In our next chapter, we'll explore how to embrace change and growth as natural expressions of your authentic identity. You'll discover that understanding who you are provides the foundation for becoming who God is calling you to be, and that growth and authenticity work together rather than in opposition.

But for now, celebrate the courage it takes to look honestly at yourself and the grace that makes authentic living possible. Trust that the God who created you with such intention and care will guide your journey of discovery and support your growth in authenticity.

8

Change & Growth

Change is the soil in which growth takes root.

WHILE MANY OF US CRAVE STABILITY AND PREDICTABILITY, the truth is that transformation—both personal and professional—requires us to embrace change, not resist it. Growth is rarely comfortable, but it is always worthwhile. Whether you are navigating a career transition, deepening your faith, or simply seeking to become a better version of yourself, every step forward begins with a willingness to let go of the familiar and step into the new.

The world's most resilient leaders and fulfilled individuals are not those who avoid change, but those who learn to welcome it as a teacher. They recognize that every new challenge, every unexpected turn, is an invitation to expand their perspective, skills, and capacity to serve. As Wayne Stiles writes, "Transformation happens when we choose to wait on God instead of pushing our own agenda". It's in the moments of uncertainty—when our plans are disrupted or our comfort zones are stretched—that we discover what we are truly capable of.

Spiritual growth, much like professional development, is a process of continual renewal. The Bible urges us, "Be transformed by the renewing of your mind" (Romans 12:2). This transformation is not just about gaining new knowledge, but about allowing the truths we learn to shape our hearts, decisions, and relationships. Habits like prayer, worship, reflection, and serving others create space for God's Spirit to work in us, molding us into people who reflect His love and wisdom. As we grow, we become more patient, compassionate, and generous—qualities that enrich not only our own lives, but also the lives of those we serve.

Change also requires humility and trust. Sometimes, the path to growth leads through seasons of uncertainty or loss. In these moments, faith reminds us that God's plans for us are good, even when we cannot see the outcome (Jeremiah 29:11). By surrendering our need for control and opening ourselves to God's guidance, we allow Him to shape us for greater purpose. As we serve others—whether through acts of kindness, mentorship, or simply showing up with a listening ear—we find that our own hearts are transformed in the process.

The Nature of Transformational Change

Understanding the difference between superficial change and transformational change is crucial for anyone seeking authentic growth. Superficial change involves modifying behaviors, circumstances, or external conditions without addressing underlying beliefs, values, or identity. Transformational change, however, involves fundamental shifts in how we see ourselves, others, and the world around us—changes that naturally result in new behaviors, different choices, and altered trajectories.

Transformational change operates at multiple levels simultaneously. At the cognitive level, it involves new ways of thinking, updated mental models, and expanded perspectives. At the emotional level, it includes shifts in what we feel, value, and desire. At the behavioral level, it produces new actions, habits, and patterns of living. At the spiritual level, it deepens our relationship with God and aligns us more closely with His purposes.

The Bible describes this kind of comprehensive transformation through the concept of being "born again" (John 3:3) and becoming "new creatures" (2 Corinthians 5:17). These metaphors suggest that authentic spiritual growth involves fundamental identity shifts, not merely behavior modification. The transformed person doesn't just act differently—they have become different at their core.

This understanding challenges the common approach of trying to change from the outside in—focusing primarily on behavior modification while leaving underlying beliefs and identity unchanged. While external changes may produce temporary improvements, they rarely create lasting transformation because they don't address the root systems that drive behavior.

Transformational change typically begins with what Richard Rohr calls "necessary suffering"—experiences that disrupt our current way of being and create openness to new possibilities. This might include failure, loss, disappointment, or simply the recognition that our current approach isn't producing the results we desire. Rather than avoiding these disruptions, we can learn to see them as invitations to growth and transformation.

The process is rarely linear or predictable. Transformation often involves periods of confusion, regression, and apparent setback before breakthrough occurs. Understanding this normalizes the messy middle of change and prevents us from abandoning growth processes when they become difficult.

Most importantly, transformational change requires what Dallas Willard called "divine transformation"—the recognition that authentic growth involves cooperation with God's Spirit rather than merely human effort. We position ourselves for transformation through spiritual disciplines and surrender, but the actual changing is God's work within us.

The Biblical Framework for Growth and Sanctification

Scripture provides a comprehensive framework for understanding spiritual growth that balances human responsibility with divine sovereignty. The biblical concept of sanctification—the process of becoming more like Christ—offers crucial insights for anyone seeking authentic transformation.

The foundation of biblical growth is justification—our right standing with God through faith in Christ. This provides the security necessary for healthy change because our identity and worth are established before we begin growing, not earned through our transformation. We grow not to become acceptable to God but because we are already accepted by Him.

The process of sanctification involves both instantaneous and progressive elements. At conversion, believers are declared holy and receive a new nature, but the working out of this new reality takes a lifetime. This explains why even mature believers continue to struggle with sin and imperfection while simultaneously experiencing genuine transformation.

Scripture describes growth using various metaphors that illuminate different aspects of the process. The agricultural metaphors of planting, growing, and harvesting emphasize the gradual, seasonal nature of development. The construction metaphors of building and foundation-laying highlight the importance of solid groundwork and careful attention to structure. The athletic metaphors of running races and fighting battles stress the need for discipline, training, and perseverance.

The apostle Paul's writings reveal that spiritual growth involves both "putting off" old patterns and "putting on" new ones (Ephesians 4:22-24). This suggests that transformation requires both elimination and addition—removing unhealthy patterns while establishing beneficial ones. This dual process explains why change often feels like loss before it feels like gain.

Scripture also emphasizes that growth occurs in community rather than isolation. The "one another" passages in the New Testament—love one another, encourage one another, bear one another's burdens—indicate that transformation happens through relationships. Iron sharpens iron (Proverbs 27:17), and we need others to see our blind spots, challenge our assumptions, and support our growth.

The ultimate goal of biblical growth is not personal perfection but conformity to the image of Christ (Romans 8:29). This Christ-likeness includes both character qualities (love, joy, peace, patience) and functional capacities (wisdom, compassion, leadership, service). The goal is not to become perfect individuals but to become effective servants who reflect God's character while advancing His kingdom purposes.

The Psychology of Change: Understanding Resistance and Breakthrough

Modern psychology has identified predictable patterns in how people experience and navigate change, providing valuable insights that complement biblical wisdom about transformation. Understanding these patterns helps us cooperate more effectively with natural change processes while avoiding common pitfalls.

The change curve, developed by Elisabeth Kübler-Ross and William Bridges, reveals that all significant change involves loss—even positive changes require letting go of familiar patterns, relationships, or identities. This explains why even desired changes often produce grief, anxiety, or resistance. The person starting a new job grieves the loss of their previous role's familiarity. The individual pursuing health changes may mourn the loss of comfort foods or sedentary habits.

Recognizing this loss dimension helps normalize the emotional complexity of change. It's not weakness or lack of faith to feel sadness about what you're leaving behind, even when you're excited about where you're going. Healthy change processes include time and space for grieving what's ending while celebrating what's beginning.

The stages of change model (pre-contemplation, contemplation, preparation, action, maintenance) reveals that sustainable transformation typically involves preparation and contemplation phases before action becomes effective. Many change attempts fail because people jump immediately to action without adequate preparation or motivation development.

This suggests that effective change often requires patience with the process rather than rushing toward immediate results. The person contemplating career change may need months of exploration and preparation before taking action. The individual considering relationship changes may require extended reflection and planning before making commitments.

Psychological research also reveals that change is easier when it aligns with existing values and identity rather than contradicting them. This is why identity-based change approaches (focusing on becoming the type of person who naturally engages in desired behaviors) tend to be more sustainable than behavior-focused approaches alone.

The concept of "implementation intentions"—specific if-then plans for handling obstacles and setbacks—significantly increases the likelihood of successful change. Rather than relying on willpower alone, successful change involves anticipating difficulties and pre-deciding how to respond when challenges arise.

Finally, the social dimension of change cannot be overlooked. Our behavior is heavily influenced by the people around us, and sustainable change often requires finding or creating communities that support our growth direction. This might mean joining new groups, finding accountability partners, or even limiting time with people who undermine our transformation efforts.

Growth Mindset vs. Fixed Mindset in Spiritual Development

Carol Dweck's research on mindset provides profound insights for spiritual growth and character development. The distinction between fixed mindset (believing abilities are static) and growth mindset (believing abilities can be developed) has significant implications for how we approach transformation and navigate challenges in our faith journey.

A fixed mindset in spiritual development leads to several problematic patterns. People with fixed spiritual mindsets often avoid challenges that might reveal limitations, interpret setbacks as evidence of spiritual inadequacy, feel threatened by others' spiritual growth, and focus more on appearing mature than on actually growing. This mindset can create spiritual pride in those who are naturally gifted or spiritual despair in those who struggle.

In contrast, a growth mindset in spiritual development embraces challenges as opportunities for development, views setbacks as learning experiences, finds inspiration in others' spiritual progress, and focuses on the process of becoming rather than the appearance of having arrived. This mindset creates both humility (recognizing ongoing need for growth) and hope (believing that growth is possible).

The growth mindset aligns beautifully with biblical teaching about spiritual development. Scripture consistently emphasizes process over position, becoming over being, and progress over perfection. The biblical heroes are not presented as spiritually perfect individuals but as growing people who learned to trust God more deeply through various experiences.

Jesus' teaching methods reflected growth mindset principles. He used parables to stretch people's thinking, asked questions that revealed assumptions, provided challenges that required faith development, and celebrated small steps of progress rather than demanding immediate perfection. His approach to the disciples was patient and developmental, working with their current capacity while consistently calling them toward greater maturity.

Developing a growth mindset in spiritual development involves several practical shifts.

Instead of asking "Am I spiritual enough?" we ask "How is God growing me?" Instead of hiding struggles out of shame, we share them as opportunities for prayer and support. Instead of comparing our progress to others', we focus on our own journey with God. Instead of avoiding spiritual challenges, we embrace them as means of grace.

This mindset transformation has profound implications for how we approach prayer, Bible study, service, and relationships. Prayer becomes experimentation and conversation rather than performance. Bible study becomes exploration and discovery rather than obligation. Service becomes learning and contribution rather than duty. Relationships become opportunities for mutual growth rather than platforms for spiritual comparison.

The growth mindset also changes how we handle spiritual dryness, doubt, or failure. These experiences become normal parts of the growth process rather than evidence of spiritual deficiency. This perspective enables us to persevere through difficult seasons and extract learning from challenging experiences.

The Role of Crisis and Disruption in Transformation

While we naturally prefer comfort and stability, some of the most significant growth occurs during seasons of crisis, disruption, and upheaval. Understanding how to navigate these challenging periods can transform them from mere survival experiences into profound opportunities for development and transformation.

Crisis serves several important functions in the growth process. First, it disrupts established patterns that may have become rigid or ineffective. The comfortable routines that provide stability can also create stagnation if they prevent us from adapting to new circumstances or opportunities. Crisis forces us out of autopilot and requires conscious decision-making about how to respond.

Second, crisis reveals what we really believe versus what we think we believe. When life is smooth, we can maintain spiritual beliefs that we've never truly tested. Difficult seasons force us to grapple with fundamental questions about God's character, our identity, and what really matters in life. This testing often strengthens authentic faith while exposing superficial beliefs.

Third, crisis develops capacities that cannot be cultivated in comfortable circumstances. Resilience is built through recovering from setbacks. Compassion grows through experiencing suffering. Faith deepens through navigating uncertainty. Leadership emerges through guiding others through difficulties. These qualities can only be developed through actual challenges.

Fourth, crisis often redirects us toward our authentic calling and priorities. When external structures are disrupted, we're forced to examine what we really value and what we want to rebuild. Many people discover their true purpose during or immediately following significant disruptions because crisis strips away non-essentials and reveals what actually matters.

The biblical narrative is filled with examples of crisis-catalyzed growth. Joseph's understanding of his calling emerged through betrayal and imprisonment. Moses' leadership development occurred through failure and exile. David's psalmic wisdom was forged through persecution and loss. Paul's apostolic ministry began with blindness and identity crisis.

However, crisis doesn't automatically produce growth—it creates opportunities for growth that can be either embraced or wasted. The difference often depends on our response to difficulty. Do we become bitter or better? Do we close down or open up? Do we blame others or take responsibility? Do we lose faith or deepen trust?

Navigating crisis productively involves several key practices. First, accepting the reality of the situation without immediately trying to fix or escape it. Second, seeking support from others rather than trying to handle everything alone. Third, maintaining spiritual practices even when they feel difficult or meaningless. Fourth, looking for lessons and growth opportunities within the challenge. Fifth, serving others even while experiencing personal difficulty.

The goal is not to seek crisis but to respond redemptively when it inevitably comes. This perspective transforms our relationship with difficulty from something to be avoided at all costs to something that can be navigated with purpose and hope.

Incremental Growth: The Power of Small, Consistent Changes

While crisis can catalyze rapid transformation, most sustainable growth occurs through small, consistent changes that compound over time. Understanding how to leverage incremental improvement can create dramatic life change without the disruption and overwhelm that often accompanies attempts at radical transformation.

The mathematics of marginal gains reveals why small improvements can create extraordinary results. Improving by just 1% consistently leads to being 37 times better over the course of a year. This principle applies to character development, skill acquisition, relationship building, and spiritual growth. The person who improves their patience by 1% daily becomes remarkably more patient over time.

Small changes work because they don't trigger the psychological resistance that major changes often provoke. Our brains are wired to resist dramatic departures from established patterns, but they readily accept minor adjustments. This makes incremental approaches more sustainable than revolutionary ones.

Incremental growth also allows for course correction along the way. When we make small changes, we can quickly assess what's working and what isn't, adjusting our approach based on real-world feedback. This iterative process leads to better outcomes than trying to perfect a plan before taking any action.

The key is focusing on systems rather than goals. Goals provide direction, but systems provide progress. The person who wants to become more generous doesn't just set a giving goal—they establish systems for regular giving, gratitude practice, and awareness of others' needs. The individual seeking spiritual growth doesn't just commit to reading the Bible more—they create systems for daily Scripture engagement, reflection, and application.

Incremental spiritual growth might involve adding five minutes to daily prayer time, memorizing one verse per month, performing one additional act of service per week, or practicing gratitude for three specific things each day. These small additions compound over time to create significant character transformation.

The biblical principle of faithfulness in little things leading to responsibility for great things (Luke 16:10) reflects this incremental approach to growth. God typically develops our capacity gradually rather than suddenly, building our character through many small tests and opportunities before entrusting us with larger responsibilities.

Incremental growth requires patience with the process and faith that small actions matter. In our instant-gratification culture, this can be challenging because results aren't immediately visible. However, the cumulative effect of consistent small improvements often produces more dramatic and sustainable transformation than attempts at rapid change.

The key is choosing the right small changes—ones that align with your values, support your long-term vision, and feel sustainable given your current circumstances. The most effective incremental changes are often keystone habits that naturally trigger other positive behaviors, creating a cascade of improvement across multiple life areas.

The Community Dimension of Growth and Change

Personal transformation, while involving individual choices and commitments, rarely occurs in isolation. Community plays crucial roles in supporting, challenging, and sustaining growth processes. Understanding how to leverage community for transformation while maintaining individual responsibility creates optimal conditions for authentic change.

Community provides several essential elements for growth. First, perspective—others can often see our patterns, blind spots, and potential more clearly than we can ourselves. The person stuck in a particular mindset may not recognize their limitations until others offer alternative viewpoints. Friends and mentors can help us see possibilities we might miss and identify obstacles we might overlook.

Second, community offers encouragement during difficult seasons of growth. Change is often uncomfortable and discouraging, particularly when progress seems slow or setbacks occur. Having others who believe in our capacity for transformation and celebrate our progress provides motivation to continue when we might otherwise quit.

Third, community provides accountability that helps bridge the gap between intention and action. When we share our growth commitments with others and ask them to check on our progress, we create external motivation that supplements internal drive. This accountability works best when it's supportive rather than judgmental, focused on encouragement rather than criticism.

Fourth, community offers modeling and inspiration through others' growth journeys. Seeing how other people have navigated similar challenges provides both hope and practical strategies. The person struggling with forgiveness can learn from someone who has successfully released bitterness. The individual working on leadership skills can observe how mature leaders handle difficult situations.

Scripture emphasizes the community dimension of spiritual growth through metaphors like the body of Christ (1 Corinthians 12) and the household of faith (Galatians 6:10). These images suggest that individual growth and community health are interconnected—we grow together or we struggle together.

However, community support for growth requires wisdom in selection and boundaries in engagement. Not all relationships are equally supportive of transformation. Some people may feel threatened by your growth and attempt to pull you back toward old patterns. Others may offer support that's more enabling than empowering, preventing you from developing your own capacity.

Effective growth communities share certain characteristics. They celebrate progress rather than demanding perfection. They offer both support and challenge, encouragement and honest feedback. They focus on becoming rather than performing, process rather than just outcomes. They provide both safety for vulnerability and challenge for growth.

Building or finding these communities often requires intentional effort. This might involve joining formal groups (small groups, support groups, mastermind groups), developing informal relationships with like-minded individuals, or even creating new communities around shared growth goals.

The most effective growth communities often include people at different stages of development—some who are ahead of you who can provide guidance and inspiration, some who are at similar stages who can provide mutual support, and some who are behind you who can benefit from your experience and insights.

Embracing the Seasons of Growth

Understanding that growth occurs in seasons helps us navigate the natural rhythms of development without becoming discouraged during slower periods or overwhelmed during intense growth phases. Like agricultural seasons, spiritual and personal growth involves times of planting, growing, harvesting, and rest.

The planting season involves preparation, learning, and establishing foundations for future growth. This might include reading, training, seeking mentorship, or developing spiritual disciplines. During planting seasons, visible results are minimal, but crucial groundwork is being laid. The person preparing for ministry might spend years in study and character development before seeing significant impact.

The growing season involves active development, skill-building, and character formation. Progress is often visible during these periods, though it may still feel slow. This is the season of steady practice, consistent choices, and gradual improvement. The individual developing leadership skills might be taking on increasing responsibilities and receiving feedback that helps them improve.

The harvesting season brings visible results, increased impact, and recognition of growth that has occurred. These are the periods when preparation and development pay off in obvious ways. The person who has been faithfully developing their gifts might find new opportunities opening up, increased effectiveness in their service, or recognition from others.

The rest season involves reflection, evaluation, and renewal preparation for the next cycle. This isn't stagnation but intentional pause that allows for integration of learning and restoration of energy for continued growth. The leader who has completed a major project might take time to reflect on lessons learned before beginning the next initiative.

Each season has its own challenges and opportunities. Planting seasons can feel frustrating because of the lack of visible progress. Growing seasons can feel overwhelming because of the constant demands for change and development. Harvesting seasons can create pressure to perform or temptation toward pride. Rest seasons can generate anxiety about productivity or fear about losing momentum.

Understanding seasonal patterns helps us adjust our expectations and strategies appropriately. During planting seasons, we focus on consistency and foundation-building rather than demanding immediate results. During growing seasons, we embrace the discomfort of development and seek support for the challenges. During harvesting seasons, we enjoy the fruits while remaining humble and grateful. During rest seasons, we resist the urge to force progress and instead focus on renewal and reflection.

Seasonal awareness also helps us prepare for transitions between seasons. The end of a harvesting season doesn't mean failure—it may simply mean it's time for rest and preparation for the next cycle. The end of a rest season doesn't mean laziness—it may indicate readiness for new planting and growth.

Most importantly, understanding seasons helps us appreciate the current stage of our growth journey rather than constantly longing for a different phase. Each season has its own gifts and purposes in the larger process of transformation and development.

PRACTICAL APPLICATIONS
The Change Readiness Assessment: Evaluating Your Growth Capacity

Before embarking on any significant change or growth initiative, it's crucial to honestly assess your current readiness and capacity for transformation. This assessment helps you choose appropriate challenges and support systems while avoiding the common mistake of attempting changes you're not prepared to sustain.

Internal Readiness Evaluation

Motivation Assessment:

- What specific outcomes are you hoping to achieve through this change?
- Are you pursuing this growth because of internal conviction or external pressure?
- How will you know when you've been successful in this area?
- What are you willing to sacrifice or give up to achieve this transformation?
- Rate your motivation level on a scale of 1-10, and identify what would need to change to make it a 10

Capacity Analysis:

- What other major changes or stressors are currently happening in your life?
- How much time and energy can you realistically devote to growth efforts?
- What resources (financial, emotional, relational) do you have available for this change?
- What skills, knowledge, or support do you need that you don't currently possess?
- How have you handled similar changes in the past, and what can you learn from those experiences?

Resistance Recognition:

- What aspects of your current situation might you be reluctant to change?
- Who in your life might not support this transformation, and how will you handle that?
- What fears or concerns do you have about the change process or outcomes?
- What have been your typical patterns when facing difficulty or setbacks?
- How will you distinguish between normal change discomfort and indicators that you need to adjust your approach?

External Support Evaluation

Relationship Inventory:

- Who in your life would be most supportive of your growth efforts?
- What relationships might be challenged or strained by your transformation?
- Who could provide practical help, encouragement, or accountability?
- What mentors, coaches, or counselors might you need to support this process?
- How will you communicate your growth goals to important people in your life?

Environmental Assessment:

- What aspects of your physical environment support or hinder your desired changes?
- How do your work, home, and social environments align with your growth goals?
- What changes to your schedule, routines, or habits would support your transformation?
- What triggers in your environment might undermine your progress?
- How can you modify your surroundings to make success more likely?

The Growth Goal Setting Framework: SMART-ER-EST Goals for Transformation

Traditional goal-setting approaches often fall short when applied to character development and spiritual growth because they focus primarily on external outcomes rather than internal transformation. This enhanced framework addresses both internal and external dimensions of growth.

S - Specific and Soul-Centered. Rather than vague intentions, create specific goals that address both external behaviors and internal transformation:

- External: "I will pray for 15 minutes each morning"
- Internal: "I will cultivate a heart of dependence on God and awareness of His presence"
- Integration: "I will spend 15 minutes each morning in prayer, focusing on surrendering my day to God and asking for wisdom in my interactions with others"

M - Measurable and Meaningful. Identify both quantitative measures and qualitative indicators of progress:

- Quantitative: Number of days, duration of practice, frequency of behaviors
- Qualitative: Changes in attitude, increased peace, improved relationships
- Questions to assess progress: "How is this change affecting my character?" "What are others noticing about my growth?"

A - Achievable and Aligned. Ensure goals stretch you appropriately while aligning with your values and current capacity:

- Consider your current spiritual maturity and life circumstances
- Choose challenges that require faith but don't overwhelm your capacity
- Align growth goals with your authentic identity and calling
- Build on existing strengths while addressing key growth areas

R - Relevant and Relational. Connect individual growth to service of others and relationship health:

- How will this transformation benefit others in your life?
- What relationships will be strengthened through your growth?
- How does this change serve your larger calling and purpose?
- What community support will enhance your growth process?

T - Time-bound and Trust-centered. Set appropriate timelines while maintaining dependence on God's timing:

- Create specific deadlines for habit establishment and milestone achievement
- Include regular review periods for assessment and adjustment
- Balance personal effort with trust in God's transforming work
- Allow flexibility for God's timing while maintaining personal responsibility

E - Encouraging and Eternal. Frame goals in ways that inspire hope and connect to eternal significance:

- Focus on progress rather than perfection
- Celebrate small victories and incremental improvement
- Connect daily growth activities to your eternal identity and calling
- Maintain perspective on temporary setbacks within the larger growth journey

R - Reviewed and Refined. Establish regular evaluation and adjustment processes:

- Weekly check-ins on progress and obstacles
- Monthly assessment of goal relevance and approach effectiveness
- Quarterly major reviews and goal refinement
- Annual evaluation of character development and growth patterns

E - Environmental and Systematic. Consider how your environment and systems support goal achievement:

- Modify physical environment to reduce barriers and increase cues
- Establish routines and habits that support growth goals
- Create accountability systems and support structures
- Address obstacles systematically rather than relying on willpower alone

S - Spiritual and Surrendered. Ground all growth efforts in spiritual foundation and divine de-

pendence:
- Begin goal-setting with prayer and seeking God's direction
- Incorporate spiritual disciplines that support character transformation
- Maintain awareness that God is the ultimate source of growth and change
- Hold goals with open hands, willing to adjust as God leads

T - Transformational and Testifying. Focus on internal transformation that naturally produces external testimony:
- Prioritize heart change over behavior modification
- Allow growth to create authentic testimony to others
- Share your journey appropriately to encourage others' growth
- View your transformation as part of God's larger work in the world

The Daily Growth Practices: Micro-Habits for Macro-Transformation

Sustainable growth often occurs through small, daily practices that compound over time rather than dramatic, sporadic efforts. These micro-habits create consistent forward momentum while being small enough to maintain during busy or difficult seasons.

Morning Growth Rituals (10-15 minutes)

The Growth-Oriented Morning Check-in:
- Surrender: "God, I surrender this day to You and ask for Your guidance"
- Identity: "I am Your beloved child, created for good works and growing in grace"
- Growth Intent: "Today I will practice [specific growth focus] through [specific action]"
- Service Awareness: "Help me notice opportunities to serve others today"
- Gratitude: "Thank You for [three specific things from yesterday]"

Character Quality Focus: Choose one character quality to focus on each month:
- Week 1: Define the quality and identify how it looks in daily life
- Week 2: Notice when you demonstrate this quality and when you fall short
- Week 3: Practice specific behaviors that express this quality
- Week 4: Reflect on growth and plan how to integrate insights going forward

Scripture-Based Growth:
- Choose one verse related to your growth focus to meditate on throughout the day
- Write the verse on a card and review it during transition moments
- Ask throughout the day: "How does this truth apply to my current situation?"

- End the day by journaling about how you saw this truth at work

Evening Growth Reflection (5-10 minutes)

The Growth Inventory:

- Growth Moments: When did I choose growth over comfort today?
- Learning Opportunities: What did challenging situations teach me about myself?
- Character Development: How did I practice the character quality I'm developing?
- Service Impact: How did I serve others, and what did I learn through serving?
- Tomorrow's Intention: Based on today's learning, how do I want to grow tomorrow?

Gratitude and Grace Practice:

- Identify three specific ways you grew or were challenged to grow today
- Thank God for both the easy growth moments and the difficult ones
- Extend grace to yourself for areas where you fell short of your ideals
- Pray for wisdom and strength for continued growth

The Growth Planning Cycles: Weekly, Monthly, and Quarterly Reviews

Consistent growth requires regular evaluation and course correction. These planning cycles help you maintain momentum while adapting your approach based on experience and changing circumstances.

Weekly Growth Planning Session (30 minutes every Sunday)

Previous Week Assessment:

- What growth commitments did I keep consistently this week?
- Where did I struggle, and what factors contributed to those struggles?
- What unexpected growth opportunities arose, and how did I respond?
- How did my growth efforts affect my relationships and service to others?
- What patterns am I noticing in my growth journey?

Coming Week Preparation:

- What are my top 3 growth priorities for the coming week?
- What obstacles might I face, and how will I prepare for them?
- Who can provide support or accountability for my growth goals?

- How will I integrate growth practices with my scheduled activities?
- What would success look like in my growth areas this week?

Monthly Growth Intensive
(2 hours on the last Saturday of each month)

Character Development Review:
- How have I grown in character over the past month?
- What qualities are developing, and what areas need more attention?
- How are others experiencing the changes in my life?
- What feedback have I received about my growth or transformation?
- What evidence do I see of God's work in my life?

Growth Strategy Refinement:
- Which growth practices are working well and should be continued?
- What approaches need modification or replacement?
- How do I need to adjust my growth goals based on what I've learned?
- What new growth areas is God highlighting for my attention?
- How can I better align my growth efforts with my calling and purpose?

Quarterly Growth Retreat (Half-day every three months)

Comprehensive Growth Assessment:
- Review your growth goals from the beginning of the quarter
- Assess progress in character development, spiritual disciplines, and service capacity
- Identify major lessons learned and breakthrough moments
- Evaluate how your growth has affected your relationships and influence
- Consider how God has been working in your life through various experiences

Vision and Goal Realignment:
- How has your understanding of your calling or purpose evolved?
- What new growth areas is God calling you to explore?
- How do your growth goals align with your larger life vision?
- What major changes or adjustments do you need to make?
- How can you better integrate growth and service in the coming quarter?

Support System Evaluation:
- Which relationships have been most supportive of your growth?

- What additional support, mentoring, or accountability do you need?
- How can you better contribute to others' growth journeys?
- What communities or resources would enhance your transformation process?
- How can you create better environmental support for your growth goals?

The Change Navigation Toolkit: Handling Resistance and Setbacks

Even well-planned growth efforts encounter obstacles, resistance, and setbacks. Having a toolkit for navigating these challenges prevents temporary difficulties from becoming permanent derailments.

Internal Resistance Management

The Resistance Inquiry Process: When you notice internal resistance to growth activities, use these questions:

- What specifically am I resisting, and what might that resistance be trying to protect?
- What fears, beliefs, or past experiences might be driving this resistance?
- How might this resistance actually contain wisdom about my approach or timing?
- What would it look like to honor the resistance while still moving forward?
- How can I address the underlying concerns while maintaining my growth commitment?

The Compassionate Reset Method: When you experience setbacks or failures in your growth journey:

1. Acknowledge the setback without minimizing or dramatizing it
2. Accept that setbacks are normal parts of the growth process
3. Analyze what contributed to the setback and what you can learn from it
4. Adjust your approach based on what you've learned
5. Advance by taking one small step forward immediately

External Challenge Response

The Relationship Navigation Strategy: When others resist or undermine your growth efforts:

- Distinguish between people who are genuinely concerned versus those who feel threatened
- Communicate your growth goals clearly while remaining open to legitimate feedback
- Set appropriate boundaries with people who consistently discourage your development
- Find or create communities that support your transformation
- Remember that your calling comes from God, not from others' approval

The Environmental Adaptation Approach: When circumstances make growth difficult:
- Identify which aspects of your environment you can control versus those you cannot
- Make whatever modifications are possible to support your growth
- Develop strategies for maintaining growth practices in challenging environments
- Create portable practices that can be maintained regardless of circumstances
- Focus on internal transformation that doesn't depend on external conditions

This comprehensive practical application system provides both daily practices for consistent growth and tools for navigating the inevitable challenges that arise during transformation processes.

CHAPTER CONCLUSION
The Beautiful Dance of Becoming

As we conclude this exploration of change and growth, it's essential to recognize the profound truth you've encountered: transformation is not a destination but a way of traveling through life. You haven't just learned techniques for self-improvement—you've discovered the sacred rhythm of becoming, the divine dance between human effort and God's grace that

creates authentic, lasting change. This dance requires both surrender and action, both patience and persistence, both acceptance of who you are and excitement about who you're becoming.

The most liberating aspect of understanding biblical growth is recognizing that you're not trying to earn God's love through your transformation—you're responding to His love by becoming more fully the person He created you to be. Your growth is not about proving your worth but about expressing your worth. Your changes are not about gaining acceptance but about living from acceptance. This foundation of grace makes growth joyful rather than burdensome, hopeful rather than anxious.

Growth as Worship and Witness

Perhaps the most transformative perspective on personal growth is understanding it as both worship and witness. When you choose to grow in character, develop your gifts, and expand your capacity to serve, you're offering your life as a living sacrifice to God (Romans 12:1). Your willingness to be transformed demonstrates your trust in His goodness and your gratitude for His grace.

Simultaneously, your growth becomes a witness to others about the reality of God's transforming power. When people see authentic change in your life—increased patience, deeper compassion, greater wisdom, enhanced effectiveness—they witness that transformation is possible. Your journey from who you were to who you're becoming creates hope for others who long for change but doubt its possibility.

This dual nature of growth as worship and witness elevates every step of your transformation journey. The daily choice to practice patience becomes an act of worship. The decision to extend forgiveness becomes a testimony. The commitment to develop your gifts becomes both service to God and inspiration to others. Your growth ripples outward, creating permission and possibility for others to begin their own transformation journeys.

The Paradox of Effort and Grace

One of the most profound mysteries of spiritual growth is the paradox between human effort and divine grace. You must work diligently at your transformation while recognizing that God is the ultimate source of all authentic change. You must take responsibility for your choices while trusting that "it is God which worketh in you both to will and to do of his good pleasure" (Philippians 2:13).

This paradox prevents both the pride that comes from thinking you've achieved growth through your own strength and the passivity that comes from thinking God will change you without your participation. You cooperate with God's transforming work by positioning yourself for His grace—through spiritual disciplines, community engagement, service to others, and openness to His leading. You provide the willingness; He provides the power.

Understanding this paradox also brings comfort during difficult seasons of growth. When transformation feels slow or stalled, you can trust that God is working even when you can't see evidence of change. When growth requires painful surrender or difficult choices, you can draw on His strength rather than relying solely on your own willpower. The burden of transformation rests ultimately on His shoulders, not yours, and yet your active participation in that transformation is being a faithful follower of God.

The Generational Impact of Your Growth

Remember that your commitment to growth creates impact far beyond your personal development. The character qualities you develop, the wisdom you gain, and the capacity you build become legacies you pass on to the next generation. Your children, students, colleagues, and community members are watching how you handle challenges, navigate changes, and pursue transformation. Your example teaches them that growth is possible and worthwhile.

The patience you develop today teaches others that emotional regulation is learnable. The generosity you cultivate demonstrates that selfishness can be overcome. The wisdom you gain through experience becomes counsel you can offer to others facing similar challenges. The resilience you build through weathering storms becomes strength you can share with others in their difficulties.

Years from now, people may not remember the specific techniques you used or the particular goals you achieved, but they will remember how your commitment to growth affected them. They'll recall how your transformation gave them hope for their own possibilities. They'll treasure how your authentic development created safety for them to be real about their own struggles and aspirations.

Your Next Growth Edge

As you move forward from this chapter, carry with you the Change Readiness Assessment from our practical applications. Take time this week to honestly evaluate your current capacity for growth and identify the specific area where God is calling you to transformation. Remember, you don't need to change everything at once—sustainable growth happens one step at a time, one choice at a time, one day at a time.

Choose one micro-habit from our daily growth practices and commit to it for the next 30 days. Whether it's a morning surrender practice, an evening reflection routine, or a daily character quality focus, begin building the rhythms that will support your ongoing transformation. Start small, be consistent, and trust that God will multiply your faithful efforts.

Looking Ahead

In our next chapter, we'll explore how to build resilience and endurance for the long journey of serving and growing richly. You'll discover that the growth mindset you're developing now becomes the foundation for weathering storms, overcoming obstacles, and maintaining hope during challenging seasons.

But for now, embrace the adventure of becoming. Trust that the God who began this good work in you will be faithful to complete it (Philippians 1:6). Believe that every step of growth, no matter how small, matters deeply to Him and serves His larger purposes. And begin living as if transformation is not only possible but inevitable for those who surrender to His loving work in their lives.

9

Resilience & Endurance

Resilience and endurance are the silent strengths that carry us through life's toughest storms.

EVERY JOURNEY OF SERVICE AND GROWTH will encounter seasons of hardship, disappointment, or uncertainty. What distinguishes those who flourish is not the absence of adversity, but the presence of an inner resolve—a willingness to keep going, no matter how rough the road becomes. Endurance is more than just surviving; it is about pressing on with hope, faith, and integrity, even when the finish line feels far away.

Endurance, in its truest sense, is a skill and a virtue. It is built through practice, patience, and a willingness to face discomfort without giving up. As the psychologist Angela Duckworth describes, grit combines passion and perseverance for long-term goals. In business, relationships, and faith, those who endure become the ones who inspire others, not because their path was easy, but because they refused to let setbacks define them. "Success is not final, failure is not fatal: It is the courage to continue that counts," Winston Churchill once said.

Faith traditions offer profound insight into the nature of resilience. The Bible teaches that endurance is not just about getting through trials, but about being transformed by them. "We rejoice in our sufferings, knowing that suffering produces perseverance; perseverance, character; and character, hope" (Romans 5:3-4). James echoes this: "Consider it pure joy... when you encounter trials... because you know that the testing of your faith develops perseverance. Allow perseverance to finish its work, so that you may be mature and complete, not lacking anything" (James 1:2-4). This perspective reframes challenges as opportunities for spiritual and personal growth, shaping us into people of depth and compassion.

Resilience is not about perfection or never stumbling. It's about getting up, again and again, and trusting that even in weakness, we are not alone. True resilience is rooted in faith—knowing that God's strength is made perfect in our weakness, and that His love never fails. Community also plays a crucial role: sharing our burdens, seeking encouragement, and offering support to others strengthens our resolve and reminds us that endurance is a shared journey.

Practical strategies for building resilience include breaking overwhelming challenges into manageable steps, focusing on what you can control, and practicing gratitude even in difficulty. Leaning on faith, prayer, and supportive relationships transforms adversity from something to be endured alone into a shared opportunity for growth and testimony. Remember, endurance is a muscle—the more you use it, the stronger it becomes.

The Anatomy of Resilience: Understanding Your Inner Shock Absorbers

Resilience is not a single trait but a complex system of mental, emotional, spiritual, and relational capacities that work together to help us navigate adversity and recover from setbacks. Understanding the components of this system helps us identify areas for development and maintain our capacity for endurance during challenging seasons.

Cognitive resilience involves our thought patterns, beliefs, and mental frameworks for interpreting difficulty. Resilient people develop what psychologists call "explanatory style"—the tendency to view setbacks as temporary rather than permanent, specific rather than pervasive, and surmountable rather than insurmountable. When facing a business failure, the resilient entrepreneur thinks "This venture didn't work" rather than "I'm a failure." When experiencing relationship conflict, the resilient individual considers "We're having a disagreement" rather than "Our relationship is doomed."

This cognitive dimension includes what Viktor Frankl called "meaning-making"—the ability to find purpose and significance even in difficult circumstances. People who can extract lessons, identify growth opportunities, or connect their suffering to larger purposes tend to recover more quickly and completely from adversity. The parent caring for a special needs child might find meaning in becoming an advocate for other families. The cancer survivor might discover purpose in supporting others facing similar diagnoses.

Emotional resilience encompasses our capacity to experience, process, and regulate emotions during stress without being overwhelmed or shutting down completely. This doesn't mean avoiding or suppressing difficult emotions but rather developing the skills to feel them fully while maintaining functionality and perspective. Emotionally resilient people allow themselves to grieve losses, feel doubt, and experience fear about uncertainties while not being controlled by these emotions.

This emotional capacity includes what researchers call "emotional granularity"—the ability to distinguish between similar emotions and identify their specific triggers and messages. Instead of just feeling "bad," the emotionally resilient person recognizes "I'm feeling disappointed about the project outcome, anxious about the upcoming presentation, and frustrated with my colleague's response." This specificity enables more targeted and effective responses.

Spiritual resilience involves our relationship with God, our understanding of His character and purposes, and our ability to maintain faith during times when His presence feels distant or His plans seem unclear. This dimension includes trust in God's sovereignty, confidence in His love, and hope in His ultimate goodness regardless of current circumstances.

Spiritual resilience also encompasses what Henri Nouwen called "spiritual fecundity"—the ability to find God's presence and purposes even in barren seasons. The spiritually resilient person can worship during loss, serve during suffering, and love during loneliness because their connection to God transcends their circumstances.

Relational resilience refers to our capacity to maintain and draw strength from relationships during difficult times. This includes both the skill of receiving support from others and the ability to continue contributing to relationships even when we're struggling. Relationally resilient people neither isolate themselves during difficulty nor become burdens that drain others' resources.

This dimension also includes what researchers call "social capital"—the network of relationships that can provide various types of support during adversity. Some relationships offer emotional support, others provide practical assistance, and still others contribute expertise or perspective. Building and maintaining diverse relationship networks creates multiple resources for navigating challenges.

Understanding resilience as a multi-dimensional system helps us avoid the common mistake of trying to build toughness through willpower alone. True resilience requires development across all dimensions, creating redundancy and interconnection that supports us when individual capacities are strained.

The Biblical Foundation of Endurance and Perseverance

Scripture consistently presents endurance not as grim survival but as a virtue that produces character, deepens faith, and prepares us for greater service. The biblical understanding of perseverance is anchored in God's character and promises, providing both motivation and methodology for sustained faithfulness during difficulty.

The Hebrew concept of "qavah" (often translated as "wait" or "hope") combines active expectation with patient endurance. This is not passive resignation but confident perseverance based on God's faithfulness. "But they that wait upon the Lord shall renew their strength; they shall mount up with wings as eagles; they shall run, and not be weary; and they shall walk, and not faint" (Isaiah 40:31). This waiting involves both trust in God's timing and continued action in faithfulness to His calling.

The Greek word "hupomone" (usually translated as "patience" or "endurance") literally means "to remain under"—the capacity to stay faithful under pressure without being crushed or abandoning our position. This endurance is not mere stubbornness but active perseverance toward worthy goals despite obstacles and opposition.

Jesus modeled this kind of endurance throughout His ministry, particularly in His approach to the cross. "Who for the joy that was set before him endured the cross, despising the shame, and is set down at the right hand of the throne of God" (Hebrews 12:2). His endurance was motivated not by grim duty but by joy in anticipated outcomes and confidence in the Father's plan.

The apostle Paul's writings reveal that endurance develops through practice and produces increasingly greater capacity for service. "And not only so, but we glory in tribulations also: knowing that tribulation worketh patience; And patience, experience; and experience, hope" (Romans 5:3-4). This progression suggests that endurance is not just about surviving difficulty but about being transformed through it in ways that enhance our effectiveness and deepen our hope.

Scripture also reveals that endurance is both individual and corporate. The early church faced persecution, internal conflicts, and doctrinal challenges together, supporting one another's faith and sharing the burden of faithfulness. "Bear ye one another's burdens, and so fulfil the law of Christ" (Galatians 6:2). Individual endurance is strengthened through community support and commitment to others' well-being.

The ultimate foundation for biblical endurance is confidence in God's character and promises. Because God is faithful, just, and loving, we can endure present difficulties with hope for future resolution. Because His plans are good and His timing is perfect, we can persevere through seasons when His purposes are unclear. Because His strength is made perfect in our weakness, we can continue when our own resources are exhausted.

This theological foundation transforms endurance from mere human determination into divine partnership. We endure not only through our own strength but through God's power working within us. We persevere not only for our own goals but for His kingdom purposes. We continue not only because we're tough but because He is faithful.

The Neuroscience of Resilience: How Difficulty Develops Strength

Modern neuroscience has revealed fascinating insights about how our brains respond to and recover from stress, providing scientific validation for biblical principles about growth through adversity. Understanding these mechanisms helps us cooperate more effectively with our brain's natural resilience-building processes.

Neuroplasticity and Stress Response. Our brains are remarkably adaptable, constantly forming new neural pathways and strengthening existing ones based on our experiences and responses. When we face challenges and choose resilient responses—problem-solving instead of panic, hope instead of despair, action instead of withdrawal—we literally rewire our brains for greater resilience.

The stress response system, when functioning properly, is designed to mobilize resources for dealing with challenges and then return to baseline functioning once the threat has passed. However, chronic stress or trauma can dysregulate this system, leading to either hypervigilance (constantly expecting danger) or numbness (shutting down emotional responsiveness).

Resilience training helps regulate this system by developing what researchers call "stress inoculation"—controlled exposure to manageable challenges that build capacity for handling larger difficulties. This is similar to how vaccines work—introducing small amounts of a pathogen to build immunity against larger infections.

The Role of Cognitive Reframing. Neuroscience confirms that how we interpret events significantly affects our stress response and recovery. The same situation can be devastating or manageable depending on how we frame it mentally. When we practice cognitive reframing—consciously choosing helpful interpretations of difficult circumstances—we strengthen neural pathways associated with resilience and weaken those associated with helplessness.

This doesn't mean denying reality or engaging in false positivity, but rather choosing the most helpful and accurate perspective available. The person facing job loss can focus either on the rejection and uncertainty (which activates stress pathways) or on the opportunity for new direction and the skills they've developed (which activates resilience pathways).

Post-Traumatic Growth. Perhaps most encouraging is the research on post-traumatic growth—the tendency for people to develop greater capacity, deeper wisdom, and stronger relationships as a result of navigating significant challenges. This growth often includes increased appreciation for life, deeper spiritual understanding, stronger relationships, greater personal strength, and clearer priorities.

This aligns perfectly with biblical teaching about God's ability to work all things together for good (Romans 8:28) and to give beauty for ashes (Isaiah 61:3). Neuroscience helps us understand the mechanisms through which difficulty can produce development, while Scripture provides the theological framework for trusting these processes even when outcomes are uncertain.

The Importance of Recovery and Renewal. Just as physical muscles need rest between workouts to grow stronger, our resilience capacity requires periods of recovery and renewal. The brain's stress response system is designed for episodic activation, not chronic engagement. Building resilience requires both challenging ourselves appropriately and creating space for restoration.

This scientific understanding validates biblical principles about Sabbath rest, the importance of community support, and the value of spiritual disciplines. Prayer, worship, meditation, and community fellowship provide the mental and emotional rest needed for resilience development.

Grit vs. Grace: The Balance of Human Effort and Divine Strength

One of the most important distinctions in building biblical resilience is understanding the difference between "grit" (human determination and persistence) and "grace" (divine strength and enabling). Both are necessary, but they serve different functions and must be held in proper balance to avoid either presumption or passivity.

The Value and Limits of Grit. Angela Duckworth's research on grit—passion and perseverance for long-term goals—has highlighted the importance of determination and sustained effort in achieving significant outcomes. Gritty people don't give up when facing obstacles, maintain effort despite setbacks, and stay committed to their goals even when progress is slow.

This quality aligns with biblical teaching about faithfulness, diligence, and perseverance. Scripture consistently commends those who continue faithful service despite difficulty and warns against giving up when facing opposition. The parable of the persistent widow (Luke 18:1-8) and Jesus' teaching about enduring to the end (Matthew 24:13) emphasize the importance of sustained effort.

However, grit alone can become problematic when it leads to self-reliance, stubborn persistence in wrong directions, or burnout from trying to accomplish everything through human effort. The person who depends only on grit may achieve impressive results but miss opportunities for deeper transformation and community support.

The Necessity of Grace. Grace provides what grit cannot: supernatural strength for superhuman challenges, wisdom for navigating complex situations, peace during uncertainty, and hope when circumstances seem hopeless. Grace enables us to persevere not just through our own determination but through God's power working within us.

This divine enabling doesn't eliminate the need for human effort but transforms its character. Instead of striving from emptiness, we labor from fullness. Instead of working to earn God's favor, we work from His acceptance. Instead of depending solely on our own resources, we draw from His unlimited supply.

Grace also provides what psychologists call "meaning-making"—the ability to find purpose and significance in difficulty that transcends immediate circumstances. This meaning can sustain us through challenges that would overwhelm mere grit.

The Integration of Grit and Grace. The healthiest approach to resilience integrates both human effort and divine dependence. We work diligently while trusting ultimately in God's power. We plan carefully while remaining open to His redirection. We persevere persistently while drawing on His strength.

This integration is beautifully illustrated in Paul's statement: "I laboured more abundantly than they all: yet not I, but the grace of God which was with me" (1 Corinthians 15:10). Paul worked harder than anyone else but recognized that his ability to work came from God's grace rather than his own strength.

Practically, this means approaching challenges with both careful preparation and earnest prayer, both strategic planning and surrendered trust, both determined effort and dependence on God's enabling. We do our part while recognizing that ultimate outcomes depend on God's sovereignty and goodness.

This balance prevents both the pride that comes from believing our success depends entirely on our effort and the passivity that comes from thinking God will accomplish everything without our participation. We cooperate with God's work rather than either competing with it or abdicating our responsibility.

The Seasons of Endurance: Different Challenges for Different Phases

Understanding that endurance requirements change throughout different life seasons and circumstances helps us adjust our strategies and expectations appropriately. What works for building resilience during one phase may need modification during another, and recognizing these differences prevents discouragement when familiar approaches seem less effective.

Crisis Endurance: Surviving Acute Challenges. During acute crises—sudden loss, health emergencies, financial catastrophes, or relationship breakdowns—endurance focuses primarily on survival and basic functioning. The goal is getting through each day while maintaining essential responsibilities and relationships. Long-term planning takes a backseat to immediate stability.

Crisis endurance requires simplifying expectations, accepting help from others, focusing on basic needs (physical, emotional, spiritual), and trusting God for daily strength rather than trying to see the entire path forward. This is the endurance of walking by faith through the valley of the shadow of death (Psalm 23:4).

During these seasons, normal spiritual disciplines may feel impossible or meaningless. The person doesn't need to maintain their usual prayer schedule or Bible reading routine—they need to cry out to God for help and accept that His grace is sufficient even when they feel spiritually dry.

Chronic Endurance: Sustaining Through Long-term Difficulties. Some challenges are not acute crises but ongoing realities—chronic illness, difficult relationships, financial limitations, or challenging work environments. These situations require different endurance strategies focused on sustainability rather than just survival.

Chronic endurance involves finding rhythms that can be maintained over time, building support systems for the long haul, developing meaning and purpose within limitations, and creating joy and growth opportunities despite constraints. This endurance is less about dramatic perseverance and more about faithful consistency.

The key is accepting reality without resigning hope, adapting dreams without abandoning them, and finding ways to serve and grow within constraints rather than waiting for circumstances to change before engaging fully with life.

Growth Endurance: Persisting Through Development Challenges. The endurance required for personal growth and character development is different from crisis survival. Growth endurance involves pushing through comfort zones, persisting when progress feels slow, maintaining hope when change seems impossible, and continuing effort when results aren't immediately visible.

This type of endurance is more voluntary than crisis endurance—we choose growth challenges rather than having them imposed upon us. However, this choice doesn't make the endurance easier, just different. Growth endurance requires patience with process, commitment to long-term vision, and willingness to invest effort for delayed gratification.

Growth endurance also involves what Carol Dweck calls "productive struggle"—the willingness to work at the edge of our capacity where learning and development occur. This requires tolerating discomfort and uncertainty while maintaining confidence that effort leads to improvement.

Service Endurance: Sustaining Ministry and Impact. Long-term service to others requires its own form of endurance, particularly when results are slow, resources are limited, or opposition is encountered. Service endurance involves maintaining compassion when people disappoint you, continuing generosity when resources are strained, and persisting in love when responses are negative.

This endurance is fueled primarily by love for God and others rather than by personal achievement or recognition. It requires finding fulfillment in faithfulness rather than just outcomes, and measuring success by obedience rather than only results.

Service endurance also involves managing what researchers call "compassion fatigue"—the emotional and physical exhaustion that can result from sustained caregiving or helping behaviors. This requires setting healthy boundaries, seeking support and renewal, and maintaining perspective on long-term impact.

Building Your Resilience Portfolio: Diversifying Your Strength Sources

Just as financial advisors recommend diversifying investment portfolios to manage risk, building resilience requires developing multiple sources of strength so that if one area is compromised, others can provide support. This diversification prevents over-dependence on any single resilience strategy and creates redundancy for challenging seasons.

Physical Resilience Foundation. Physical health provides the foundational capacity for all other forms of resilience. When our bodies are strong, well-rested, and properly nourished, we have greater capacity for handling emotional, mental, and spiritual challenges. Conversely, when physical resources are depleted, everything else becomes more difficult.

Building physical resilience involves regular exercise appropriate to your capacity, adequate sleep and rest, proper nutrition that supports brain and body function, and stress management practices that regulate your nervous system. This also includes managing chronic health conditions proactively and seeking medical care when needed.

The goal is not perfect health—which isn't possible for everyone—but optimal function within your current constraints. The person with chronic illness can still build physical resilience by managing their condition well, maximizing their capacity within limitations, and preventing additional health problems through lifestyle choices.

Emotional Resilience Capacity. Emotional resilience involves developing skills for recognizing, processing, and regulating emotions during stress. This includes building emotional vocabulary (being able to name and distinguish between different emotions), developing self-awareness (recognizing your emotional patterns and triggers), and practicing emotional regulation (managing intensity and duration of emotional responses).

Emotional resilience also requires what Brené Brown calls "vulnerability courage"—the willingness to feel and express emotions appropriately rather than numbing or avoiding them. This includes grieving losses fully and sharing fears and concerns with trusted people.

Building emotional resilience often involves healing from past wounds that might compromise your current capacity, developing better communication skills for expressing emotions clearly, and learning to receive comfort and support from others during difficult times.

Mental Resilience Development. Mental resilience encompasses cognitive skills for problem-solving, decision-making, and perspective maintenance during adversity. This includes developing critical thinking skills that help you assess situations accurately, creativity for generating multiple solutions to problems, and cognitive flexibility for adapting your approach when circumstances change.

Mental resilience also involves what psychologists call "cognitive restructuring"—the ability to identify and challenge unhelpful thought patterns that increase stress or decrease hope. This includes recognizing catastrophic thinking, all-or-nothing perspectives, and other mental habits that amplify difficulty unnecessarily.

Building mental resilience requires regular intellectual stimulation through reading, learning, and engaging with challenging ideas. It also involves seeking wise counsel from mentors and advisors who can provide perspective during difficult decisions.

Spiritual Resilience Grounding. Spiritual resilience provides the deepest and most sustainable source of strength during adversity. This involves developing confidence in God's character and promises, maintaining regular spiritual disciplines that connect you to His presence, and building theological understanding that helps you interpret difficulty within the larger context of His purposes.

Spiritual resilience includes what Dallas Willard called "the withness of God"—the cultivated awareness that you are never alone in your struggles because God is always present and engaged in your circumstances. This presence provides both comfort during suffering and strength for persevering.

Building spiritual resilience requires consistent investment in prayer, Scripture study, worship, and community fellowship. It also involves developing spiritual friendships with people who encourage your faith and help you discern God's leading during difficult seasons.

Relational Resilience Network. No one endures alone, and building a network of supportive relationships is crucial for sustained resilience. This network should include different types of relationships that provide various forms of support: emotional support (people who care about your feelings), informational support (people who can provide advice and guidance), instrumental support (people who can offer practical help), and spiritual support (people who can encourage your faith).

Building relational resilience involves both giving and receiving support, being vulnerable about your needs while also contributing to others' well-being. It requires maintaining relationships during good times so they're available during difficult seasons, and investing in community rather than trying to be completely self-sufficient.

This network should be diverse enough to provide multiple perspectives and types of support while being trustworthy enough to share honestly about your struggles and needs. Quality matters more than quantity—a few deep, supportive relationships are more valuable than many superficial connections.

PRACTICAL APPLICATIONS
The Resilience Assessment and Development Plan

Before building resilience, it's crucial to understand your current capacity and identify specific areas for development. This comprehensive assessment helps you create a targeted plan for strengthening your ability to endure and thrive through adversity.

Current Resilience Inventory

Physical Resilience Assessment:

- Energy Levels: Rate your typical energy throughout the day (1-10 scale)
- Sleep Quality: How well do you sleep, and how rested do you feel upon waking?
- Stress Response: How does your body typically respond to stress (tension, fatigue, illness)?
- Recovery Capacity: How quickly do you bounce back from physical demands or illness?
- Health Management: How proactively do you manage your physical health and any chronic conditions?

Emotional Resilience Evaluation:

- Emotional Awareness: How well can you identify and name your emotions as they arise?
- Emotional Regulation: How effectively do you manage emotional intensity during stress?
- Emotional Recovery: How long does it typically take you to process and move through difficult emotions?
- Emotional Expression: How comfortable are you sharing your feelings with trusted people?
- Emotional Boundaries: How well do you protect yourself from others' emotional chaos while remaining compassionate?

Mental Resilience Analysis:

- Problem-Solving: How confident are you in your ability to find solutions to challenges?
- Perspective Maintenance: How well do you maintain balanced thinking during stress?
- Cognitive Flexibility: How easily can you adapt your thinking when circumstances change?
- Decision-Making: How effectively do you make decisions under pressure?
- Learning from Setbacks: How well do you extract lessons and wisdom from difficult experiences?

Spiritual Resilience Review:
- Faith Stability: How stable is your trust in God during difficult seasons?
- Spiritual Practices: How consistent are you with prayer, Scripture reading, and worship?
- Meaning-Making: How well do you find purpose and significance in challenging circumstances?
- Divine Connection: How aware are you of God's presence and involvement in your daily life?
- Hope Maintenance: How well do you maintain hope when circumstances seem hopeless?

Relational Resilience Audit:
- Support Network: How many people can you turn to for different types of support?
- Vulnerability: How comfortable are you being honest about your struggles and needs?
- Support Giving: How effectively do you provide support to others during their difficulties?
- Boundary Setting: How well do you balance helping others with protecting your own well-being?
- Community Integration: How connected are you to communities that share your values and support your growth?

The Daily Resilience Building Practices

Resilience is built through consistent daily practices that strengthen your capacity incrementally over time. These micro-practices require minimal time but create significant cumulative impact when maintained consistently.

Morning Resilience Preparation (10 minutes)

Physical Foundation Setting:
- Take 5 deep breaths while stretching your body gently
- Drink a full glass of water to begin hydration for the day
- Do 2 minutes of light movement (walking, stretching, or gentle exercises)
- Set an intention to care for your body throughout the day

Mental Resilience Priming:
- Review your schedule and identify potential challenges or stressors
- For each anticipated challenge, mentally rehearse one positive response strategy
- Remind yourself of one problem you've successfully solved in the past
- Set an intention to approach difficulties with curiosity rather than anxiety

Emotional Resilience Centering:
- Acknowledge any emotions you're currently feeling without judgment
- Practice gratitude by identifying three specific things you appreciate
- Send loving thoughts to one person who might be struggling today
- Set an intention to respond rather than react to emotional triggers

Spiritual Resilience Grounding:
- Spend 3 minutes in prayer, surrendering your day to God's care
- Read one verse or brief devotional passage for guidance and encouragement
- Remember one way you've seen God's faithfulness in your life
- Set an intention to look for God's presence in ordinary moments

Evening Resilience Review (10 minutes)

Stress Processing:
- Identify the most stressful moment of your day and how you handled it
- Acknowledge any emotions that arose without trying to fix or change them
- Consider what you learned about yourself through the day's challenges
- Release any tension through prayer, journaling, or gentle movement

Gratitude and Growth Recognition:
- Write down three specific things you're grateful for from today
- Identify one way you demonstrated resilience during a difficult moment
- Note one area where you'd like to respond differently in the future
- Celebrate any progress, no matter how small, in your resilience development

Relationship and Service Reflection:
- Consider how you supported or encouraged someone today
- Acknowledge any support or encouragement you received from others
- Identify one person you can bless or serve tomorrow

The Resilience Workout:
Specific Exercises for Different Types of Endurance

Just as physical fitness requires targeted exercises for different muscle groups, resilience requires specific practices for developing different types of endurance capacity.

Stress Inoculation Training

Controlled Challenge Exposure:
- Week 1-2: Practice small discomforts (cold showers, uncomfortable conversations,

physical challenges)

- Week 3-4: Take on slightly larger challenges (public speaking, new social situations, learning difficult skills)
- Week 5-6: Engage in meaningful but stretching service opportunities (volunteering in unfamiliar settings, helping with complex problems)
- Week 7-8: Accept leadership responsibilities that require you to support others through difficulties

Cognitive Resilience Training:

- Practice the "worst case scenario" exercise: identify your biggest current worry, imagine the worst possible outcome, and create specific plans for handling that situation
- Develop "alternative explanation" skills: when something goes wrong, brainstorm three different possible explanations beyond the most negative one
- Use "zoom out" perspective practice: when facing current stress, imagine how this situation will look in 1 year, 5 years, and 10 years
- Create "past success" reminders: write down 10 difficult situations you've successfully navigated and refer to this list during current challenges

Emotional Endurance Building:

- Practice "emotional surfing": when experiencing difficult emotions, commit to feeling them fully for 5 minutes without trying to escape or fix them
- Develop "compassion practices": spend time each week actively serving or encouraging people who are struggling
- Create "emotional expression" opportunities: find safe places and people where you can share your struggles honestly
- Build "empathy without absorption" skills: practice caring about others' pain without taking on their emotional burden as your own

The Support System Architecture: Building Your Resilience Network

Resilience is enhanced through community, and building an effective support system requires intentional strategy and ongoing investment. This network should provide different types of support for various kinds of challenges.

Mapping Your Current Network

Support Type Analysis: Create a visual map identifying people in your life who provide:

- Emotional Support: People who care about your feelings and offer comfort during difficulty
- Informational Support: People who can provide advice, wisdom, or expertise for problem-solving

- Instrumental Support: People who can offer practical help (time, money, resources, skills)
- Spiritual Support: People who encourage your faith and help you discern God's leading
- Social Support: People who provide belonging, fun, and normal social connection during stressful times

Network Gap Identification:
- Which types of support are well-covered in your current network?
- Where do you have gaps that leave you vulnerable during certain types of challenges?
- Are you over-dependent on any one person or relationship for too many types of support?
- How well-distributed is your network across different life areas (work, home, church, community)?
- Do you have enough reciprocal relationships where you both give and receive support?

Relationship Investment Strategy

Deepening Existing Relationships:
- Choose 3-5 current relationships that could provide better mutual support
- Schedule regular check-ins with these people to maintain connection
- Practice vulnerability by sharing appropriate struggles and growth areas
- Look for opportunities to provide support to these individuals when they face challenges
- Express gratitude for the support they provide and how they contribute to your life

Building New Connections:
- Identify communities or groups where you might find like-minded people (church small groups, professional organizations, volunteer opportunities, hobby groups)
- Take initiative in reaching out and building relationships rather than waiting for others to approach you
- Practice being genuinely interested in others' lives, challenges, and growth
- Offer help and support before asking for it, creating a foundation of giving in new relationships
- Be patient with relationship development, understanding that deep supportive friendships take time to build

Creating Resilience Partnerships

Accountability and Encouragement Partners: Find one or two people who will commit to mutual support for resilience building:

- Meeting Schedule: Meet weekly or bi-weekly for 60-90 minutes
- Check-in Structure: Share current challenges, stress levels, and resilience goals
- Accountability Elements: Report on resilience practices and progress toward endurance goals
- Encouragement Focus: Celebrate growth, offer hope during discouragement, and remind each other of past successes
- Prayer and Spiritual Support: Pray together for wisdom, strength, and faithfulness during difficult seasons

Crisis Response Team: Identify 3-4 people who would be your "first call" during different types of emergencies:

- Someone who can provide immediate practical help (transportation, childcare, financial assistance)
- Someone who can offer emotional support and comfort during trauma or loss
- Someone who can provide wise counsel and help with important decisions during crisis
- Someone who can coordinate care from others and help manage logistics during overwhelming situations

The Seasonal Resilience Strategies: Adapting Your Approach

Different seasons of life and types of challenges require different resilience strategies. Having a toolkit of approaches allows you to adapt your methods based on current circumstances and needs.

Crisis Season Resilience

Immediate Stabilization:

- Simplify all non-essential commitments and focus only on basic necessities
- Activate your support network immediately and accept help graciously
- Establish daily routines that provide structure and predictability
- Focus on one day at a time rather than trying to plan far into the future
- Maintain minimal spiritual practices even if normal disciplines feel impossible

Resource Management:

- Conserve emotional and physical energy for essential activities

- Delegate responsibilities wherever possible to trusted family members or friends
- Seek professional help (counseling, medical care, financial advice) as needed
- Communicate clearly with employers, family, and others about your current limitations
- Practice saying no to additional commitments until the crisis stabilizes

Chronic Challenge Resilience

Sustainable Pace Development:

- Accept the reality of limitations while maintaining hope for adaptation and growth
- Create rhythms that can be maintained long-term rather than sprinting unsustainably
- Find meaning and purpose within constraints rather than waiting for circumstances to change
- Develop expertise in managing your specific challenge and share that wisdom with others
- Build joy and celebration into routine activities to prevent life from becoming purely about survival

Long-term Vision Maintenance:

- Regularly revisit and adjust your life vision to align with current realities
- Find ways to contribute meaningfully within your constraints
- Connect with others facing similar challenges for mutual support and encouragement
- Invest in relationships and activities that provide fulfillment independent of your challenge
- Maintain spiritual practices that remind you of your identity beyond your circumstances

Growth Season Resilience

Productive Discomfort Management:

- Distinguish between healthy growing pains and signs that you need to slow down or seek help
- Set realistic expectations for the pace of change and progress
- Celebrate small victories and incremental improvements rather than demanding dramatic transformation
- Seek feedback and guidance from mentors or coaches who can provide perspective on your development

- Balance challenge with adequate rest and recovery to prevent burnout

Momentum Maintenance:
- Track progress regularly to maintain motivation during slow periods
- Connect with others who are pursuing similar growth goals for mutual encouragement
- Adjust goals and strategies based on what you learn about yourself through the process
- Remember your "why"—the deeper purposes that motivated your growth commitment
- Share your journey appropriately with others who can benefit from your experience and insights

This comprehensive approach to resilience building recognizes that endurance is both a skill to be developed and a grace to be received, requiring both human effort and divine enabling for sustainable strength during life's inevitable challenges.

CHAPTER CONCLUSION
The Sacred Art of Enduring Well

As we conclude this exploration of resilience and endurance, it's vital to understand the profound transformation that has occurred in your perspective. You haven't simply learned techniques for surviving difficult times—you've discovered the sacred art of enduring well, of persisting with purpose, and of finding strength that transcends human capacity. True resilience is not about becoming invulnerable to pain but about developing the capacity to remain faithful, hopeful, and loving even when circumstances would justify bitterness, despair, or withdrawal.

The most beautiful aspect of biblical endurance is that it transforms suffering from meaningless hardship into purposeful development. When you endure with faith, patience, and love, you don't just survive your trials—you are shaped by them into someone with greater capacity for compassion, deeper wisdom, and stronger character. Your resilience becomes not just personal strength but a gift you offer to others who are struggling, a living testimony that it's possible to remain faithful when life becomes difficult.

Endurance as Worship and Witness

Perhaps the most transformative understanding of resilience is recognizing that how you handle adversity becomes both worship and witness. When you choose hope over despair during loss, when you extend love despite being hurt, when you serve others while you're struggling, you're offering your endurance as an act of worship to God. Your faithfulness during difficulty declares your trust in His character more powerfully than praise during prosperity ever could.

Simultaneously, your resilience becomes a witness to others about the reality of God's sustaining grace. When people see you maintaining joy in sorrow, peace in chaos, and love in conflict, they witness that supernatural strength is available to ordinary people. Your endurance gives others permission to hope that they too can survive their storms, and your example provides a roadmap for how faith can sustain us through any difficulty.

This dual nature of endurance as worship and witness elevates every moment of perseverance from mere survival to sacred service. The parent caring for a special needs child demonstrates God's patient love. The caregiver serving an aging family member reflects divine compassion. The entrepreneur persisting through business challenges models faithful stewardship. Every act of faithful endurance becomes a sermon about God's sustaining grace.

The Community of Endurance

Remember that you were never meant to endure alone. God has designed us for community precisely because some burdens are too heavy for individual shoulders and some journeys are too long for solitary travelers. Your resilience is both strengthened by others' support and becomes a source of strength for their struggles. The endurance you develop today prepares you to carry others when their strength fails tomorrow.

This interconnectedness means that investing in your own resilience is not selfish but generous. When you build emotional, spiritual, and physical capacity for handling difficulty, you become better able to support others during their challenges. When you develop skills for finding hope in hopeless situations, you can share that hope with those who are struggling to believe. When you learn to trust God's faithfulness through your own dark seasons, you can remind others of His character when they can't see it for themselves.

The community of endurance spans generations as well. The resilience you model today teaches the next generation that faith can sustain us through any trial. The perseverance you demonstrate creates a legacy of faithfulness that will strengthen your children, grandchildren, and spiritual offspring long after your own struggles are past.

The Eternal Perspective on Temporary Trials

As you continue your journey, remember that every trial you endure with faith has eternal significance, while every hardship you face is ultimately temporary. This perspective doesn't minimize present pain but provides hope that transcends current circumstances. "For our light affliction, which is but for a moment, worketh for us a far more exceeding and eternal weight of glory" (2 Corinthians 4:17).

Understanding the temporary nature of earthly trials enables you to persevere through situations that might otherwise seem unbearable. The cancer diagnosis, job loss, relationship breakdown, or financial crisis that feels overwhelming today will eventually pass, but the character you develop through enduring it faithfully will last forever. The strength you gain, the wisdom you acquire, and the compassion you develop through suffering become permanent additions to your capacity for serving others.

This eternal perspective also provides comfort during seasons when you can't see purpose in your pain. God is working in ways that may not be visible until heaven, creating beauty from ashes and redemption from ruin in patterns too complex for our current understanding. Your faithful endurance participates in this divine artistry, even when you can't see the full picture.

Your Resilience Assignment

As you move forward from this chapter, carry with you the Resilience Assessment from our practical applications. This week, honestly evaluate your current capacity across all dimensions—physical, emotional, mental, spiritual, and relational. Identify your strongest areas and your most vulnerable spots, understanding that resilience building requires both leveraging strengths and addressing weaknesses.

Choose one daily resilience practice from our toolkit and commit to it for the next 30 days. Whether it's a morning preparation routine, evening reflection practice, or specific endurance exercise, begin building the muscle of faithful perseverance through small, consistent choices. Remember, resilience is developed gradually through practice, not instantly through crisis.

Looking Ahead

In our next chapter, we'll explore how to build meaningful relationships and expand your positive influence in the lives of others. You'll discover that the resilience you're developing now becomes the foundation for sustainable service and leadership that can weather any storm while continuing to bless those around you.

But for now, embrace your calling to endure well. Trust that the God who has sustained you through past difficulties will provide strength for future challenges. Believe that your faithful perseverance matters more than you can imagine, both for your own character development and for the encouragement of others who are watching your journey.

10

Relationships & Influence

No one grows richly—or serves deeply—in isolation.
Relationships are the currency of a meaningful life, and influence is the natural outflow of authentic connection.

WHETHER IN BUSINESS, FAITH, OR EVERYDAY LIFE, the people we surround ourselves with shape our character, our choices, and the legacy we leave behind. The most successful leaders and fulfilled individuals understand that influence is not about authority or status, but about the trust and respect earned through genuine care and service.

At the heart of every thriving organization or community is a network of strong, supportive relationships. These bonds are built on trust, honesty, and shared values. In business, teams that communicate openly and value each member's contribution outperform those that operate in silos. In faith communities, relationships become the foundation for encouragement, accountability, and spiritual growth. As research shows, developmental relationships—those characterized by care, mentorship, and shared purpose—help both young people and adults thrive, shaping not only our faith but our confidence and sense of agency.

Jesus modeled the power of intentional, life-on-life relationships. He invested deeply in a small group of disciples, teaching, encouraging, and even challenging them. He prayed with them, shared meals, and walked through both triumphs and trials together. His relationships were marked by love, patience, and a willingness to serve. "By this shall all men know that ye are my disciples, if ye have love one to another" (John 13:35). The Bible reminds us that we are created for relationship—with God, and with one another—and that our influence grows as we invest in others with humility and grace.

Building strong relationships requires intentionality. It means choosing friends and partners who share your vision and values, being open to mentorship and accountability, and practicing patience and forgiveness as you grow together. It also means welcoming differences as opportunities for growth, and facing conflict with honesty and a desire for understanding. Prayer, shared service, and honest conversation are practical ways to deepen bonds and nurture a supportive community.

Influence is not about manipulation, but about inspiring others through your example. When you serve others and invest in their growth, your impact multiplies far beyond what you can achieve alone. As you build relationships rooted in trust and encouragement, you become a catalyst for positive change—in your workplace, your family, your faith community, and beyond.

The Architecture of Meaningful Relationships

Understanding the structure and dynamics of meaningful relationships provides a foundation for building connections that enrich your life while serving others effectively. Not all relationships are designed to function at the same level of intimacy or serve the same purposes, and recognizing these differences helps you invest appropriately in each type of connection.

Concentric Circles of Relationship. Healthy relationship architecture resembles concentric circles, with different levels of intimacy, commitment, and mutual investment. At the center are your most intimate relationships—spouse, closest family members, and perhaps one or two best friends. These relationships involve complete vulnerability, mutual accountability, and shared life direction. They require the highest investment of time, energy, and emotional resources but also provide the greatest support, encouragement, and growth opportunities.

The next circle includes close friends and family members with whom you share significant but not complete intimacy. These relationships involve regular communication, mutual support during challenges, and shared experiences that create lasting bonds. You might have 8-12 relationships in this category, providing a strong foundation of connection without overwhelming your capacity for deep relationship investment.

The third circle encompasses broader friendships, colleagues, and community connections. These relationships are characterized by mutual respect, shared interests or values, and occasional deeper interaction. While less intimate than inner circles, these relationships provide social support, professional collaboration, and opportunities for service and influence.

The outer circle includes acquaintances, neighbors, and people you encounter regularly but with limited depth. While these relationships may seem less important, they often provide opportunities for service, witness, and unexpected connection. Many meaningful relationships begin in this outer circle and move inward through intentional investment over time.

Relationship Purposes and Functions. Different relationships serve different purposes in our lives, and understanding these functions helps us appreciate each connection appropriately without expecting every relationship to meet every need.

Support relationships provide emotional encouragement, practical help, and presence during difficult times. These people celebrate your successes, comfort you during losses, and offer assistance when you're overwhelmed. Support relationships require mutual care and availability, creating networks of reciprocal help and encouragement.

Growth relationships challenge you to become better, offer honest feedback about blind spots, and encourage you to pursue your potential. These relationships include mentors, coaches, accountability partners, and friends who love you enough to speak truth even when it's difficult to hear. Growth relationships require humility, openness to feedback, and commitment to development.

Collaborative relationships focus on shared goals, projects, or purposes. These might include business partners, ministry teammates, or community volunteers working together on common causes. Collaborative relationships require clear communication, mutual respect for different strengths, and commitment to shared vision over personal agenda.

Inspirational relationships expose you to different perspectives, challenge your assumptions, and expand your vision of what's possible. These relationships include thought leaders, creative individuals, or people whose lives demonstrate qualities you want to develop. Inspirational relationships often involve more receiving than giving, at least initially.

The Biblical Foundation of Transformational Relationships

Scripture provides a comprehensive framework for understanding how relationships can facilitate mutual growth, spiritual development, and effective service. The biblical approach to relationships emphasizes both personal benefit and others' welfare, creating connections that serve kingdom purposes while meeting human needs for love and belonging.

The Trinity as Relationship Model. The doctrine of the Trinity reveals that relationship is fundamental to God's nature. The Father, Son, and Holy Spirit exist in perfect unity while maintaining distinct personalities and roles. This divine relationship model demonstrates several principles for human relationships: unity without uniformity, mutual honor and submission, shared purpose with individual contribution, and love that seeks the other's glory rather than personal advancement.

This Trinitarian model suggests that the healthiest human relationships involve both deep connection and individual identity, shared values with diverse perspectives, and mutual service rather than competitive self-interest. Just as the persons of the Trinity work together for common purposes while maintaining their unique roles, healthy relationships allow each person to contribute their distinctive gifts while supporting shared goals.

Jesus' Relational Ministry Model. Jesus' approach to relationships provides a practical blueprint for building connections that transform lives. He invested in different people at different levels—intimate relationships with the twelve disciples, closer relationships with Peter, James, and John, and his closest relationship with John the Beloved. He also maintained broader relationships with followers like Mary, Martha, and Lazarus, and engaged meaningfully with many others he encountered.

Jesus' relationships were characterized by intentionality, authenticity, and service. He chose his disciples purposefully, called them into specific relationships, and invested in their development over time. He was genuine about his emotions, needs, and struggles while maintaining appropriate boundaries. He consistently served others' interests, even when it required personal sacrifice.

Perhaps most importantly, Jesus' relationships were developmental—he focused on helping others become who God created them to be rather than using them for his own purposes. He saw potential in unlikely people, called out their gifts, and provided opportunities for growth and service. His relational investment multiplied his influence.

The "One Another" Passages. The New Testament contains numerous "one another" commands that describe how believers should relate to each other: love one another, encourage one another, serve one another, bear one another's burdens, forgive one another, and many others.

These passages reveal that spiritual growth and effective ministry happen primarily through relationships rather than individual effort.

These relational commands suggest that Christian community should be characterized by mutual care, shared responsibility, and reciprocal service. No one person has all the gifts or wisdom needed for spiritual maturity—we are better when we can lean of each other's contributions, perspectives, and support. This interdependence creates both opportunity and responsibility for building relationships that facilitate growth and service. And yet ultimately all we need is a loving relationship with God the Father and His Son Our Lord and Savior Jesus Christ.

The "one another" passages also imply that influence is reciprocal rather than unidirectional. Even in relationships with clear authority structures (like parent-child or mentor-mentee), both parties have opportunities to serve and influence each other. This mutuality prevents relationships from becoming exploitative or one-sided.

The Psychology of Influence and Persuasion

Understanding how influence actually works in human relationships helps us become more effective at inspiring positive change while avoiding manipulative or coercive approaches. True influence is based on trust, authenticity, and genuine care for others' welfare rather than personal agenda or control.

Authority vs. Influence. Authority is position-based power—the ability to compel compliance through formal role, control of resources, or threat of consequences. Influence is relationship-based power—the ability to inspire voluntary cooperation through trust, respect, and shared vision. While authority can produce immediate compliance, influence creates lasting change and enthusiastic participation.

The most effective leaders combine appropriate authority with genuine influence, using their position to serve others' development rather than merely securing their own objectives. They earn the right to be heard through demonstrated competence, integrity, and care for others' welfare. This approach creates what researchers call "referent power"—people follow not because they have to but because they want to.

Authority without influence often produces resentment, minimal compliance, and resistance when oversight is reduced. Influence without authority can create frustration when good ideas cannot be implemented due to structural constraints. The ideal combination leverages position appropriately while building genuine relationships that inspire voluntary cooperation.

The Trust Foundation. All genuine influence is built on trust, which researcher Charles Feltman defines as "choosing to risk making something you value vulnerable to another person's actions." Trust has four core components: sincerity (honesty about motives and feelings), reliability (consistency in words and actions), competence (ability to deliver on commitments), and care (genuine concern for others' welfare).

Building trust requires time, consistency, and vulnerability. People need to observe your character across various situations before they're willing to be influenced by your ideas or follow your leadership. This means that influence is often a long-term investment rather than a short-term achievement.

Trust can be destroyed quickly but takes significant time to rebuild. This makes integrity and consistency crucial for maintaining influence over time. People will forgive occasional mistakes or failures, but they struggle to trust those who are consistently unreliable or who demonstrate selfish motives.

Reciprocity and Social Exchange. Human relationships operate on principles of reciprocity—we tend to respond to others' actions with similar behaviors. When someone serves us, we feel obligated to serve them. When someone trusts us, we're more likely to be trustworthy. When someone invests in our growth, we want to contribute to theirs.

Understanding reciprocity helps explain why servant leadership is so effective at building influence. When leaders consistently serve others' interests, those being served naturally want to support the leader's objectives. This creates what researchers call "idiosyncrasy credits"—permission to make difficult requests or challenge others because you've demonstrated consistent care for their welfare.

However, reciprocity-based influence must be authentic rather than manipulative. If people sense that your service is merely a strategy to gain compliance, the reciprocity dynamic backfires and creates resistance rather than cooperation. Genuine service that flows from love and care naturally creates influence, but calculated service designed to create obligation often produces cynicism.

Emotional Intelligence in Relationships

Emotional intelligence—the ability to recognize, understand, and manage emotions in yourself and others—is crucial for building meaningful relationships and exercising positive influence. This capacity involves both intrapersonal skills (managing your own emotions) and interpersonal skills (understanding and responding appropriately to others' emotions).

Self-Awareness and Self-Regulation. Effective relationship building begins with understanding your own emotional patterns, triggers, and responses. Self-aware people recognize when they're feeling defensive, anxious, frustrated, or excited, and they understand how these emotions affect their communication and decision-making. This awareness enables them to choose their responses rather than simply reacting automatically.

Self-regulation involves managing your emotional responses in ways that serve relationships rather than damage them. This doesn't mean suppressing or denying emotions but rather expressing them appropriately and constructively.

Self-regulation also includes managing your impact on others' emotions. Emotions are contagious—your anxiety can increase others' stress, your enthusiasm can energize a team, and your peace can calm a tense situation. Understanding this emotional impact helps you become more intentional about the emotional tone you bring to relationships and interactions.

Empathy and Social Awareness. Empathy involves understanding others' emotions, perspectives, and experiences without necessarily agreeing with them or taking responsibility for fixing them. Empathetic people can accurately read emotional cues, understand underlying concerns, and respond in ways that make others feel heard and understood.

Social awareness extends empathy to group dynamics, organizational culture, and community patterns. Socially aware people understand how different individuals relate to each other, what unspoken rules govern group behavior, and how to navigate complex social systems effectively.

These skills are crucial for influence because people are more likely to be influenced by those who understand them. When someone feels truly seen and understood, they become more open to that person's ideas, feedback, and direction. Conversely, people resist influence from those who seem oblivious to their concerns, emotions, or perspectives.

Relationship Management. Relationship management involves using emotional intelligence to build stronger connections, resolve conflicts constructively, and inspire others toward shared goals. This includes skills like active listening, clear communication, conflict resolution, and collaborative problem-solving.

Effective relationship management requires adapting your communication style to others' preferences and needs. Some people need detailed information before making decisions, while others prefer broad concepts. Some respond well to direct challenges, while others need gentle encouragement. Emotionally intelligent people adjust their approach based on what will be most effective for each individual.

Relationship management also involves understanding and working with others' motivations, strengths, and developmental needs. Instead of trying to influence everyone the same way, emotionally intelligent people tailor their approach to what will genuinely serve each person's growth and contribution.

The Mentoring and Discipleship Model

One of the most powerful forms of relationship-based influence is mentoring—the intentional investment in others' development through relationship, guidance, and shared experience. This model, exemplified by Jesus' relationship with his disciples, creates multiplication of impact as those being mentored eventually mentor others.

Characteristics of Effective Mentoring. Effective mentoring relationships are characterized by several key elements. Intentionality means both parties are clear about the purpose and goals of the relationship. Mutual commitment involves agreed-upon expectations for time, communication, and investment. Developmental focus prioritizes the mentee's growth over the mentor's convenience or agenda. Trust and safety create an environment where honest conversation and vulnerability are possible.

Reciprocal learning recognizes that mentors also learn and grow through the relationship, even while providing primary guidance. Gradual release involves progressively giving the mentee more responsibility and independence. Multiplication vision anticipates that the mentee will eventually mentor others, creating exponential impact.

Biblical mentoring relationships like Moses and Joshua, Elijah and Elisha, and Paul and Timothy demonstrate these characteristics while showing how mentoring serves God's larger purposes rather than just individual development.

The Mentoring Process. Effective mentoring typically follows a predictable process that moves from dependence to independence to interdependence. The modeling phase involves the mentor demonstrating skills, character qualities, or approaches while the mentee observes and learns. The coaching phase provides opportunities for the mentee to practice with guidance, feedback, and support. The releasing phase gives the mentee increasing independence while maintaining relationship and availability for consultation.

This process requires wisdom about timing and individual readiness. Some people need extended modeling before they're ready for coaching, while others learn better through trial and experience. Effective mentors adjust their approach based on the mentee's learning style, confidence level, and specific developmental needs.

The goal is not to create dependency but to develop capacity. Successful mentoring produces people who become effective mentors themselves, multiplying impact across generations and communities.

Discipleship as Life-on-Life Influence. Christian discipleship represents the highest form of mentoring, focusing not just on skill development but on spiritual formation and character transformation. Discipleship involves modeling Christ-like character, teaching biblical truth, providing spiritual guidance, and creating opportunities for ministry and service.

Jesus' discipleship model involved both formal teaching and informal life sharing. He taught in synagogues and crowds, but he also lived with his disciples, shared meals, faced challenges together, and processed experiences through conversation and prayer. This life-on-life approach created deep formation that classroom instruction alone could not achieve.

Modern discipleship often lacks this life-sharing component, limiting its effectiveness. The most transformational discipleship relationships involve spending time together in various contexts—work, family, recreation, service, and worship—so that spiritual formation happens through shared experience rather than just formal instruction.

Building Influence Networks and Communities

Sustainable influence rarely depends on individual relationships alone but rather on networks and communities that share values, vision, and commitment to mutual growth and service. Understanding how to build and participate in such networks multiplies your impact while providing support for your own development.

Network Types and Functions. Different types of networks serve different purposes in your influence strategy. Professional networks focus on career development, business collaboration, and industry advancement. Ministry networks center on spiritual growth, service opportunities, and kingdom impact. Learning networks emphasize skill development, knowledge sharing, and intellectual growth. Support networks prioritize encouragement, accountability, and mutual care.

Most effective leaders participate in multiple networks that serve different aspects of their calling and development. This diversity prevents over-dependence on any single community while providing various perspectives and resources for different challenges and opportunities.

Network Building Strategies. Building influence networks requires both strategic thinking and genuine relationship investment. Value creation involves consistently contributing to others' success rather than just seeking personal benefit. Connector mindset focuses on introducing people who could benefit from knowing each other. Authentic engagement emphasizes genuine interest in others over self-promotion.

Consistency in participation and follow-through builds trust and reliability within networks. Reciprocity ensures that you both give and receive support rather than just taking from network relationships. Long-term perspective recognizes that network building is an investment that pays dividends over years rather than immediate returns.

Community Leadership and Influence. Leading within communities and networks requires understanding group dynamics, consensus building, and collaborative decision-making. Community leaders serve as facilitators rather than dictators, helping groups discover shared vision and coordinate efforts toward common goals.

Effective community leadership involves vision casting that helps people see possibilities for collective impact. Conflict resolution skills enable groups to work through disagreements constructively. Resource coordination ensures that people's gifts and contributions are utilized effectively. Culture creation establishes norms and values that support the community's purposes.

Community influence often operates differently than individual influence, requiring patience with group processes, willingness to share credit and recognition, and commitment to consensus-building rather than unilateral decision-making.

Digital Age Relationships and Virtual Influence

The digital revolution has created new opportunities and challenges for building relationships and exercising influence. Understanding how to leverage technology for meaningful connection while avoiding its pitfalls is crucial for modern relationship building and influence development.

Digital Relationship Building. Technology can enhance relationship building through increased communication frequency, broader geographic reach, and new forms of shared experience. Social media platforms, video calls, messaging apps, and collaborative tools enable relationships that would be impossible through face-to-face interaction alone.

However, digital relationships require different skills and awareness than in-person connections. Digital presence involves being intentional about how you present yourself online and how your communications affect others. Virtual empathy requires developing sensitivity to others' emotions and needs even without physical presence cues. Boundary management becomes crucial when digital communication can intrude on personal time and space.

Online Influence Strategies. Digital platforms provide unprecedented opportunities for influence through content creation, thought leadership, and community building. Content strategy involves sharing insights, experiences, and resources that genuinely help others. Platform optimization requires understanding how different digital environments work and adapting your approach accordingly.

Authentic voice remains crucial in digital influence—people can sense when online communication is genuine versus manufactured. Engagement quality matters more than quantity—meaningful interactions with smaller audiences often create more influence than superficial contact with large numbers.

Balancing Digital and In-Person Connection. The most effective relationship builders and influencers combine digital tools with face-to-face interaction, using technology to enhance rather than replace personal connection. Hybrid approaches might include online communication between in-person meetings, digital content that supplements live events, or virtual platforms that facilitate real-world collaboration.

Digital detox practices help maintain the capacity for deep, focused relationship building in an environment of constant connectivity and distraction. Intentional presence in both digital and physical interactions creates more meaningful connections than divided attention across multiple platforms.

The goal is using technology as a tool for genuine relationship building rather than a substitute for authentic human connection. Digital platforms work best when they facilitate real relationships rather than replacing them with virtual substitutes.

PRACTICAL APPLICATIONS
The Relationship Audit and Investment Strategy

Before building new relationships or expanding your influence, it's crucial to assess your current relational landscape and identify areas for strategic investment. This audit helps you understand where your relationships are thriving, where they need attention, and where new connections might serve both your growth and others' benefit.

Current Relationship Mapping Exercise

Concentric Circle Analysis: Draw four concentric circles and place people in your life according to their relational proximity:

- Inner Circle (5-7 people): Spouse, closest family, best friends who know you completely

- Close Circle (10-15 people): Good friends, close family members, trusted colleagues
- Broader Circle (20-30 people): Regular friends, extended family, respected colleagues
- Outer Circle (50+ people): Acquaintances, neighbors, casual colleagues, community connections

Relationship Function Assessment: For each person in your inner and close circles, identify what role they play:

- Support Provider: Offers emotional encouragement and practical help
- Growth Catalyst: Challenges you to improve and provides honest feedback
- Wisdom Source: Provides guidance based on experience and insight
- Collaboration Partner: Works with you on shared goals and projects
- Joy Bringer: Adds fun, laughter, and lightness to your life
- Service Opportunity: Someone you primarily serve or mentor

Relationship Health Evaluation: Rate each significant relationship on these dimensions (1-5 scale):

- Mutual Investment: Both parties contribute time and energy
- Trust Level: Degree of vulnerability and reliability present
- Growth Impact: How much this relationship helps you become better
- Alignment: How well your values and directions complement each other
- Communication Quality: Honesty, clarity, and respect in interactions
- Conflict Resolution: Ability to work through disagreements constructively

Investment Priority Identification

Relationship Investment Matrix: Plot your relationships on a matrix with two axes:

- Vertical Axis: High Impact on Your Growth/Service vs. Low Impact
- Horizontal Axis: High Investment Required vs. Low Investment Required

This creates four quadrants:

- High Impact, Low Investment: Maintain these relationships consistently
- High Impact, High Investment: These are your priority development relationships
- Low Impact, Low Investment: Maintain these casually without guilt
- Low Impact, High Investment: Consider whether these relationships are worth the cost

Strategic Investment Planning: Based on your analysis, identify:

- 3 relationships to deepen through increased time and vulnerability

- 2 relationships that need repair or renewed attention
- 1 new relationship you'd like to develop for mutual growth
- 1 relationship where you can increase your service and contribution
- 2-3 relationships where you need to establish better boundaries

The Influence Development Toolkit

Building positive influence requires developing specific skills and practices that earn trust, create value for others, and inspire voluntary cooperation. This toolkit provides concrete strategies for developing authentic influence in various contexts.

Trust-Building Practices

Reliability Development:

- Commitment Management: Only make promises you can keep, and keep every promise you make
- Time Respect: Arrive on time for appointments and meetings, and honor others' time constraints
- Follow-Through Systems: Create reminders and accountability systems to ensure you complete what you start
- Consistency: Maintain the same character and values across different situations and relationships
- Transparent Communication: Share your reasoning for decisions and be honest about limitations or mistakes

Competence Demonstration:

- Skill Development: Continuously improve abilities that serve others and advance shared goals
- Preparation: Come to interactions and meetings well-prepared and ready to contribute value
- Quality Work: Deliver excellent results in whatever responsibilities you accept
- Learning Mindset: Acknowledge when you don't know something and commit to finding answers
- Resource Sharing: Offer knowledge, connections, or tools that help others succeed

Care Expression:

- Active Listening: Focus completely on understanding others' perspectives and concerns
- Personal Interest: Remember and ask about things that matter to others (family, goals, challenges)
- Celebration: Acknowledge others' successes and milestones genuinely

- Support Offering: Provide help during difficult times without being asked
- Advocacy: Speak positively about others when they're not present

Value Creation Strategies

Problem-Solving Contribution:
- Identify challenges that others are facing and offer practical solutions
- Share resources, connections, or expertise that address real needs
- Volunteer for difficult tasks that others are avoiding or unable to handle
- Bring different perspectives to complex problems
- Follow up to ensure your contributions were actually helpful

Growth Facilitation:
- Provide feedback that helps others improve without damaging their confidence
- Create opportunities for others to develop new skills or gain experience
- Connect people with mentors, resources, or opportunities that serve their development
- Share your own failures and lessons learned to help others avoid similar mistakes
- Celebrate others' growth and acknowledge their progress publicly

Vision Casting and Inspiration:
- Help others see possibilities they might not recognize in themselves
- Share stories and examples that expand others' sense of what's possible
- Connect individual contributions to larger purposes and meanings
- Maintain hope and optimism during difficult seasons
- Challenge others to pursue worthy goals that stretch their capacity

The Mentoring and Discipleship Framework

Whether you're mentoring others or seeking mentorship yourself, having a clear framework helps ensure these relationships are productive and transformational for all parties involved.

Becoming an Effective Mentor

Mentee Selection and Preparation: Look for people who demonstrate:
- Genuine desire for growth rather than just wanting easy answers
- Willingness to receive feedback and implement suggestions
- Respect for your time and expertise shown through preparation and follow-through

- Character qualities that align with your values and calling
- Potential for impact in their sphere of influence

Prepare for mentoring by:
- Clarifying what you can and cannot offer based on your experience and availability
- Establishing clear expectations for time commitment, communication, and goals
- Developing a loose curriculum or framework based on what you've learned
- Identifying your own ongoing learning needs to prevent stagnation
- Seeking accountability for your mentoring effectiveness

Mentoring Process and Practices:

Relationship Building Phase (First 1-2 meetings):
- Get to know each other's backgrounds, goals, and expectations
- Establish communication preferences and meeting schedules
- Clarify confidentiality boundaries and other relationship guidelines
- Begin with low-risk sharing to build trust gradually
- Assess learning style and developmental needs

Development Phase (Ongoing):
- Share relevant experiences and lessons learned without dominating conversation
- Ask questions that help mentees discover insights rather than just giving answers
- Provide specific, actionable feedback based on observation and interaction
- Create opportunities for mentees to practice new skills with your support
- Connect mentees with other resources, people, and experiences that support their growth

Release Phase (As appropriate):
- Gradually reduce frequency of formal meetings while maintaining relationship
- Encourage mentees to begin mentoring others to multiply impact
- Celebrate growth and achievements while acknowledging ongoing development needs
- Transition to peer-level relationship when appropriate
- Maintain availability for consultation while fostering independence

Seeking and Maximizing Mentorship

Mentor Identification and Approach: Look for potential mentors who:

- Demonstrate character qualities you want to develop
- Have achieved goals similar to what you're pursuing
- Show willingness to invest in others' development
- Maintain healthy relationships and balanced perspectives
- Align with your values even if their methods differ from yours

Approach potential mentors by:
- Researching their background and current commitments before reaching out
- Explaining specifically what you hope to learn and why you chose them
- Offering to meet their schedule and location preferences
- Suggesting a trial period to see if the relationship is mutually beneficial
- Expressing gratitude for their time regardless of their response

Maximizing Mentoring Relationships:
- Come prepared with specific questions and challenges you're facing
- Take notes during conversations and follow up on suggestions
- Report back on progress and lessons learned from previous conversations
- Ask for introductions to other people who could contribute to your development
- Look for ways to serve your mentor's interests and goals
- Practice what you're learning by beginning to mentor others

Digital Relationship Building and Online Influence

In our connected world, developing skills for building meaningful relationships and exercising positive influence through digital platforms is essential for expanding your reach and impact.

Digital Presence Development

Platform Strategy and Optimization:
- Choose 1-2 primary platforms where your target audience is most active
- Develop a consistent voice and message across all digital communications
- Create valuable content that serves others rather than just promoting yourself
- Engage authentically with others' content through thoughtful comments and shares
- Use professional photos and clear, compelling descriptions of who you are and what you offer

Content Creation for Influence:

- Share insights and lessons learned from your experiences
- Ask thoughtful questions that generate meaningful discussion
- Provide practical tips and resources that help others solve problems
- Tell stories that illustrate important principles without being preachy
- Highlight others' achievements and contributions to build community

Online Community Building:
- Create or participate in groups focused on shared interests or goals
- Host virtual events, discussions, or learning opportunities
- Connect people who could benefit from knowing each other
- Facilitate conversations that help people learn and grow
- Maintain consistent participation rather than sporadic posting

Digital Relationship Maintenance

Virtual Communication Best Practices:
- Respond promptly to messages and comments to show respect for others' engagement
- Use video calls when possible for important conversations to maintain personal connection
- Remember and reference previous conversations to show you value the relationship
- Share appropriate personal updates to maintain authenticity and vulnerability
- Celebrate others' milestones and achievements publicly when appropriate

Balancing Digital and In-Person Connection:
- Use digital communication to enhance rather than replace face-to-face interaction
- Transition online relationships to in-person meetings when geographically possible
- Create opportunities for your online community to connect with each other offline
- Maintain digital sabbaths or boundaries to preserve capacity for deep relationships
- Prioritize quality of digital interactions over quantity of followers or connections

Conflict Resolution and Relationship Repair

Even the best relationships encounter misunderstandings, disagreements, and conflicts. Having skills for navigating these challenges constructively can deepen relationships rather than damage them.

Conflict Prevention Strategies:
- Clear Communication: Say what you mean directly but kindly, and ask clarifying

questions when you're uncertain about others' intentions

- Expectation Management: Discuss roles, responsibilities, and expectations explicitly rather than assuming others understand
- Regular Check-ins: Schedule periodic conversations to address small issues before they become larger problems
- Assumption Challenging: When you feel hurt or frustrated, consider alternative explanations before concluding others acted with negative intent
- Boundary Setting: Communicate your limits clearly and respectfully before resentment builds

Conflict Resolution Process:

Preparation Phase:

- Examine your own contribution to the conflict before addressing others' actions
- Pray for wisdom, humility, and love for the other person
- Choose an appropriate time and setting for the conversation
- Prepare to listen as much as you speak
- Focus on specific behaviors rather than character attacks

Conversation Phase:

- Start by affirming your commitment to the relationship
- Share your perspective using "I" statements rather than accusations
- Listen actively to understand the other person's viewpoint
- Acknowledge valid points in their perspective
- Work together to identify solutions that serve both parties' legitimate needs

Resolution Phase:

- Agree on specific actions each person will take going forward
- Establish accountability measures to ensure follow-through
- Schedule a follow-up conversation to assess progress
- Extend and request forgiveness for mistakes made
- Celebrate the relationship's resilience and growth through the conflict

This comprehensive approach to relationship building and influence development recognizes that meaningful connections require intentional investment, authentic care, and consistent character, while influence flows naturally from genuine service to others' growth and well-being.

CHAPTER CONCLUSION
The Multiplication of Love Through Relationship

As we conclude this exploration of relationships and influence, it's essential to recognize the profound truth you've encountered: meaningful relationships are not just pleasant additions to life—they are the primary vehicles through which love, growth, and service multiply in the world. You haven't simply learned techniques for networking or strategies for persuasion—you've discovered the sacred art of human connection that transforms both individuals and communities. True influence flows not from position or manipulation but from authentic love expressed through consistent service to others' growth and well-being.

The most beautiful aspect of relationship-based influence is its exponential nature. When you invest in someone's development, you're not just helping one person—you're empowering them to help others, creating ripple effects that extend far beyond your direct involvement. The person you mentor today becomes the mentor who shapes others tomorrow. The encouragement you offer in someone's difficult season becomes the hope they share with others facing similar struggles. Your relationship investments become multiplying legacies that touch lives you may never know about.

Relationships as Sacred Trust

Perhaps the most transformative perspective on relationships is understanding them as sacred trusts—opportunities to steward God's love in human form. When someone allows you into their life, shares their struggles, or seeks your guidance, they're entrusting you with something precious and vulnerable. This trust creates both privilege and responsibility to handle their confidence with care, respect their dignity, and serve their highest good rather than your own agenda.

This understanding elevates every relationship interaction from casual exchange to holy ground. The conversation with a struggling colleague becomes an opportunity to embody God's compassion. The time spent with a friend in crisis becomes a chance to demonstrate His faithfulness. The investment in a younger person's development becomes participation in His ongoing work of forming human beings for His purposes. Your relationships become both worship and ministry, expressing your love for God through love for others.

When you approach relationships as sacred trusts, you naturally become more careful with others' hearts, more intentional about your influence, and more committed to their welfare. This perspective prevents the subtle selfishness that can creep into even well-intentioned relationships and keeps your focus on serving rather than using others for your own benefit.

The Legacy of Relational Investment

Remember that the relationships you build and the influence you exercise create legacies that extend far beyond your lifetime. The character qualities you model, the wisdom you share, and the love you demonstrate become patterns that others carry forward into their own relationships. The young person you mentor today may mentor hundreds of others throughout their lifetime. The colleague you encourage during a difficult season may become a source of hope for many others facing similar challenges.

This generational perspective transforms how you approach every relationship interaction. The patience you demonstrate with a difficult family member teaches everyone watching about unconditional love. The way you handle conflict with a friend provides a model for healthy disagreement. The forgiveness you extend to someone who has hurt you demonstrates the possibility of redemption and restoration. Your relational example becomes curriculum for those who observe your life.

Years from now, people may not remember your specific words or achievements, but they will remember how you made them feel, how you treated them during difficult times, and how your presence in their lives helped them become better people. This relational legacy becomes one of the most meaningful forms of service you can offer to the world.

The Divine Partnership in Human Connection

As you continue building relationships and exercising influence, remember that you're never working alone in these endeavors. The same God who created us for relationship and designed us to need each other is actively involved in every authentic connection you make and every positive influence you exercise. He works through your relationships to accomplish His purposes while using them to shape your own character and expand your capacity for love.

This divine partnership means that even your relational failures and mistakes can be redeemed for good purposes. The relationship conflict that teaches you humility, the influence attempt that fails but shows you your pride, the friendship that ends painfully but develops your capacity for forgiveness—all of these experiences contribute to your growth and preparation for future relationships. God wastes nothing in the economy of relationship development.

Understanding this partnership also provides comfort during seasons when relationships feel difficult or influence seems limited. You can trust that God is working through your faithful investment in others even when you can't see immediate results. You can persevere through relationship challenges knowing that He is using these difficulties to develop both your character and theirs. You can extend love and service without demanding reciprocation because your ultimate relationship is with Him.

Your Relational Assignment

As you move forward from this chapter, carry with you the Relationship Audit from our practical applications. This week, honestly assess your current relational landscape and identify specific areas for strategic investment. Choose one relationship to deepen, one to repair, and one new connection to develop. Remember, meaningful relationships are built through consistent investment over time, not dramatic gestures or intensive effort.

Begin implementing one trust-building practice from our toolkit consistently across all your relationships. Whether it's improved listening, more reliable follow-through, or increased care expression, start developing the relational muscles that will enhance your capacity for meaningful connection and positive influence. Small, consistent improvements in your relational skills create significant cumulative impact over time.

Looking Ahead

In our next chapter, we'll explore how to cultivate love and compassion as the foundation for all meaningful service and relationship. You'll discover that the influence skills you're developing now reach their full potential when grounded in genuine care for others' welfare and authentic expression of God's love.

But for now, embrace your calling to be a person of deep relationships and positive influence. Trust that God will use your investment in others to accomplish purposes greater than you can imagine. Believe that every act of love, every moment of authentic connection, and every effort to serve others' growth matters more than you can comprehend.

11

Love & Compassion

*At the core of every life that serves and grows richly
is a heart shaped by love and compassion.*

THESE ARE NOT PASSIVE EMOTIONS, BUT ACTIVE FORCES—choices we make, day after day, to see the world through the eyes of empathy, kindness, and grace. In business, leadership, and daily life, love and compassion are the qualities that turn transactions into relationships, teams into communities, and challenges into opportunities for healing and hope.

Love, as Jesus taught, is not just a feeling but a way of living. "Be ye therefore merciful, as your Father also is merciful" (Luke 6:36). Compassion moves us beyond sympathy into action; it compels us to reach out, to heal, and to uphold the dignity of every person we encounter. The parable of the Good Samaritan reminds us that love knows no boundaries, and that true compassion is measured not by sentiment but by our willingness to serve, even when it's inconvenient or costly. This is the love that forgives, the love that lifts up the broken, and the love that welcomes the stranger as a neighbor.

In the teachings of Jesus, love and compassion are inseparable from leadership and influence. He calls us to love our neighbors as ourselves, to forgive not just once but "seventy times seven" (Matthew 18:22), and to extend kindness even to those who may never return it. This radical, selfless love is the gold standard for all our interactions—at home, at work, and in the wider world. It is the kind of love that seeks the highest good of others, expecting nothing in return, and is always aligned with God's truth and grace.

But love and compassion are not only outward acts; they begin within. To love others well, we must first accept the love and compassion God has for us, and extend that same kindness to ourselves. Cultivating a heart of loving-kindness—through prayer, meditation, or simple gratitude—grounds us in the reality that we are loved, forgiven, and called to be agents of that love in the world. As we receive, so we give.

Practicing compassion is not always easy. It requires humility, patience, and a willingness to see beyond our own needs. Sometimes, it means loving those who are difficult, forgiving those who have hurt us, or offering help when it goes unnoticed. Yet, every act of compassion—no matter how small—ripples outward, creating a more loving, just, and connected world. As Ephesians 5:2 reminds us, "Walk in love, as Christ also hath loved us, and hath given himself for us".

The Anatomy of Compassion: From Feeling to Action

Compassion involves both emotional and cognitive responses to others' suffering, but true compassion moves beyond feeling to effective action. Understanding the components of compassion helps us develop this capacity more intentionally while avoiding the pitfalls of either cold duty or overwhelming emotion.

Compassionate Awareness. The foundation of compassion is awareness—the ability to recognize and acknowledge others' pain, struggles, and needs. This requires developing what Buddhist teachers call "beginner's mind"—approaching others with fresh eyes rather than assumptions or preconceptions about their experiences or needs.

Compassionate awareness involves several skills. Emotional attunement enables us to recognize when others are struggling, even when they don't explicitly express their pain. Perspective-taking allows us to understand others' experiences from their viewpoint rather than imposing our own interpretations. Non-judgmental observation helps us see others' situations clearly without immediately evaluating or trying to fix them.

Developing compassionate awareness often requires slowing down enough to truly see others rather than rushing through interactions focused primarily on our own agenda. It means asking better questions, listening more carefully, and paying attention to non-verbal cues that reveal others' emotional and spiritual needs.

Emotional Resonance and Regulation. Healthy compassion involves feeling with others without being overwhelmed by their emotions. This requires what researchers call "emotional resonance"—the ability to understand and share others' feelings—combined with "emotional regulation"—the capacity to maintain your own emotional stability while caring deeply about others' welfare.

Emotional resonance without regulation leads to what social workers call "compassion fatigue"—becoming so overwhelmed by others' pain that we become unable to help effectively. Emotional regulation without resonance leads to cold, duty-based service that lacks the warmth and understanding that people need during difficult times.

The balance involves learning to feel others' pain without taking responsibility for fixing it, to care deeply without becoming anxious or depressed, and to maintain hope for others even when they cannot hope for themselves. This often requires developing strong spiritual practices and support systems that help us process the emotional weight of caring for others.

Compassionate Action. True compassion always moves toward action, but effective compassionate action requires wisdom, skill, and often patience. Not every impulse to help actually helps, and sometimes our desire to alleviate others' suffering quickly prevents us from addressing underlying causes or respecting their autonomy and dignity.

Compassionate action involves several key principles. Respectful engagement honors others' dignity and decision-making capacity rather than treating them as helpless victims.

Appropriate boundaries enable us to help without enabling dependency or compromising our own well-being. Long-term thinking considers what will truly serve others' welfare over time rather than just providing immediate relief.

Skillful means involves developing the practical abilities needed to help effectively—whether that's counseling skills, practical resources, or simply the wisdom to know when to act and when to simply be present. Collaborative approach engages others as partners in addressing their challenges rather than assuming we know what they need.

The Neuroscience of Love and Empathy

Modern neuroscience has revealed fascinating insights about how love and compassion affect both our brains and our bodies, providing scientific validation for the biblical teaching that love is not just morally good but actually beneficial for human flourishing.

The Biology of Attachment and Bonding. Human beings are neurologically wired for connection and relationship. The release of oxytocin (often called the "bonding hormone") during positive social interactions creates feelings of trust, empathy, and connection while reducing stress and promoting physical healing. This biological foundation for love suggests that compassionate relationships are not just nice additions to life but fundamental requirements for optimal human functioning.

Research shows that people with strong, loving relationships have better immune function, lower rates of depression and anxiety, and even longer lifespans than those who are socially isolated. This validates the biblical teaching that "it is not good that the man should be alone" (Genesis 2:18) and suggests that our capacity for love and compassion directly affects our overall well-being.

Understanding the biology of bonding also helps explain why love and compassion must be practiced consistently over time to be most effective. Neural pathways associated with empathy, trust, and cooperation are strengthened through repeated positive interactions, creating what researchers call "positive spirals" of increasing connection and mutual care.

Mirror Neurons and Empathetic Response. Mirror neurons fire both when we perform an action and when we observe others performing the same action, creating the neurological foundation for empathy and emotional contagion. This explains why we naturally "catch" others' emotions and why spending time with compassionate people tends to increase our own capacity for compassion.

This mirror neuron system means that our emotional state significantly affects others, often unconsciously. When we approach others with genuine love and compassion, we create neurological conditions that make them more likely to respond positively and feel understood. Conversely, when we approach others with judgment, anxiety, or irritation, we trigger defensive responses that make positive interaction more difficult.

Understanding mirror neurons reinforces the importance of internal emotional work in developing compassion. We cannot fake genuine care—others' brains will pick up on our authentic emotional state regardless of our words or actions. This means that developing true compassion requires addressing our own heart attitudes rather than just learning compassionate behaviors.

The Prefrontal Cortex and Cognitive Empathy. While emotional empathy (feeling others' emotions) is largely automatic through mirror neuron systems, cognitive empathy (understanding others' perspectives) involves higher-order thinking in the prefrontal cortex. This form of empathy can be developed through practice and conscious effort, even when natural emotional empathy is limited.

Cognitive empathy involves skills like perspective-taking, theory of mind (understanding that others have different thoughts and feelings than we do), and contextual awareness (recognizing how circumstances affect others' experiences). These skills can be learned and improved through practice, making compassion partly a matter of intellectual development rather than just emotional capacity.

This understanding provides hope for people who struggle with natural emotional empathy due to personality differences, trauma history, or neurological variations. Even those who don't naturally "feel" others' emotions can learn to understand and respond to others' needs through cognitive empathy and chosen compassionate actions.

Self-Compassion: The Foundation for Loving Others

One of the most overlooked aspects of developing love and compassion for others is learning to extend love and compassion to ourselves. Self-compassion is not selfishness or self-indulgence but rather the foundation that enables sustainable, authentic care for others.

The Components of Self-Compassion. Kristin Neff's research identifies three core components of self-compassion: self-kindness (treating yourself with the same gentleness you would offer a good friend), common humanity (recognizing that struggle and imperfection are part of the human experience rather than personal failures), and mindfulness (acknowledging your pain without being overwhelmed by it or trying to suppress it).

Self-kindness involves speaking to yourself with encouragement rather than harsh criticism, offering yourself grace during failures and mistakes, and caring for your physical and emotional needs rather than ignoring or neglecting them. This doesn't mean avoiding accountability or lowering standards, but rather maintaining a supportive inner voice that motivates growth rather than paralyzing with shame.

Common humanity helps us recognize that everyone struggles, makes mistakes, and faces challenges. This perspective prevents the isolation that often accompanies difficulty and helps us maintain connection with others even during our own painful seasons. When we understand that struggle is universal, we're less likely to waste energy on self-pity and more likely to seek appropriate support and learning from our experiences.

Mindfulness in self-compassion involves acknowledging our emotions and experiences without either suppressing them or being consumed by them. This creates the emotional balance needed to respond to our own needs wisely while maintaining capacity to care for others.

Why Self-Compassion Enables Other-Compassion. People who are harsh, critical, or neglectful toward themselves often struggle to offer authentic compassion to others. Internal self-criticism creates a scarcity mindset that makes it difficult to be generous with others. Self-neglect depletes the emotional and physical resources needed for sustainable service. Self-rejection makes it hard to believe that others could truly be valuable if we ourselves are not.

Conversely, people who practice healthy self-compassion tend to be more patient, understanding, and generous with others. They have emotional resources available for caring because they're not constantly depleted by internal criticism. They can offer grace to others because they've experienced the healing power of grace in their own lives.

Self-compassion also provides the emotional stability needed for setting healthy boundaries in helping relationships. People who practice self-compassion are more likely to help others in sustainable ways rather than burning out from over-giving or becoming resentful from under-caring.

Developing Self-Compassion Practices Self-Kindness Practices: Notice your internal dialogue and consciously choose encouraging words over critical ones. Ask yourself, "What would I say to a good friend in this situation?" and offer yourself the same encouragement. Practice physical self-care as an expression of self-respect rather than just practical necessity.

Common Humanity Practices: When facing difficulties, remind yourself that "this is part of the human experience" rather than "why is this happening to me?" Connect with others who have faced similar challenges rather than isolating yourself. Practice gratitude for the ways your struggles have developed empathy and wisdom.

Mindfulness Practices: Acknowledge your emotions without judgment ("I notice that I'm feeling anxious about this presentation"). Practice self-compassion breaks when you're struggling—place your hand on your heart, acknowledge your pain, and offer yourself kindness. Develop the ability to sit with difficult emotions without immediately trying to fix or escape them.

Love in Action: Practical Expressions of Compassion

While love and compassion begin in the heart, they must be expressed through concrete actions to have transformative impact. Understanding how to translate compassionate feelings into effective helping behaviors enables us to serve others more meaningfully while avoiding common pitfalls that can actually harm those we're trying to help.

The Art of Presence. Sometimes the most powerful expression of love and compassion is simply being fully present with others in their pain, joy, or ordinary experiences. Presence involves bringing our complete attention, acceptance, and care to others without trying to fix, change, or improve them in the moment.

Attentive presence means putting aside distractions, agenda, and internal commentary to focus entirely on the other person. This might involve turning off phones, maintaining eye contact, and listening with our whole being rather than just waiting for our turn to speak.

Accepting presence involves being with others as they are rather than as we think they should be. This means not immediately trying to cheer up someone who is sad, convince someone who is angry to calm down, or rush someone through their processing time to reach resolution.

Compassionate presence brings warmth, care, and love into the space we share with others. This doesn't require saying anything profound or doing anything dramatic—often it simply means communicating through our demeanor that we care about their welfare and are honored to share this moment with them.

Active Listening as Love. Deep listening is one of the most generous gifts we can offer others because it communicates value, respect, and care more powerfully than advice or solutions. Active listening involves several key skills that can be developed through practice.

Reflective listening involves paraphrasing what we've heard to ensure understanding and demonstrate that we're truly paying attention. "It sounds like you're feeling overwhelmed by all the responsibilities you're carrying right now." This gives the speaker opportunity to correct misunderstandings while feeling heard and understood.

Empathetic listening involves trying to understand not just the content of what someone is sharing but the emotions and underlying needs behind their words. "I can hear how frustrated you are that your efforts aren't being recognized." This validates others' emotional experiences and helps them feel less alone in their struggles.

Curious listening involves asking questions that help others explore their own thoughts and feelings more deeply rather than questions that serve our curiosity or push toward our preferred solutions. "What's been most difficult about this situation for you?" This honors others' capacity for insight while providing support for their own discovery process.

Service as Worship. When we serve others with love and compassion, we participate in God's character and purposes in ways that become both worship and ministry. This perspective transforms ordinary acts of service into sacred offerings while ensuring that our motivation remains pure.

Humble service recognizes that we serve not because we're superior to those we help but because we're privileged to participate in God's care for His children. This prevents the condescension that can creep into helping relationships and maintains respect for others' dignity and worth.

Joyful service flows from gratitude for God's love rather than obligation or guilt. When we serve from joy, others experience blessing rather than burden, and we avoid the resentment that often accompanies duty-based helping.

Skillful service involves developing the practical abilities needed to help effectively rather than just having good intentions. This might mean learning counseling skills, developing cultural competency, or building expertise in areas where we want to serve. Love without skill can sometimes cause harm despite good intentions.

Forgiveness: Love's Response to Hurt

Perhaps no aspect of love and compassion is more challenging or more transformative than forgiveness—the choice to release others from debts they owe us and to seek their good despite their harmful actions toward us. Understanding forgiveness properly helps us extend this grace while protecting ourselves and others from continued harm.

What Forgiveness Is and Isn't. Forgiveness is often misunderstood in ways that make it seem either impossible or unwise. Forgiveness is not forgetting—we may remember harmful actions while choosing not to hold them against the offender. Forgiveness is not excusing—we can acknowledge that others' actions were wrong while choosing not to seek revenge. Forgiveness is not reconciliation—we can forgive people without returning to the same relationship dynamic, especially if they remain dangerous or unrepentant.

Forgiveness is not enabling—we can forgive while still maintaining appropriate boundaries and consequences. Forgiveness is not a feeling—it's a choice we make regardless of our emotions, though feelings often follow eventually. Forgiveness is not a one-time event—it's often a process that requires repeated choices, especially for deep hurts.

Forgiveness is fundamentally a choice to release our right to revenge, to seek the offender's good rather than their harm, and to entrust justice to God rather than taking it into our own hands. This choice frees us from the burden of carrying others' debts while opening possibilities for healing and restoration.

The Process of Forgiveness. Forgiveness typically unfolds through several stages that cannot be rushed but can be supported through intentional practices and community support.

Acknowledgment involves facing the reality of what happened and how it affected us rather than minimizing, denying, or excusing harmful actions. This stage often requires grieving the losses we've experienced and feeling the full weight of betrayal or injury.

Understanding seeks to comprehend what motivated the offender's actions without excusing them. This doesn't mean agreement or approval but rather recognizing the human factors that contributed to their choices. Understanding often helps us see offenders as flawed humans rather than evil monsters, making forgiveness more possible.

Choice is the central moment of forgiveness when we decide to release the debt and seek the offender's good. This choice is independent of our feelings and their response—we forgive because it's right and beneficial, not because it's easy or appreciated.

Process acknowledges that forgiveness is usually not a one-time decision but an ongoing choice, especially for significant hurts. We may need to choose forgiveness repeatedly as memories resurface, triggers occur, or new layers of pain are discovered.

The Benefits and Challenges of Forgiveness. Research consistently shows that people who practice forgiveness experience lower rates of depression, anxiety, and stress-related illness while enjoying better relationships and greater life satisfaction. Forgiveness benefits the forgiver more than the forgiven, releasing us from the emotional prison of resentment and revenge.

However, forgiveness is not always the same as reconciliation or trust restoration. We can forgive someone while maintaining boundaries for our protection or others' safety. We can seek their good while recognizing that continued relationship may not be wise or possible.

Forgiveness also doesn't eliminate the need for justice or consequences. We can forgive while still supporting appropriate legal action, therapeutic intervention, or other measures designed to prevent future harm and encourage accountability.

Compassion in Leadership and Service

Leadership infused with genuine love and compassion creates environments where people thrive, grow, and contribute their best efforts. Understanding how to lead with compassion while maintaining appropriate authority and accountability transforms both the leader's effectiveness and the organization's culture.

Compassionate Authority. True authority flows from service rather than domination, seeking others' development rather than compliance. Compassionate leaders use their position and influence to empower others rather than to control them, creating what researchers call "servant leadership" that benefits both individuals and organizations.

Compassionate authority involves several key practices. Clear expectations communicate standards and requirements with kindness rather than harshness, helping people succeed rather than setting them up for failure. Consistent boundaries provide safety and structure while being enforced with care rather than punishment. Growth-oriented feedback focuses on development and improvement rather than criticism and judgment.

Supportive accountability holds people responsible for their commitments while providing resources and encouragement for success. Humble power recognizes that authority is a trust to be stewarded for others' benefit rather than a privilege to be enjoyed for personal advantage.

Creating Cultures of Compassion. Leaders who consistently model love and compassion create organizational cultures where these values become normative rather than exceptional. This requires intentional effort to establish systems, practices, and rewards that support compassionate behavior throughout the organization.

Value-based hiring seeks people who demonstrate character qualities that align with compassionate leadership rather than just technical competence. Compassion training helps people develop skills for empathy, conflict resolution, and mutual support. Recognition systems celebrate acts of service, kindness, and care rather than just individual achievement.

Restorative practices focus on learning and improvement when mistakes occur rather than just punishment. Mutual support structures create opportunities for people to help each other during personal and professional challenges. Stress management policies acknowledge human limitations and provide resources for maintaining well-being during demanding seasons.

Sustainable Compassion in Service. People in helping professions or intensive service roles face unique challenges in maintaining compassion over time. Understanding how to practice sustainable compassion prevents burnout while ensuring continued effectiveness in serving others.

Boundaries and self-care are not selfish but necessary for long-term service capacity. Professional development builds skills that increase helping effectiveness while reducing emotional strain. Team support creates communities of care for those who serve others professionally. Spiritual practices provide renewal and perspective that sustains motivation and hope during difficult seasons.

Realistic expectations acknowledge that we cannot fix everyone or solve every problem, freeing us to focus on our specific calling and capacity. Celebration practices acknowledge the positive impact we do have rather than focusing only on ongoing needs and problems.

PRACTICAL APPLICATIONS
The Love and Compassion Assessment:
Understanding Your Current Capacity

Before developing greater capacity for love and compassion, it's important to honestly assess your current strengths, limitations, and growth areas. This assessment helps you identify specific areas for development while celebrating the compassionate qualities you already demonstrate.

Self-Compassion Evaluation

Internal Dialogue Assessment:

- How do you typically speak to yourself when you make mistakes or face challenges?
- What percentage of your self-talk would you characterize as encouraging versus critical?
- When you're struggling, do you tend to isolate yourself or seek support from others?
- How do you respond to your own emotional needs (physical comfort, rest, encouragement)?
- Rate your ability to forgive yourself for past mistakes (1-10 scale)

Self-Care Practice Review:

- How consistently do you attend to your physical needs (nutrition, exercise, sleep, medical care)?
- What practices do you use to process difficult emotions healthily?
- How well do you maintain boundaries that protect your well-being?

- What activities or relationships consistently restore your energy and hope?
- How do you balance caring for others with caring for yourself?

Other-Compassion Assessment

Empathy and Understanding Capacity:

- How accurately can you identify others' emotions, even when they don't explicitly express them?
- How well do you listen to understand rather than to respond or fix?
- How comfortable are you sitting with others' pain without trying to immediately solve it?
- How effectively do you show care for people whose backgrounds or values differ from yours?
- Rate your ability to see situations from others' perspectives (1-10 scale)

Compassionate Action Evaluation:

- How consistently do you follow through on impulses to help others?
- What barriers typically prevent you from acting on compassionate feelings?
- How skilled are you at helping others in ways they actually find helpful?
- How well do you balance offering support with respecting others' autonomy?
- What types of people or situations most challenge your compassion?

Forgiveness Capacity Review:

- How quickly do you typically move through the forgiveness process when hurt by others?
- What factors make forgiveness easier or more difficult for you?
- How well do you distinguish between forgiveness and reconciliation?
- How effectively do you forgive while maintaining appropriate boundaries?
- What unresolved hurts might be limiting your current capacity for love?

Daily Love and Compassion Practices

Building greater capacity for love and compassion requires consistent daily practices that strengthen your emotional muscles and create habits of caring response to others' needs.

Morning Compassion Preparation (10 minutes)

Heart-Centering Practice:

- Begin with three deep breaths while placing your hand on your heart

- Recall God's love for you: "I am beloved, forgiven, and called to love others"
- Set an intention for the day: "Today I will look for opportunities to show love and kindness"
- Visualize yourself responding with patience and kindness to potential challenges

Compassion Focus Selection: Each week, choose one specific aspect of compassion to practice:

- Week 1: Active listening - Focus on truly hearing others before responding
- Week 2: Encouragement - Look for opportunities to build others up with words
- Week 3: Practical help - Offer tangible assistance when you notice needs
- Week 4: Patience - Practice extending grace when others are difficult or slow

Midday Compassion Check-in (5 minutes)

Love Temperature Reading:

- How am I doing with showing love and compassion so far today?
- What opportunities have I noticed to serve others, and how have I responded?
- Where have I been reactive or self-focused instead of compassionate?
- Who around me seems to be struggling and might need encouragement?
- How can I adjust my approach for the rest of the day?

Reset and Refocus:

- Take three deep breaths and reconnect with your intention to love others
- Extend forgiveness to yourself for any missed opportunities or reactive responses
- Look ahead to remaining interactions and plan how to show care
- Say a quick prayer for wisdom and kindness in upcoming encounters

Evening Compassion Review (10 minutes)

Love Impact Reflection:

- When did I show genuine love and compassion today?
- How did others respond to my attempts to be caring and kind?
- What did I learn about myself through today's compassion challenges?
- Where did I miss opportunities to love others well?
- How did practicing compassion affect my own emotional state?

Gratitude and Growth Planning:

- Thank God for opportunities to express His love through my actions

- Identify one specific way I grew in compassion today
- Note one area where I want to improve tomorrow
- Set an intention for how I want to show love tomorrow

The Emotional Regulation Toolkit for Sustainable Compassion

Maintaining compassion over time requires developing skills for managing your own emotions so that you can respond to others from a place of strength rather than depletion or reactivity.

Stress and Overwhelm Management

The STOP Technique: When feeling overwhelmed by others' needs or your own emotional reactions:

- S - Stop what you're doing and pause
- T - Take three deep breaths to center yourself
- O - Observe what you're feeling and thinking without judgment
- P - Proceed with intention rather than reaction

Boundary Setting for Compassion Sustainability:

- Identify your emotional capacity limits and communicate them honestly
- Practice saying "I care about you, and I need to take care of myself so I can continue helping"
- Set specific times for availability versus personal restoration
- Distinguish between empathy (feeling with others) and sympathy (taking on others' emotions)
- Create physical and emotional space when needed without guilt

The Compassion Fatigue Prevention System:

- Weekly Compassion Inventory: Assess how much emotional energy you're investing in others versus receiving
- Monthly Support Check: Evaluate whether you have adequate support for your own challenges and growth
- Quarterly Calling Review: Ensure your service activities align with your gifts and calling rather than just others' expectations
- Annual Sabbatical Planning: Schedule extended times for personal renewal and spiritual refreshment

Conflict Resolution and Difficult Relationship Navigation

Love and compassion are most challenged in difficult relationships and conflict situations. Having specific skills for these scenarios helps you maintain love even when others are unloving.

The Compassionate Conflict Response Model

Preparation Phase:

- Examine your own contribution to the conflict before addressing theirs
- Choose to seek understanding and resolution rather than winning or punishment
- Prepare to listen as much as you speak
- Set realistic expectations about outcomes while hoping for the best

Engagement Phase:

- Begin by affirming your care for the person and the relationship
- Use "I" statements to share your experience without attacking their character
- Listen actively to understand their perspective, even if you disagree
- Look for valid points in their position and acknowledge them
- Focus on specific behaviors and their impact rather than character judgments

Resolution Phase:

- Work together to identify solutions that address both parties' legitimate needs
- Agree on specific actions each person will take going forward
- Establish ways to rebuild trust gradually if it has been damaged
- Plan follow-up conversations to assess progress and address ongoing issues
- Extend and request forgiveness for mistakes made during the conflict

Loving Difficult People Strategies

The Compassion Challenge Approach: When someone consistently triggers negative reactions in you:

- Look for evidence of their struggles or pain that might explain their behavior
- Practice finding one positive quality to appreciate about them
- Set boundaries that protect you while still treating them with dignity
- Remember that loving someone doesn't mean allowing them to harm you or others

The Growth Opportunity Perspective:

- View difficult people as opportunities to develop patience, forgiveness, and unconditional love
- Ask "What might God want to teach me through this relationship?"
- Consider how this person might be serving your character development
- Look for ways their challenges might be developing empathy for others who struggle similarly
- Practice responding from your values rather than reacting from your emotions

Service and Ministry Applications

Translating love and compassion into effective service requires practical skills and wisdom about how to help others in ways they actually find helpful.

The Effective Helping Framework

Assessment Before Action:
- Ask people what they actually need rather than assuming you know
- Consider their dignity, autonomy, and capacity for self-determination
- Evaluate whether your help addresses symptoms or underlying issues
- Assess your own competence to provide the type of help needed
- Determine appropriate boundaries and expectations for your involvement

Collaborative Helping Approach:
- Work with people rather than doing things for them when possible
- Respect their goals and values even if they differ from yours
- Provide resources and support rather than taking over their responsibilities
- Encourage their own problem-solving capacity while offering assistance
- Maintain hope for their ability to grow and change

Follow-up and Accountability:
- Check back to see if your help was actually helpful
- Adjust your approach based on feedback and results
- Celebrate progress and growth rather than just focusing on remaining needs
- Know when to refer people to others with greater expertise
- Maintain appropriate boundaries around your helping relationships

Community Compassion Building

Creating Cultures of Care:
- Model the love and compassion you want to see in your community
- Celebrate and recognize others when they demonstrate caring behavior
- Create opportunities for people to serve others and experience the joy of giving
- Establish systems that make it easy for people to help each other
- Address barriers that prevent compassionate responses in your environment

Compassion Multiplication Strategy:
- Teach others the compassion skills you're developing
- Share stories of how love and kindness have impacted your life
- Invite others to join you in service activities and compassionate responses
- Mentor people who want to develop greater capacity for caring
- Create ripple effects by loving people who will then love others

CHAPTER CONCLUSION
The Transforming Power of Love

As we conclude this exploration of love and compassion, it's crucial to understand the profound truth you've encountered: love is not merely a nice addition to an effective life—it is the very essence of what makes life meaningful and service transformational. You haven't just learned strategies for being kinder or techniques for helping others—you've discovered the divine force that has the power to heal broken hearts, restore damaged relationships, and create communities of hope in a wounded world. Love is both the motivation for all meaningful service and the method by which that service becomes truly effective.

The most beautiful aspect of love and compassion is their self-multiplying nature. When you love someone authentically, you don't diminish your capacity for loving others—you actually increase it. Every act of genuine compassion strengthens your emotional muscles and expands your heart's capacity. Every choice to forgive frees you from the burden of resentment and creates space for deeper relationships. Every moment of authentic care for another person connects you more deeply to the source of all love, making even greater love possible.

Love as the Ultimate Influence

Perhaps the most transformative understanding about love and compassion is recognizing that they represent the highest form of influence. While authority can compel compliance and manipulation can create temporary cooperation, love inspires lasting transformation. When people experience genuine care, they don't just change their behavior—they begin to believe different things about themselves, others, and what's possible in relationships.

This love-based influence operates differently from other forms of power because it serves the influenced person's good rather than the influencer's agenda. When you love someone well, you give them a glimpse of their true worth and potential. You create safety for them to be vulnerable, to grow, and to become more authentically themselves. This kind of influence doesn't control people—it liberates them to become who God created them to be.

The ripple effects of love-based influence extend far beyond immediate relationships. The person who experiences genuine care often becomes more caring toward others. The individual who receives forgiveness becomes more forgiving. The one who feels truly valued begins to value others more highly. Your love becomes a gift that keeps giving, touching lives you may never know about through the people you've touched directly.

The Eternal Dimension of Temporal Love

Remember that every act of love and compassion you offer in this life has eternal significance. When you choose to love difficult people, forgive those who hurt you, or serve others sacrificially, you participate in God's character and purposes in ways that transcend earthly time and circumstance. The love you show today creates reverberations that echo in eternity, touching not only the immediate recipients but all those they will influence throughout their lives.

This eternal perspective transforms how you view seemingly small acts of kindness. The encouraging word you speak to a discouraged colleague may be exactly what they need to persevere through a difficult season. The patience you show with a challenging family member may model grace they've never experienced before. The compassion you extend to someone who doesn't deserve it may be the catalyst that begins their journey toward healing and wholeness.

Understanding the eternal dimension of love also provides motivation during seasons when love feels costly or unrewarded. Even when your compassion is rejected, your forgiveness is spurned, or your service goes unnoticed, you can trust that God sees every act of love and that nothing given in genuine care is ever wasted in His economy.

Love as Worship and Mission

As you continue developing your capacity for love and compassion, remember that these qualities are both worship and mission. When you love others well, you reflect God's character to a world that desperately needs to see what divine love looks like in human form. Your compassion becomes a sermon about God's care, your forgiveness becomes a testimony to His grace, and your service becomes a demonstration of His kingdom values.

This understanding elevates every loving action from nice behavior to sacred ministry. The parent showing patience with a difficult child is modeling God's patience with His difficult children. The friend providing comfort during loss is channeling God's comfort to those who mourn. The leader serving employees' development is demonstrating how God invests in our growth and potential.

When you approach love and compassion as worship and mission, you find motivation that transcends reciprocity or appreciation. You love because God first loved you, serve because He first served you, and forgive because He first forgave you. This foundation makes your love sustainable even when others don't respond positively and meaningful even when results aren't immediately visible.

Your Love Assignment

As you move forward from this chapter, carry with you the Love and Compassion Assessment from our practical applications. This week, honestly evaluate your current capacity for self-compassion and other-compassion, identifying specific areas where God is calling you to grow in love. Choose one daily practice from our toolkit and commit to it for the next 30 days, whether it's the morning compassion preparation, midday check-ins, or evening reflection.

Pay particular attention to relationships or situations where love feels most challenging. These difficult areas often represent your greatest opportunities for growth and your most significant potential impact. Remember, love is most powerful precisely when it's most costly, and compassion is most transformational when it's extended to those who seem least deserving.

Looking Ahead

In our next chapter, we'll explore how to take responsibility and ownership for your life, choices, and impact. You'll discover that the love and compassion you're developing now provide the foundation for authentic accountability that serves others rather than just protecting yourself.

But for now, embrace your calling to be a person of extraordinary love in an ordinary world. Trust that every choice to love, every act of compassion, and every decision to forgive matters more than you can imagine. Believe that God delights in using willing hearts to channel His love to a world that needs to experience it desperately.

12

Responsibility & Ownership

True growth and authentic service flourish where responsibility is embraced and ownership is practiced.

IN EVERY SPHERE—BUSINESS, MINISTRY, OR DAILY LIFE—those who take responsibility for their actions, decisions, and influence become catalysts for lasting change. Ownership is not about control or pride; it is about stewardship, humility, and a willingness to be accountable for what has been entrusted to us.

In business and leadership, the most respected individuals are those who "own everything"—who acknowledge mistakes, admit failures, and develop plans to improve rather than shifting blame or making excuses. This principle, often called "extreme ownership," means accepting that every outcome, good or bad, is an opportunity to learn, grow, and set a higher standard for yourself and your team. Leaders who model responsibility inspire trust, foster accountability, and create cultures where others are empowered to do the same. As you lead, remember: your words and actions set the tone for those around you.

Yet, responsibility goes deeper than professional standards. From a faith perspective, we are reminded that everything we have—our talents, resources, opportunities—ultimately belongs to God. We are not owners, but stewards, entrusted to manage these gifts wisely and for purposes greater than ourselves. "The earth is the Lord's, and everything in it," declares Psalm 24:1. This truth reframes our sense of ownership: what matters most is not what we possess, but how we use what we've been given to serve others and honor God. Stewardship calls us to humility, gratitude, and a deep sense of purpose in every decision we make.

Integrity is the foundation of responsible leadership. To live and lead with integrity means aligning your actions with your values, keeping your promises, and being honest—even when it's difficult or costly. The Bible teaches, "To do righteousness and justice is more acceptable to the Lord than sacrifice" (Proverbs 21:3). When we act with integrity, we not only build trust with others, but also witness to the transformative power of faith in action.

Taking responsibility also means being proactive—anticipating needs, addressing problems before they escalate, and seeking solutions rather than waiting for someone else to act. It requires courage to admit when you're wrong, humility to seek forgiveness, and wisdom to learn from every experience. As Oswald Sanders writes, "Leadership is influence, and the best leaders are those who accept responsibility for both their successes and their failures".

The Foundation of Personal Responsibility

Personal responsibility forms the bedrock of character development and effective service. It represents the recognition that while we cannot control all circumstances, we can always choose our responses, and these choices ultimately determine our character and impact more than external events ever could.

The Locus of Control Principle. Psychologist Julian Rotter's research on locus of control reveals that people generally operate from either an internal or external orientation when explaining life events. Those with an internal locus of control believe their actions significantly influence outcomes, while those with an external locus attribute results primarily to luck, fate, or others' actions.

People with internal locus of control tend to be more proactive, persistent, and successful across various life domains because they focus energy on factors they can influence rather than feeling victimized by circumstances beyond their control. This doesn't mean ignoring real external constraints or denying the impact of systemic issues, but rather recognizing that personal agency exists within any situation.

From a biblical perspective, this aligns with the principle that while God is sovereign over all circumstances, humans are responsible for their choices within those circumstances. Joseph couldn't control being sold into slavery or falsely imprisoned, but he could choose how to respond with integrity, excellence, and trust in God. His personal responsibility within difficult circumstances eventually positioned him for extraordinary influence and service.

Response vs. Reaction. One of the most crucial distinctions in personal responsibility is understanding the difference between responding and reacting. Reactions are automatic, emotional, and often regrettable responses to triggers or challenges. Responses are thoughtful, intentional, and values-driven choices about how to handle situations.

Between any stimulus and our behavioral choice lies what Viktor Frankl called "the space of freedom"—the moment where we can choose our response based on our values rather than our emotions. This space can be expanded through practices like mindfulness, prayer, and conscious value clarification that help us pause and choose rather than simply react automatically.

Taking responsibility for our responses rather than just our reactions means developing the capacity to choose behavior that aligns with our character and goals even when we feel angry, hurt, scared, or frustrated. This is perhaps the highest form of personal responsibility because it involves governing our internal world rather than just managing external behaviors.

Accountability vs. Blame. Healthy responsibility culture distinguishes clearly between accountability and blame. Accountability focuses on learning, improvement, and prevention of future problems. Blame focuses on punishment, shame, and finding someone to hold responsible for past failures.

Accountability asks questions like "What can we learn from this?" "How can we prevent this problem in the future?" and "What systems or processes need improvement?" Blame asks "Whose fault is this?" and "Who should be punished for this failure?"

Personal responsibility involves embracing accountability while rejecting both blame of others and self-condemnation. When we make mistakes, we acknowledge them honestly, learn from them thoroughly, make necessary amends, and develop better systems or skills to prevent repetition. This accountability-based approach to responsibility creates learning and growth rather than shame and stagnation.

Stewardship:
The Biblical Framework for Ownership

The biblical concept of stewardship provides a comprehensive framework for understanding responsibility and ownership that transcends merely personal accountability to encompass our role in God's larger purposes and kingdom work.

Everything Belongs to God. The foundation of biblical stewardship is the recognition that God is the ultimate owner of everything, and humans are entrusted with managing His resources for His purposes. "The earth is the Lord's, and the fulness thereof; the world, and they that dwell therein" (Psalm 24:1). This includes not just material possessions but also our time, talents, relationships, opportunities, and influence.

This perspective radically reframes how we approach ownership and responsibility. Instead of asking "How can I use my resources for my benefit?" we ask "How can I steward God's resources for His glory and others' good?" Instead of viewing our abilities as personal assets, we see them as divine gifts entrusted to us for kingdom purposes.

This stewardship mindset prevents both the pride that comes from thinking we've achieved everything through our own effort and the despair that comes from feeling we lack sufficient resources. We steward faithfully what we've been given while trusting God for outcomes beyond our control.

Faithful Stewardship Principles. Jesus' parable of the talents (Matthew 25:14-30) reveals several key principles of faithful stewardship. Proportional expectation means God expects return proportional to what we've been given rather than equal results from everyone. Active investment involves using our resources purposefully rather than merely preserving them safely. Risk-taking faith requires stepping beyond comfort zones to multiply our impact.

Accountability to the Master reminds us that we will give account for how we've stewarded what was entrusted to us. Multiplication reward shows that faithful stewardship leads to increased responsibility and opportunity. Trust-based allocation reveals that God gives greater resources to those who prove faithful with smaller ones.

These principles apply to every aspect of life—our finances, relationships, professional opportunities, spiritual gifts, and influence. Faithful stewardship involves actively developing and deploying these resources for maximum kingdom impact rather than minimum personal risk.

Stewardship vs. Ownership Mentality. The difference between stewardship and ownership mentality affects every decision and relationship. Ownership mentality asks "What's in this for me?" while stewardship mentality asks "How can this serve God's purposes?" Ownership focuses on accumulation and control; stewardship focuses on multiplication and service.

Ownership creates anxiety about loss and competition with others; stewardship creates peace about outcomes and collaboration with others. Ownership leads to hoarding and self-protection; stewardship leads to generosity and investment in others' development.

This shift in mentality transforms how we approach career decisions, financial planning, relationship building, and service opportunities. Instead of maximizing personal benefit, we optimize for kingdom impact. Instead of protecting our interests, we invest in God's purposes through others' welfare.

The Psychology of Ownership and Agency

Understanding the psychological dynamics of ownership and personal agency helps us develop healthier patterns of responsibility while avoiding common pitfalls that can undermine our effectiveness and well-being.

Learned Helplessness vs. Learned Optimism. Martin Seligman's research on learned helplessness reveals that people can develop persistent feelings of powerlessness when they repeatedly experience situations where their actions don't influence outcomes. This learned helplessness can generalize to situations where they actually do have agency, creating chronic patterns of passivity and victimization.

Conversely, learned optimism involves developing explanatory styles that maintain hope and motivation even during difficult circumstances. Optimistic people tend to view setbacks as temporary, specific, and surmountable rather than permanent, pervasive, and insurmountable.

Taking responsibility involves developing learned optimism while acknowledging real constraints and limitations. This means focusing energy on areas where we have influence while accepting areas where we don't, distinguishing between what we can change and what we must endure.

The Paradox of Control. One of the most sophisticated aspects of personal responsibility is learning to hold the paradox of control—taking complete responsibility for our choices and efforts while surrendering control over outcomes and others' responses. This paradox prevents both the paralysis that comes from feeling overwhelmed by responsibility for everything and the passivity that comes from feeling responsible for nothing.

We control our preparation but not whether opportunities arise. We control our communication but not whether others understand or respond positively. We control our character development but not whether others recognize or appreciate our growth. We control our service but not whether others receive it gratefully.

Mastering this paradox enables us to invest fully in what we can influence while maintaining peace about what we cannot control. This creates both maximum effort and minimum anxiety, maximum responsibility and minimum overwhelm.

Growth Mindset and Responsibility. Carol Dweck's research on growth mindset has significant implications for how we approach responsibility and ownership. People with growth mindset believe abilities can be developed through effort and learning, while those with fixed mindset believe abilities are static traits.

Growth mindset individuals take responsibility for developing their capacities rather than just performing with existing abilities. They view failures as learning opportunities rather than evidence of inadequacy. They seek challenges that stretch their abilities rather than avoiding situations where they might not excel immediately.

This growth-oriented approach to responsibility creates resilience, curiosity, and continuous improvement rather than defensiveness, excuse-making, and stagnation. It enables us to take ownership of our development while maintaining humility about our current limitations.

Extreme Ownership in Leadership and Life

The concept of extreme ownership, popularized by former Navy SEALs Jocko Willink and Leif Babin, provides a framework for taking maximum responsibility as a tool for maximum effectiveness and influence. This approach goes beyond personal accountability to embrace responsibility for outcomes in any situation where we have influence.

Taking Ownership of Everything in Your Sphere. Extreme ownership means accepting responsibility not just for your own actions but for all outcomes within your sphere of influence. If your team fails to meet objectives, you take responsibility for inadequate communication, training, or support rather than blaming team members. If a project fails, you examine your planning, resource allocation, and risk management rather than focusing on external factors.

This doesn't mean ignoring others' contributions to problems or accepting blame for things genuinely beyond your control. Rather, it means focusing first and most intensively on what you could have done differently to influence better outcomes. This approach maximizes learning and improvement while minimizing the energy wasted on blame and excuse-making.

From a biblical perspective, this aligns with Jesus' teaching to remove the plank from your own eye before addressing the speck in others' eyes (Matthew 7:3-5). By taking maximum responsibility for our contribution to problems, we position ourselves to influence solutions most effectively.

The Power of Ownership Language. The language we use to describe problems and failures significantly affects our ability to learn from them and influence better outcomes in the future. Ownership language focuses on our role and agency: "What could I have done differently?" "How can I better support my team next time?" "What systems do I need to improve?"

Blame language focuses on others' faults and external factors: "They didn't follow instructions." "The circumstances were impossible." "We didn't have enough resources." While these factors may be true, focusing on them doesn't position us to influence change.

Ownership language creates psychological and practical empowerment by directing attention toward areas where we have agency. Even when external factors genuinely contributed to problems, focusing on our sphere of influence enables us to prepare better for similar challenges in the future.

Ownership Culture Creation. Leaders who practice extreme ownership tend to create cultures where others also take responsibility rather than making excuses. This happens through several mechanisms. Modeling demonstrates that taking ownership is safe and valued rather than punished. Problem-solving focus creates environments where energy goes toward solutions rather than blame.

Learning orientation frames failures as development opportunities rather than grounds for criticism. Support systems provide resources and training that enable people to take ownership successfully rather than setting them up for failure. Recognition systems celebrate accountability and improvement rather than just perfect performance.

Creating ownership culture requires patience and consistency because many people have learned to avoid responsibility due to previous experiences with blame-focused environments. Building trust that ownership will be rewarded rather than punished takes time but creates extraordinary results in terms of team performance and individual development.

Responsibility in Relationships and Community

Taking responsibility in relationships involves understanding our role in relationship dynamics while maintaining appropriate boundaries and expectations for others' behavior. This creates healthier connections and more effective conflict resolution.

Owning Your Contribution to Relationship Dynamics. Every relationship involves mutual influence, and taking responsibility means examining how our communication style, emotional patterns, and behavioral choices contribute to relationship health or dysfunction. This doesn't mean taking blame for others' actions but rather owning our part in the dance of interaction.

Communication responsibility involves speaking clearly, listening actively, and taking ownership when our words are misunderstood or hurtful. Emotional responsibility means managing our own emotional responses rather than expecting others to regulate our feelings for us. Behavioral responsibility involves aligning our actions with our stated values and commitments.

Pattern responsibility means examining recurring relationship conflicts to identify our contribution to negative cycles. If we consistently experience certain types of relationship problems across multiple connections, taking responsibility involves looking at our own patterns rather than concluding that everyone else is difficult.

Responsibility vs. Enabling. One of the challenges in relationship responsibility is distinguishing between helpful accountability and harmful enabling. Enabling involves protecting others from the natural consequences of their choices, which often prevents learning and growth. Healthy responsibility involves supporting others while allowing them to experience appropriate consequences.

Enabling behaviors include making excuses for others, cleaning up their messes repeatedly, or providing resources without requiring accountability. Healthy support includes offering encouragement, providing appropriate assistance, and maintaining boundaries that promote both parties' growth.

This distinction is particularly important in parenting, management, and helping relationships where the goal is developing others' capacity for responsibility rather than creating dependency on our intervention.

Community Responsibility and Social Stewardship. Personal responsibility extends beyond individual and immediate relationship concerns to encompass our role in community health and social justice. This includes both direct service and advocacy for systems that enable others to experience dignity, opportunity, and development.

Community stewardship involves investing in the health of organizations, neighborhoods, and groups where we have influence. Social responsibility includes using our voice, vote, and resources to promote justice and opportunity for others. Environmental stewardship encompasses caring for creation as part of our stewardship calling.

This broader view of responsibility prevents the self-focus that can make personal development merely selfish while ensuring that our growth serves larger purposes of justice, compassion, and community health.

Financial Responsibility and Resource Stewardship

How we handle money and material resources reflects our understanding of stewardship and responsibility while significantly affecting our capacity for service and generosity.

Biblical Financial Principles. Scripture provides comprehensive guidance for financial responsibility that goes far beyond mere money management to encompass heart attitudes and kingdom priorities. God's ownership means all resources ultimately belong to Him, making us managers rather than owners. Contentment involves finding satisfaction in God's provision rather than constantly seeking more.

Generosity reflects God's character and serves others' needs while protecting us from materialism. Planning demonstrates good stewardship while trust prevents anxiety about provision. Work ethic honors God through excellence while rest acknowledges our dependence on His provision rather than our own effort.

Debt avoidance preserves freedom for generous giving and opportunity response. Investment wisdom multiplies resources for greater kingdom impact. Simple living prevents lifestyle inflation that could limit generosity or create unnecessary stress.

Practical Financial Responsibility Budgeting involves planning resource allocation based on priorities and values rather than just tracking spending after the fact. Emergency funds provide security that enables generosity and risk-taking for kingdom purposes. Investment strategy considers both financial return and ethical alignment with values.

Giving practices should be systematic and generous rather than occasional and minimal. Debt management involves paying obligations responsibly while avoiding unnecessary borrowing. Lifestyle choices should reflect stewardship values rather than cultural pressure or status seeking.

Financial transparency in marriage and business builds trust and accountability. Professional development represents investment in our capacity to serve and contribute. Estate planning ensures resources continue serving kingdom purposes beyond our lifetime.

Money and Ministry Balance. One of the ongoing challenges for people of faith is balancing financial responsibility with generosity and trust in God's provision. Prudent planning demonstrates stewardship without crossing into anxious hoarding. Generous giving reflects faith and love without becoming financially irresponsible.

Career decisions should consider both provision needs and service calling rather than maximizing income at the expense of other values. Lifestyle choices should enable rather than hinder our capacity for service and relationship. Resource sharing should be wise and helpful rather than enabling or depleting.

The goal is using money as a tool for kingdom purposes rather than becoming enslaved to it or neglecting appropriate financial responsibility in the name of faith.

Responsibility for Personal Development and Growth

Taking ownership of our personal development involves actively pursuing growth rather than passively hoping for improvement, while recognizing that transformation ultimately depends on God's grace working through our faithful efforts.

Learning Responsibility Continuous learning represents stewardship of our intellectual capacity and service preparation. Skill development increases our ability to contribute value in our spheres of influence. Knowledge acquisition should serve others' benefit rather than just personal advancement or intellectual pride.

Feedback seeking demonstrates humility and commitment to improvement rather than defensiveness about current performance. Mentorship pursuit shows wisdom in recognizing we need others' input for optimal development. Teaching others multiplies our learning while serving their growth needs.

Reading habits should include materials that challenge, inspire, and equip us for better service. Conference attendance and training participation represent investment in our capacity for contribution. Reflection practices help us extract maximum learning from experience.

Character Development Ownership Self-awareness involves honest assessment of our strengths, weaknesses, and growth needs without either pride or despair. Virtue cultivation requires intentional practice of qualities like patience, kindness, and integrity. Habit formation creates automatic behaviors that support character development.

Spiritual disciplines position us for God's transforming work while requiring our active participation. Accountability relationships provide external support for internal growth goals. Service opportunities create contexts for character development through practical application.

Failure processing involves learning from mistakes without being paralyzed by shame or condemnation. Success evaluation examines how achievements align with values and serve others' welfare. Course correction demonstrates flexibility and responsiveness to feedback and changing circumstances.

Physical and Emotional Health Responsibility Health stewardship recognizes our bodies as gifts from God requiring appropriate care and maintenance. Exercise habits maintain physical capacity for service while modeling self-care for others. Nutrition choices affect energy levels and modeling for family members.

Stress management preserves long-term capacity for service while preventing burnout or health problems. Sleep prioritization enables optimal functioning and decision-making. Medical care represents responsible stewardship when health problems arise.

Emotional regulation skills enable us to respond rather than react during challenging situations. Mental health attention addresses depression, anxiety, or trauma that could limit our effectiveness or relationships. Recreation and renewal maintain joy and perspective necessary for sustainable service.

Taking responsibility for personal development creates a foundation for all other forms of service and responsibility while preventing the stagnation that can limit our impact and satisfaction over time.

PRACTICAL APPLICATIONS
The Personal Responsibility Assessment: Identifying Your Ownership Patterns

Before developing greater personal responsibility, it's important to honestly assess your current patterns of ownership and accountability across different life areas. This assessment helps you identify strengths to build upon and gaps that need attention.

Responsibility Pattern Analysis

Response vs. Reaction Evaluation:

- In what situations do you typically react emotionally rather than respond thoughtfully?
- How often do you pause to consider your values before responding to challenging circumstances?
- What triggers consistently cause you to abandon your best intentions and react poorly?
- How well do you take responsibility for your emotional responses rather than blam-

ing others for "making" you feel certain ways?

- Rate your ability to choose your response even when feeling angry, hurt, or frustrated (1-10 scale)

Accountability vs. Blame Assessment:

- When problems occur, do you first examine your contribution or look for others to blame?
- How comfortable are you admitting mistakes and taking ownership of failures?
- What patterns do you notice in how you explain successes versus failures?
- How often do you make excuses versus taking responsibility for outcomes?
- Do you focus more on learning from problems or finding someone to hold responsible?

Stewardship vs. Ownership Mindset Review:

- How often do you consider how your decisions serve purposes beyond your immediate benefit?
- Do you view your resources (time, money, talents) as yours to use or God's to steward?
- How does understanding stewardship affect your financial decisions and resource allocation?
- What evidence shows you're investing in others' development rather than just your own advancement?
- How well do you balance personal needs with service to others and God's purposes?

Sphere of Influence Analysis

Control vs. Influence Mapping: Create three circles representing:

- Direct Control: Things you can completely control (your actions, words, attitudes, choices)
- Influence: Things you can affect but not control (others' responses, team outcomes, relationship dynamics)
- Concern: Things that affect you but you cannot control or influence (weather, others' choices, economic conditions)

For each major area of your life (work, family, ministry, finances, health), identify specific concerns and place them in the appropriate circle. This exercise helps you focus energy on areas where you have agency while reducing anxiety about areas beyond your influence.

Responsibility Expansion Opportunities:

- What areas of influence could you take more ownership of?
- Where have you been waiting for others to take initiative that you could provide?
- What problems in your environment could be addressed through your leadership?
- How could you increase your positive influence in your family, workplace, or com-

munity?

- What skills or resources would enhance your capacity for responsible leadership?

The Daily Ownership Practices: Building Responsibility Muscles

Developing consistent personal responsibility requires daily practices that strengthen your ownership mindset and response patterns.

Morning Responsibility Preparation (10 minutes)

Stewardship Centering Practice:

- Begin with prayer acknowledging God's ownership of everything in your life
- Review your schedule and identify opportunities to serve others through your responsibilities
- Set specific intentions for how you want to respond to potential challenges today
- Ask for wisdom to distinguish between what you can control and what you must entrust to God
- Commit to looking for your contribution to any problems that arise

Daily Ownership Declarations:

- "Today I will focus on what I can control and influence rather than what I cannot"
- "I am a steward of God's resources, called to use them for His glory and others' good"
- "I will take responsibility for my responses while allowing others to own their choices"
- "I will look for ways to solve problems rather than assign blame"
- "I will view challenges as opportunities to demonstrate faithful stewardship"

Midday Responsibility Check-in (5 minutes)

Response Quality Assessment:

- How have I responded to challenges and frustrations so far today?
- Where have I taken appropriate ownership versus where have I made excuses or blamed others?
- What opportunities have I had to demonstrate stewardship and responsibility?
- How well am I focusing on my sphere of influence rather than worrying about things beyond my control?
- What adjustments do I need to make for the remainder of the day?

Course Correction Practice:

- If you've reacted poorly or avoided responsibility, acknowledge it honestly
- Identify what you can learn from the situation
- Make any necessary apologies or corrections
- Recommit to your values and intentions for responsible living
- Ask God for strength and wisdom for upcoming interactions

Evening Responsibility Review (10 minutes)

Ownership Reflection Questions:
- Where did I take appropriate responsibility today?
- What situations challenged my commitment to ownership and accountability?
- How did my stewardship mindset affect my decisions and interactions?
- What did I learn about myself through today's responsibility opportunities?
- How can I improve my ownership patterns tomorrow?

Growth and Gratitude Practice:
- Thank God for opportunities to exercise stewardship and responsibility
- Celebrate specific moments when you chose ownership over blame or excuse-making
- Identify one area where you want to take greater responsibility tomorrow
- Pray for wisdom to be a faithful steward of all God has entrusted to you
- Set intentions for how you want to demonstrate responsibility in tomorrow's anticipated challenges

The Extreme Ownership Implementation Framework

Applying extreme ownership principles in your daily life requires specific strategies for taking maximum responsibility while maintaining healthy boundaries and realistic expectations.

Problem-Solving Ownership Protocol

The "What Could I Have Done Differently?" Exercise: When problems occur, use this systematic approach:

1. Immediate Response: Take responsibility for any aspect of the problem within your influence
2. Analysis Phase: Examine your planning, communication, preparation, and execution
3. Learning Extraction: Identify specific lessons and improvements for future similar situations

4. System Improvement: Adjust processes, habits, or approaches to prevent similar problems

5. Team Development: Share insights with others who could benefit from your learning

The Leadership Ownership Model: For any team or relationship responsibility:

- Own the outcome even when others contributed to problems
- Focus on solutions rather than spending energy on blame or excuses
- Take responsibility for communication clarity and follow-through
- Provide resources and support needed for others' success
- Model accountability that encourages others to take ownership as well

Conflict Resolution Ownership: When relationship conflicts arise:

- Start by examining your contribution before addressing others' actions
- Take responsibility for your communication style and emotional responses
- Own the relationship dynamic you've helped create through your patterns
- Focus on what you can change rather than what others need to do differently
- Seek to understand before demanding to be understood

Stewardship Planning and Resource Management

Translating stewardship principles into practical resource management requires specific strategies for finances, time, talents, and opportunities.

Financial Stewardship Implementation

The Kingdom-Focused Budget Process:

1. Prayer and Values Alignment: Begin financial planning with prayer about God's priorities for your resources

2. Giving First: Allocate generous giving before determining spending in other categories

3. Needs vs. Wants Distinction: Carefully differentiate between genuine needs and cultural desires

4. Investment Strategy: Consider both financial return and kingdom impact in investment choices

5. Lifestyle Simplicity: Choose simplicity that enables greater generosity and service capacity

Resource Allocation Framework:

- 10% Minimum Giving: Systematic giving to church and ministries as baseline stewardship
- 10% Savings/Investment: Building resources for future kingdom opportunities and

security

- 60% Living Expenses: Modest lifestyle that enables generosity while meeting genuine needs
- 20% Flexible Fund: Resources for unexpected opportunities to serve, special gifts, or emergencies

Time Stewardship Strategies

The Priority-Based Scheduling Method:

- God Time: Daily spiritual disciplines as non-negotiable foundation
- Family Time: Invested relationships with spouse, children, and close family
- Work Time: Excellent service in professional responsibilities
- Service Time: Regular investment in others' welfare and kingdom advancement
- Rest Time: Renewal activities that restore capacity for service

Energy Management for Stewardship:

- Peak Energy: Schedule most important responsibilities during your highest energy times
- Routine Tasks: Handle administrative and maintenance activities during medium energy periods
- Relationship Investment: Engage in meaningful conversations and service during good energy times
- Rest and Renewal: Protect low-energy times for restoration rather than pushing through fatigue

Talent and Gift Development

The Faithful Stewardship Growth Plan:

1. Gift Identification: Honestly assess your natural talents and developed skills
2. Development Investment: Systematically improve abilities that serve others most effectively
3. Service Application: Use developing gifts in practical service opportunities
4. Multiplication Teaching: Share knowledge and skills with others who can benefit
5. Strategic Planning: Align gift development with opportunities for maximum kingdom impact

Opportunity Stewardship Framework:

- Evaluation Criteria: Assess opportunities based on kingdom impact potential, not just personal benefit
- Resource Requirements: Consider whether you have adequate resources to steward

opportunities well

- Timing Wisdom: Discern between opportunities to pursue now versus later
- Team Development: Include others in opportunities when possible to multiply impact
- Long-term Perspective: Choose opportunities that build capacity for greater future service

Accountability Systems and Support Structures

Building sustainable responsibility requires external accountability and support systems that encourage ownership while providing guidance and encouragement.

Personal Accountability Architecture

The Responsibility Accountability Partner: Find someone who will help you maintain ownership patterns:

- Selection Criteria: Choose someone who demonstrates personal responsibility and shares your values
- Meeting Structure: Meet weekly or bi-weekly for accountability conversations
- Discussion Topics: Share challenges in taking ownership, successes in stewardship, and areas for growth
- Mutual Responsibility: Provide accountability for each other rather than one-sided reporting

Professional and Ministry Accountability:

- Work Performance Reviews: Seek regular feedback on professional responsibility and contribution
- Ministry Evaluation: Ask for honest assessment of your service effectiveness and growth areas
- Financial Accountability: Include trusted others in major financial decisions and stewardship evaluation
- Family Feedback: Regularly ask family members how you're doing in your responsibilities to them
- Community Input: Seek feedback from community members about your contribution and areas for improvement

The Personal Responsibility Board of Directors: Assemble 3-5 people who can provide different perspectives on your responsibility development:

- The Wise Counselor: Someone with life experience who can provide perspective on responsibility challenges
- The Professional Mentor: Someone in your field who can guide career and profession-

al responsibility development

- The Spiritual Advisor: Someone who can help you discern God's calling and stewardship priorities
- The Family Representative: Someone who understands your family dynamics and responsibilities
- The Peer Partner: Someone at a similar life stage who faces comparable responsibility challenges

Responsibility Recovery Protocols

When You've Avoided Responsibility:

1. Acknowledge the avoidance honestly without making excuses
2. Assess what fear, pride, or other factor contributed to the avoidance
3. Apologize to anyone affected by your failure to take ownership
4. Act to address the problem or take the responsibility you've been avoiding
5. Adjust your systems or approaches to prevent similar avoidance in the future

When You've Over-Functioned or Enabled Others:

1. Recognize that taking inappropriate responsibility prevents others' growth
2. Communicate clearly about boundaries and expectations going forward
3. Support others in taking appropriate ownership without rescuing them from consequences
4. Maintain healthy boundaries while remaining encouraging and available
5. Trust that allowing others to experience appropriate consequences serves their development

This comprehensive approach to responsibility and ownership provides both internal development practices and external accountability structures that support faithful stewardship across all areas of life while serving others' growth and God's kingdom purposes.

CHAPTER CONCLUSION
The Sacred Trust of Stewardship

As we conclude this exploration of responsibility and ownership, it's essential to understand the profound transformation that has occurred in your perspective. You haven't simply learned techniques for better accountability or strategies for professional effectiveness—you've discovered the sacred trust of stewardship that transforms every decision, relationship, and opportunity into an expression of faithfulness to God and service to others. True responsibility is not a burden to carry but a privilege to steward, not a performance to maintain but a calling to fulfill with integrity and love.

The most beautiful aspect of biblical stewardship is that it liberates us from the anxiety of ownership while empowering us with the purpose of service. When we understand that everything we have—our talents, resources, opportunities, and influence—belongs to God and is entrusted to us for His purposes, we're freed from the pressure of protecting our own interests while being empowered to invest boldly in kingdom outcomes. This perspective transforms responsibility from self-serving obligation into other-serving opportunity.

Responsibility as Worship and Witness

Perhaps the most transformative understanding of responsibility is recognizing that how we steward what we've been given becomes both worship and witness. When you take ownership of your choices, invest in others' development, and manage resources with integrity, you're offering your life as an act of worship to God. Your faithful stewardship declares your trust in His character and your commitment to His purposes more powerfully than words ever could.

Simultaneously, your responsibility becomes a witness to others about the reality of transformation through faith. When people see you taking ownership instead of making excuses, investing in solutions rather than assigning blame, and serving others' interests alongside your own, they witness that it's possible to live with integrity and purpose. Your stewardship gives others permission to hope that they too can make a meaningful difference through faithful responsibility.

This dual nature of responsibility as worship and witness elevates every act of ownership from mere duty to sacred service. The parent taking responsibility for their family's well-being demonstrates God's faithful provision. The employee taking ownership of their work quality reflects divine excellence. The leader accepting accountability for outcomes models God's commitment to His people. Every act of faithful stewardship becomes a sermon about God's character and calling.

The Multiplication Effect of Faithful Stewardship

Remember that your commitment to responsibility and ownership creates ripple effects that extend far beyond your immediate sphere of influence. When you consistently take ownership, others learn that accountability is possible and beneficial. When you steward resources with integrity, you model that trustworthiness leads to greater opportunity. When you accept responsibility for developing others, you create leaders who will develop others in turn.

This multiplication effect means that your faithful stewardship today prepares the ground for greater kingdom impact tomorrow. The employee you develop through responsible leadership may become a leader who influences thousands. The child you raise with accountability may become an adult who models integrity for their generation. The resources you steward wisely may enable ministries and opportunities that touch lives around the world.

Years from now, people may not remember your specific achievements or possessions, but they will remember how you handled responsibility, how you treated the resources entrusted to you, and how your stewardship enabled others to flourish. This legacy of faithful responsibility becomes one of the most meaningful gifts you can offer to future generations.

The Grace Foundation of Responsible Living

As you continue developing your capacity for responsibility and ownership, remember that faithful stewardship is built on grace, not performance. Your worth and identity come from God's love, not from your effectiveness as a steward. This grace foundation actually enhances rather than undermines responsibility because it frees you from the fear of failure that can paralyze good stewardship.

When you understand that God's love for you doesn't depend on your perfect management of His resources, you can take appropriate risks, admit mistakes quickly, and learn from failures without shame. When you know that your identity is secure in Christ, you can focus on faithful service rather than self-protection. When you trust that God's purposes will ultimately prevail, you can invest boldly in kingdom outcomes without anxiety about immediate results.

The goal is not perfect stewardship but faithful partnership with God's work in the world. He provides the resources and opportunities; you provide the willingness and effort. He supplies the wisdom and strength; you supply the availability and obedience. He creates the outcomes; you create the faithfulness that positions you to participate in His purposes.

Your Stewardship Assignment

As you move forward from this chapter, carry with you the Personal Responsibility Assessment from our practical applications. This week, honestly evaluate your current patterns of ownership and accountability across different life areas. Identify one specific area where God is calling you to take greater responsibility, whether in relationships, work, finances, or personal development.

Begin implementing one daily ownership practice from our toolkit, whether it's the morning stewardship centering, midday responsibility check-ins, or evening reflection routine. Remember, responsibility muscles are built through consistent exercise over time, not through dramatic one-time efforts. Small, daily choices to take ownership compound into significant character development and increased capacity for service.

Looking Ahead

In our next chapter, we'll explore how to develop and maintain faith and spiritual strength as the foundation for all other responsibilities and service. You'll discover that the ownership principles you're developing now find their ultimate grounding in your relationship with God and dependence on His strength.

But for now, embrace your calling to be a faithful steward of everything God has entrusted to you. Trust that He has given you exactly what you need for this season of service and that faithful management of current responsibilities prepares you for greater opportunities to serve. Believe that every choice to take ownership, every decision to accept accountability, and every effort to steward well matters more than you can imagine.

13

Faith & Spiritual Strength

*At the heart of every enduring leader and servant is a wellspring of faith—
a quiet, unwavering trust that there is a purpose greater
than ourselves guiding every step.*

FAITH IS NOT JUST A PRIVATE CONVICTION; it is a living force that shapes our decisions, our resilience, and our ability to serve others with courage and integrity. In the boardroom, the community, or the home, spiritual strength is the anchor that holds us steady through uncertainty, challenge, and change.

Faith-driven leadership is distinct from worldly models of power and control. Where the world often equates leadership with authority, Jesus modeled a different way: servant leadership marked by humility, compassion, and dependence on God. He washed His disciples' feet, forgave His enemies, and led with a heart surrendered to His Father's will. This kind of leadership is not about self-promotion, but about stewarding influence for the good of others and the glory of God. As Paul writes, "When I am weak, then am I strong" (2 Corinthians 12:10). True spiritual strength is found not in self-reliance, but in reliance on God's Spirit, wisdom, and grace.

Faith also provides a moral compass, shaping our ethical framework and the way we navigate complex decisions. Leaders who ground their actions in faith are more likely to act with integrity, compassion, and justice—even when the path is difficult or unpopular. They pause and pray before making decisions, seek wise counsel, and consider not just the bottom line, but the greater good and the impact on others. This spiritual foundation builds trust, inspires teams, and creates a culture where people feel valued and empowered.

Spiritual strength is cultivated through regular practices: prayer, meditation, worship, and reflection on Scripture. These habits help us listen for God's guidance, renew our minds, and draw courage for the journey ahead. As Joshua was reminded, " Be strong and of a good courage; be not afraid, neither be thou dismayed: for the Lord thy God is with thee whithersoever thou goest " (Joshua 1:9). Faith assures us that we are never alone in our calling; God's presence goes before us, sustains us, and equips us to lead and serve with boldness.

In today's world, where ethical leadership is more vital than ever, integrating faith into our leadership is both a privilege and a responsibility. As you lead, let your faith be visible—not as a badge of superiority, but as a beacon of hope, humility, and service. Remember, your spiritual strength is not just for your own benefit, but for the blessing and encouragement of those you influence.

The Nature of Biblical Faith: Beyond Belief to Trust

Understanding faith properly requires distinguishing between intellectual belief and active trust. Biblical faith encompasses both cognitive agreement with truth and volitional commitment to act on that truth, creating a dynamic relationship with God that transforms every aspect of life and service.

Faith as Knowledge, Assent, and Trust. Theologians traditionally describe saving faith as having three components: notitia (knowledge), assensus (assent), and fiducia (trust). Knowledge involves understanding basic truths about God's character, Christ's work, and our need for salvation. Assent means agreeing intellectually that these truths are accurate and reliable. Trust involves personally relying on these truths for salvation and life direction.

However, faith extends beyond the moment of salvation to encompass ongoing relationship with God characterized by increasing trust in His character, promises, and guidance. This progressive faith enables us to make decisions based on spiritual principles rather than just human wisdom, to find hope during difficult circumstances, and to serve others with supernatural love and power.

Active versus passive faith represents a crucial distinction. Passive faith merely acknowledges God's existence and power without allowing these truths to significantly influence daily choices. Active faith consistently applies spiritual truths to practical decisions, relationships, and challenges, creating visible transformation in character and priorities.

Faith as Response to God's Faithfulness. Biblical faith is fundamentally responsive rather than generative—we don't create faith through human effort but respond to God's demonstrated faithfulness throughout history and in our personal experience. "Faith cometh by hearing, and hearing by the word of God" (Romans 10:17). As we learn about God's character and experience His faithfulness personally, our capacity for trust grows naturally.

This understanding prevents faith from becoming a burden we must manufacture through sheer willpower while making it a gift we receive through attention to God's revelation and action. The more we study Scripture, observe God's work in the world, and experience His presence in our lives, the easier it becomes to trust Him with increasing areas of responsibility and service.

Historical faith involves trusting in God's past actions recorded in Scripture and church history. Present faith means relying on God's current involvement in our circumstances and relationships. Future faith encompasses hope in God's promises about ultimate outcomes and eternal purposes. Mature spiritual strength integrates all three dimensions, creating stability that transcends immediate circumstances.

Faith and Reason Integration. Contrary to popular misconceptions, biblical faith and rational thinking are not opposites but complementary ways of understanding reality. Faith provides a framework for interpreting evidence while reason helps us understand the implications and applications of faith-based beliefs.

Faith-informed reason uses spiritual principles to evaluate information, make decisions, and solve problems. This doesn't mean abandoning critical thinking but rather applying both spiritual and natural wisdom to life challenges. Reasonable faith examines evidence for God's existence and character while remaining humble about the limitations of human understanding.

This integration enables believers to engage intellectual challenges confidently while maintaining spiritual priorities, to make practical decisions wisely while considering eternal implications, and to serve others effectively by combining spiritual insight with practical competence.

Spiritual Disciplines: Building Faith Through Practice

Spiritual strength is developed through regular practices that position us to receive God's grace while creating habits of dependence on His wisdom and power. These disciplines are not legalistic requirements but means of grace that facilitate spiritual growth and intimacy with God.

Prayer as Foundation for Spiritual Strength. Prayer serves multiple functions in developing spiritual strength. Adoration connects us to God's character and greatness, providing perspective on our challenges and circumstances. Confession maintains intimacy with God by addressing sin that could hinder our relationship and service effectiveness. Thanksgiving develops gratitude that protects against entitlement and complaining.

Supplication involves bringing our needs and others' needs to God, acknowledging our dependence on His provision and power. Intercession for others develops compassion while participating in God's work in their lives. Listening prayer creates space for God to speak through His Spirit, Scripture, and circumstances.

Conversational prayer throughout the day maintains awareness of God's presence and involvement in ordinary activities. Contemplative prayer develops deeper intimacy through focused attention on God's presence.

The goal of prayer is not perfect technique but authentic relationship with God that provides strength, wisdom, and comfort for all aspects of life and service. Regular prayer habits create a foundation of spiritual connection that supports decision-making, relationship building, and service opportunities.

Scripture Study and Meditation Bible study provides knowledge of God's character, promises, and principles that serve as resources for faith development. Systematic study ensures comprehensive understanding of biblical themes and teachings. Topical study addresses specific questions or challenges you're facing. Biographical study examines how biblical figures developed and exercised faith.

Scripture meditation involves sustained reflection on specific passages to extract practical application and spiritual insight. Memorization creates internal resources for times when external access to Scripture may be limited. Lectio divina and other contemplative reading practices slow down the study process to hear God›s voice through His Word.

Application focus ensures that Scripture study leads to life change rather than just information accumulation. Community study with others provides accountability for application while offering different perspectives on biblical truth. Teaching others what you're learning multiplies the impact while deepening your own understanding.

Regular Scripture engagement transforms thinking patterns, provides wisdom for complex decisions, and creates confidence in God's faithfulness based on His demonstrated character throughout history.

Worship and Celebration Corporate worship with other believers builds community while focusing attention on God's greatness and goodness. Music, liturgy, and sacraments engage multiple senses in spiritual experience while connecting us to historical Christian faith. Preaching and teaching provide instruction and inspiration for spiritual growth.

Private worship through music, art, nature appreciation, or simple reflection maintains spiritual focus during daily activities. Celebration of God's goodness through gratitude practices and milestone acknowledgment develops positive spiritual emotions. Sabbath observance creates regular rhythm of rest and spiritual renewal.

Service as worship transforms ordinary activities into expressions of love for God when done with proper motivation and heart attitude. Creative expression through art, music, writing, or other media can become worship when offered to God with thanksgiving and love.

Worship practices combat the natural human tendency toward self-focus and anxiety while developing spiritual perspective that supports courage, generosity, and hope during challenging circumstances.

Faith in Action:
Spiritual Strength in Leadership and Service

Spiritual strength becomes most evident and most effective when applied to practical challenges of leadership, service, and relationship building. Understanding how to integrate faith with action creates authentic spiritual influence that blesses others while honoring God.

Decision-Making with Spiritual Wisdom Prayer-based decision-making involves seeking God's guidance before major choices while using the wisdom and resources He's provided for evaluation and planning. Scripture-informed decisions apply biblical principles to specific situations while considering both immediate and eternal implications.

Wise counsel seeking from mature believers provides additional perspective and accountability for important choices. Peace confirmation involves paying attention to internal sense of God's approval or caution about potential decisions. Circumstantial guidance considers how God might be opening or closing doors through external factors.

Values-based evaluation ensures that decisions align with spiritual priorities rather than just practical considerations. Long-term perspective considers how choices affect spiritual growth, relationship health, and service capacity. Kingdom impact assessment evaluates how decisions serve God's purposes and others' welfare.

This approach to decision-making doesn't guarantee perfect choices but creates a process that honors God while utilizing both spiritual and natural wisdom for optimal outcomes.

Faith-Based Leadership Principles Servant leadership involves using authority and influence to develop others rather than just accomplish tasks. Humble confidence combines appropriate boldness about God's calling with honest acknowledgment of personal limitations. Integrity consistency ensures that private character matches public leadership persona.

Vision casting helps others see how their work serves larger spiritual purposes and kingdom objectives. Team development invests in others' growth and capacity rather than just utilizing their current abilities. Conflict resolution addresses disagreements with both truth and grace while seeking restoration and understanding.

Resource stewardship manages budgets, time, and opportunities as gifts from God entrusted for faithful management. Cultural development creates environments where spiritual values like honesty, compassion, and excellence become normative. Crisis leadership maintains hope and perspective during difficult seasons while taking appropriate action to address challenges.

Faith-based leadership often involves making decisions that prioritize long-term spiritual outcomes over short-term practical benefits, trusting that God will honor obedience even when immediate results aren't visible.

Evangelism and Spiritual Influence Lifestyle evangelism involves living in ways that attract others to faith through observed character, priorities, and relationships. Conversational evangelism creates opportunities for spiritual discussions through genuine interest in others' lives and concerns. Service evangelism demonstrates God's love through practical help and community involvement.

Story sharing involves telling others about God's work in your life in ways that are authentic and relevant to their circumstances. Question asking helps others examine their own spiritual beliefs and experiences while showing respect for their journey. Bridge building finds connections between their interests and spiritual truth.

Apologetics preparation enables you to address intellectual questions and objections to faith while maintaining humility about the limitations of human understanding. Prayer ministry offers to pray for faith in God's involvement.

The goal of spiritual influence is not converting others through argument or manipulation but demonstrating the reality and attractiveness of life with God through authentic relationship and service.

Suffering and Faith: Spiritual Strength in Adversity

One of the most challenging aspects of spiritual strength involves maintaining faith during seasons of suffering, disappointment, or apparent divine silence. Understanding how to navigate these experiences with integrity strengthens faith while providing resources for helping others through similar challenges.

The Mystery of Suffering and God's Goodness. Scripture acknowledges that suffering is a universal human experience that affects both believers and unbelievers, often in ways that seem unrelated to moral choices or spiritual maturity. The problem of pain creates theological and emotional challenges that have no easy answers but require faith responses that transcend complete understanding.

Trusting God's character when circumstances seem to contradict His goodness requires confidence in His love and wisdom that goes beyond immediate experience. Eternal perspective provides hope that current suffering serves purposes that may not be visible until heaven. Community support from other believers helps sustain faith when individual resources feel inadequate.

Honest lament following biblical examples like Job and David's psalms allows for authentic expression of pain and confusion while maintaining relationship with God. Redemptive hope believes that God can use even terrible circumstances for good outcomes, though specific benefits may not be visible immediately.

The goal is not to explain suffering satisfactorily but to maintain faith relationship with God while enduring pain and to offer hope to others who are struggling with similar questions and experiences.

Faith Development Through Trials Character formation through adversity develops qualities like patience, perseverance, and compassion that cannot be cultivated through comfortable circumstances alone. Dependence deepening occurs when human resources prove inadequate and faith in God becomes necessary for survival and hope.

Empathy expansion results from personal experience with pain that enables more effective ministry to others who are suffering. Priority clarification often occurs during crisis when non-essential concerns fall away and truly important values become clear.

Spiritual authority often develops through successfully navigating significant challenges with faith intact, creating credibility for future ministry and influence. Testimony creation provides stories of God's faithfulness that can encourage others during their own difficult seasons.

The apostle Paul's experience with his "thorn in the flesh" (2 Corinthians 12:7-10) illustrates how God's strength can be displayed through human weakness when we learn to depend on His grace rather than our own capacity.

Ministry to Others in Suffering Presence over answers often serves suffering people better than attempts to explain or fix their circumstances. Practical help meets immediate needs while demonstrating care and concern.

Hope offering shares confidence in God's ultimate goodness and purpose without minimizing present pain or difficulty. Story sharing tells about times when you or others have experienced God's faithfulness during adversity. Community connection helps suffering people maintain relationships when they might be tempted to isolate.

Long-term presence demonstrates commitment that extends beyond the acute phase of crisis into ongoing recovery and adjustment periods. Resource sharing provides practical assistance with finances, childcare, meals, or other needs that arise during difficult circumstances.

Effective ministry to suffering people requires both spiritual resources (faith, hope, prayer) and practical wisdom (timing, boundaries, appropriate help) that serve others' actual needs rather than our desire to feel helpful.

Faith and Work:
Integrating Spiritual Strength in Professional Life

One of the most challenging areas for spiritual strength involves integrating faith authentically in professional environments that may not share or support spiritual values. Understanding how to maintain spiritual integrity while serving effectively in secular contexts requires wisdom, courage, and strategic thinking.

Calling and Career Integration Work as worship involves approaching professional responsibilities as opportunities to serve God through excellence, integrity, and service to others. Skill development represents stewardship of abilities that can serve both professional success and kingdom purposes. Relationship building creates opportunities for positive spiritual influence through authentic care and service.

Ethical decision-making applies spiritual principles to business situations while respecting professional requirements and legal constraints. Cultural engagement participates constructively in workplace relationships and activities while maintaining spiritual distinctiveness. Leadership opportunities steward influence to serve others' development and welfare.

Mission alignment seeks professional roles and responsibilities that serve larger spiritual purposes when possible. Boundary maintenance protects spiritual priorities while fulfilling professional obligations conscientiously. Witness preparation develops capacity to share faith appropriately when opportunities arise naturally.

The goal is not to compartmentalize faith and work but to integrate spiritual values with professional excellence in ways that honor both God and employment responsibilities.

Marketplace Ministry and Influence Excellence as testimony demonstrates spiritual values through consistently high-quality work and professional conduct. Integrity in details shows faithfulness in small matters that builds trust and credibility for larger influence opportunities. Service attitude looks for ways to help colleagues and contribute to organizational success beyond minimum requirements.

Conflict resolution applies spiritual principles of forgiveness, understanding, and reconciliation to workplace disagreements and personality conflicts. Stress management demonstrates peace and perspective that can attract others' interest in spiritual resources. Generosity practices share resources, recognition, and opportunities with others when appropriate.

Mentoring opportunities invest in others' professional development while potentially creating space for spiritual influence and guidance. Community building helps create positive workplace culture that reflects spiritual values like respect, collaboration, and mutual support.

Crisis leadership provides stability and hope during organizational challenges through spiritual strength and perspective that serves others' welfare alongside business objectives.

Spiritual Warfare: Faith Strength in Conflict

Understanding spiritual warfare provides crucial context for developing spiritual strength, recognizing that faith development occurs within larger cosmic conflict between good and evil that affects both individual and corporate spiritual health.

The Reality of Spiritual Opposition Biblical worldview acknowledges that spiritual forces of evil actively oppose God's purposes and people's spiritual development. Personal attacks may include temptation, discouragement, confusion, and accusations designed to undermine faith and effectiveness. Corporate opposition affects churches, organizations, and communities through division, moral compromise, and misdirected priorities.

Cultural influence shapes values and assumptions in ways that often contradict spiritual truth and biblical principles. Systemic evil operates through institutions, structures, and social patterns that perpetuate injustice and opposition to God's kingdom values.

Understanding spiritual opposition helps explain why spiritual growth often feels difficult and why maintaining faith requires intentional effort and community support rather than happening automatically through good intentions alone.

Spiritual Armor and Weapons Truth foundation (Ephesians 6:14) involves grounding life and decisions in God's revealed truth rather than human opinion or cultural values. Righteousness protection maintains moral integrity that prevents spiritual vulnerability and preserves influence credibility. Peace preparation develops internal stability that enables effective response during conflicts and challenges.

Faith shield deflects accusations, temptations, and attacks that could undermine spiritual confidence and effectiveness. Salvation helmet protects thinking patterns from lies and deception that could compromise spiritual perspective. Word sword provides offensive capability through Scripture knowledge and application.

Prayer weapons include intercession, spiritual warfare prayer, and corporate prayer that addresses spiritual dimensions of personal and community challenges. Worship warfare focuses attention on God's greatness and goodness in ways that counteract fear, discouragement, and spiritual confusion.

These spiritual resources require regular cultivation and practice to be effective during times of significant spiritual opposition or challenge.

Community Spiritual Strength Corporate prayer mobilizes collective spiritual resources for challenges that exceed individual capacity or insight. Mutual accountability provides protection against moral compromise and spiritual deception through honest relationship and feedback. Shared worship builds corporate faith and reminds communities of God's character and faithfulness.

Mission focus maintains clarity about spiritual purposes that can resist distraction or misdirection toward less important objectives. Resource sharing enables communities to support members during spiritual, physical, or emotional challenges that could compromise spiritual strength.

Generational perspective considers how current spiritual choices affect future generations and long-term kingdom advancement rather than just immediate comfort or convenience.

Spiritual warfare awareness doesn't create paranoia or fear but rather wisdom and preparation that enables effective spiritual living and service in a world where opposition to God's purposes is real and significant.

PRACTICAL APPLICATIONS
The Spiritual Strength Assessment:
Evaluating Your Faith Foundation

Before developing deeper spiritual strength, it's important to honestly assess your current spiritual condition and identify areas where God is calling you to grow in faith and dependence on Him.

Faith Development Evaluation

Knowledge Foundation Assessment:
- How well do you understand basic Christian doctrines (salvation, God's character, Scripture authority, eternal life)?
- What questions or doubts about faith do you need to address through study or counsel?
- How familiar are you with biblical stories and principles that apply to daily life challenges?
- What theological topics would strengthen your faith if you understood them better?
- Rate your confidence in explaining your faith to others who ask about it (1-10 scale)

Trust Application Review:
- In what areas of life do you consistently apply faith principles to decisions and challenges?
- Where do you tend to rely on human wisdom or resources instead of seeking God's guidance?
- How often do you pray about daily decisions versus just major life choices?
- What fears or anxieties reveal areas where you're not fully trusting God's character and promises?
- How does your faith affect your handling of money, relationships, and career decisions?

Spiritual Discipline Practice Audit:
- What spiritual disciplines do you practice consistently (prayer, Bible reading, worship, fasting, service)?
- How has your spiritual discipline practice changed over the past year?
- What obstacles typically prevent you from maintaining regular spiritual practices?
- Which disciplines do you find most meaningful and life-changing?
- What new spiritual practices might strengthen your faith and intimacy with God?

Spiritual Fruit Inspection:
- What evidence of spiritual growth have others noticed in your life recently?
- How has your faith affected your character qualities (patience, kindness, self-control, etc.)?
- In what ways has spiritual strength helped you serve others more effectively?
- Where do you see gaps between your stated faith and your lived priorities?
- How well does your private spiritual life support your public spiritual witness?

Daily Spiritual Strength Building Practices

Developing spiritual strength requires consistent daily practices that position you to receive God's grace while building habits of dependence on His wisdom and power.

Morning Spiritual Foundation Routine (15-20 minutes)

Scripture and Prayer Integration:
- Begin with 5 minutes of Bible reading, focusing on one passage for application
- Spend 5 minutes in prayer: adoration (God's character), confession (sin acknowledgment), thanksgiving (grateful recognition), supplication (personal needs)
- Ask for specific wisdom and strength for the day's anticipated challenges

- Surrender your schedule and plans to God's priorities and purposes
- Set an intention to remain aware of God's presence throughout ordinary activities

Weekly Spiritual Discipline Rotation:
- Monday: Focus on gratitude and praise in your prayers and Scripture reading
- Tuesday: Emphasize confession and forgiveness in your spiritual time
- Wednesday: Practice intercession for family, friends, and community needs
- Thursday: Seek wisdom and guidance for current decisions and challenges
- Friday: Focus on mission and service opportunities in your spheres of influence
- Saturday: Practice rest and celebration of God's goodness and faithfulness
- Sunday: Emphasize worship and community connection with other believers

Midday Spiritual Check-In (5 minutes)

God's Presence Awareness Practice:
- Pause whatever you're doing and take three deep breaths
- Ask: "How have I been aware of God's presence and guidance so far today?"
- Reflect: "What opportunities have I had to demonstrate faith through my choices and interactions?"
- Pray briefly for wisdom and strength for the remainder of the day
- Recommit to living as someone who belongs to God and serves His purposes

Evening Spiritual Review (10-15 minutes)

Faith Integration Reflection:
- Where did I see God's faithfulness and provision today?
- How did my faith affect my responses to challenges and opportunities?
- What did I learn about God's character or my need for His grace?
- Where did I miss opportunities to demonstrate spiritual strength or faith-based living?
- How can I better integrate my faith with tomorrow's anticipated activities?

Gratitude and Growth Planning:
- Thank God for specific ways He showed His love and care today
- Identify one area where you grew in spiritual strength or faith application
- Note one spiritual discipline or practice you want to improve tomorrow
- Set intentions for how you want to demonstrate spiritual strength tomorrow

Spiritual Warfare and Protection Strategies

Maintaining spiritual strength requires understanding and preparing for the spiritual opposition that targets faith development and service effectiveness.

Spiritual Armor Daily Application

Truth Belt (Ephesians 6:14):

- Begin each day by reminding yourself of core truths about God's character and your identity in Christ
- When facing confusion or discouragement, return to biblical truth rather than emotional reactions
- Study Scripture regularly to build a foundation of truth that can counter lies and deception
- Practice distinguishing between thoughts that align with God's truth versus those that contradict it

Righteousness Breastplate:

- Maintain moral integrity in both major decisions and small daily choices
- Confess sin quickly to prevent spiritual vulnerability and relationship barriers with God
- Avoid situations and relationships that consistently tempt you toward moral compromise
- Practice spiritual disciplines that strengthen your capacity for holy living

Peace Shoes:

- Cultivate internal peace through trust in God's sovereignty and goodness
- Prepare to share the gospel of peace with others through both words and actions
- Practice conflict resolution skills that demonstrate God's reconciling love
- Maintain readiness to serve others and advance God's kingdom purposes

Faith Shield:

- Practice trusting God's promises during daily challenges and uncertainties
- Use Scripture and prayer to deflect attacks of doubt, fear, and discouragement
- Surround yourself with faith-building influences (books, music, people, activities)
- Regularly remind yourself of past experiences of God's faithfulness

Salvation Helmet:

- Protect your thinking patterns from lies about your identity, worth, and future
- Practice renewing your mind with Scripture and godly perspectives
- Resist thoughts that contradict what God says about you as His child

- Maintain hope in eternal perspective that transcends temporary circumstances

Word of God Sword:

- Memorize Scripture verses that address your common temptations and fears
- Use biblical truth to address lies, accusations, and distorted thinking
- Study the Bible regularly to stay sharp and prepared for spiritual battles
- Speak God's truth over situations and people as led by His Spirit

Faith Integration in Professional and Social Contexts

Living with spiritual strength in environments that may not share your faith requires wisdom, courage, and strategic approaches that honor both your beliefs and your relationships.

Workplace Faith Integration

Excellence as Witness Strategy:

- Consistently deliver high-quality work as a reflection of serving God through professional responsibilities
- Maintain integrity in all business dealings, even when shortcuts or compromises would be easier
- Treat colleagues with respect and kindness regardless of their treatment of you
- Volunteer for difficult tasks and support struggling team members when appropriate

Appropriate Faith Sharing:

- Let others initiate spiritual conversations rather than forcing religious topics into discussions
- Answer questions about your faith honestly and respectfully when asked
- Share how your faith affects your values and priorities in natural, conversational ways

Boundary Management:

- Participate in workplace social activities while maintaining personal convictions
- Decline activities that compromise your values without being judgmental of others
- Find ways to serve company goals while honoring spiritual priorities
- Seek wisdom about when to speak up regarding ethical concerns versus when to remain silent

Community Faith Leadership

Service-Based Influence:

- Volunteer in community organizations where your skills can serve others effectively
- Look for ways to address local needs through both individual action and

organizational involvement
- Build relationships with community leaders who share values of service and human dignity
- Participate in civic activities that promote justice, compassion, and community health

Cultural Engagement Principles:
- Engage with cultural issues from a perspective of love and truth rather than judgment or withdrawal
- Seek to understand different viewpoints while maintaining convictions about biblical truth
- Build bridges with people who hold different beliefs through shared concerns for human welfare
- Practice speaking truth with grace in ways that invite dialogue rather than defensiveness

Crisis Faith and Spiritual Emergency Protocols

Maintaining spiritual strength during seasons of intense difficulty requires specific strategies and resources for navigating challenges that test faith foundations.

Crisis Faith Maintenance

When God Seems Silent or Absent:
- Continue spiritual disciplines even when they feel meaningless or difficult
- Review past experiences of God's faithfulness as reminders of His character
- Focus on God's revealed character in Scripture rather than your current emotional experience
- Remember that God's presence doesn't depend on your ability to feel or sense it

When Prayers Seem Unanswered:
- Examine whether your prayers align with God's revealed will and character
- Consider that God's answers might be "not yet" or "something better" rather than "no"
- Look for ways God might be answering differently than you expected
- Pray for faith to trust God's wisdom and timing rather than demanding specific outcomes
- Continue praying while surrendering results to God's sovereignty and love

When Suffering Challenges Faith:
- Allow yourself to grieve and lament honestly without pretending everything is fine

- Seek community support from others who have faced similar challenges with faith intact

- Study biblical examples of faithful people who suffered without losing trust in God

- Focus on God's character and promises rather than trying to understand specific reasons for suffering

- Look for ways to serve others even while experiencing your own pain

Spiritual Recovery and Restoration

After Seasons of Spiritual Dryness:

- Begin with small, manageable spiritual disciplines rather than trying to restart everything at once

- Seek forgiveness for any sin that might have contributed to spiritual distance

- Reconnect with spiritual community and accountability relationships

- Be patient with the process of rebuilding spiritual momentum and intimacy with God

- Celebrate small steps of progress rather than focusing on how far you have to go

After Moral Failure or Spiritual Compromise:

- Confess sin specifically and completely to God and appropriate people

- Accept responsibility for your choices while receiving God's forgiveness and grace

- Rebuild trust gradually through consistent character demonstration over time

- Seek wise counsel about how to make amends and prevent similar failures

- Focus on God's mercy and restoration rather than shame and condemnation

Community Restoration Support:

- Connect with believers who will encourage your restoration without enabling continued sin

- Find accountability partners who will support your growth while providing honest feedback

- Participate in corporate worship and prayer even when you don't feel worthy or connected

- Serve others as a way of rebuilding confidence in your capacity for faithful living

- Share your story appropriately with others who might benefit from your experience and recovery

This comprehensive approach to spiritual strength development provides both individual practices for faith growth and community resources for maintaining spiritual health through all seasons of life and service.

CHAPTER CONCLUSION
The Unshakeable Foundation

As we conclude this exploration of faith and spiritual strength, it's essential to understand the profound transformation that has occurred in your perspective. You haven't simply learned techniques for religious practice or strategies for spiritual growth—you've discovered the unshakeable foundation that makes all other aspects of serving and growing richly not only possible but sustainable. Faith is not an add-on to an effective life; it is the bedrock upon which all meaningful service, authentic relationships, and lasting impact are built.

The most beautiful aspect of spiritual strength is that it provides what no human resource can offer: a source of power, wisdom, and hope that transcends circumstances, outlasts difficulties, and multiplies through service to others. When your strength comes from God, you can continue serving when your own resources are depleted, keep loving when others disappoint you, and maintain hope when situations seem hopeless. This spiritual foundation transforms you from someone who serves from their own limited capacity into someone who becomes a conduit for unlimited divine love and power.

Faith as the Integrating Force

Perhaps the most transformative understanding about spiritual strength is recognizing how it integrates and empowers every other element of growth and service we've explored throughout this book. Your mindset becomes anchored in eternal truth rather than shifting circumstances. Your actions flow from divine purpose rather than mere human ambition. Your goals align with kingdom priorities that outlast earthly achievements. Your courage grows from confidence in God's presence rather than personal bravery alone.

Your resilience deepens through trust in God's sovereignty and goodness rather than just human determination. Your relationships reflect divine love rather than just human affection. Your responsibility springs from stewardship of divine gifts rather than mere personal accountability. Every aspect of serving and growing richly finds its ultimate meaning and power through faith that connects temporal efforts to eternal purposes.

This integration means that spiritual strength doesn't compete with other areas of development—it completes them. The leader who combines professional competence with spiritual depth becomes more effective, not less. The servant who approaches helping others with both practical skills and divine love creates more lasting impact than either approach alone could achieve.

The Witness of Spiritual Strength

Remember that your spiritual strength becomes one of the most powerful forms of witness to a world that desperately needs to see authentic faith in action. When people observe you maintaining peace during chaos, extending forgiveness when hurt, serving others sacrificially, and finding hope during loss, they witness the reality of God's presence and power working through ordinary human lives.

This witness doesn't require dramatic spiritual performances or constant religious talk. Often the most powerful testimony comes through quiet consistency—the way you handle pressure, treat difficult people, respond to failure, and prioritize relationships over achievements. Your spiritual strength becomes a living sermon about God's character and the possibility of transformation through faith.

Years from now, people may not remember your specific words about faith, but they will remember how your spiritual strength affected them during their own difficult seasons. They'll recall how your peace gave them hope, how your integrity inspired their trust, and how your love reflected something greater than human care. Your faith becomes a gift you offer to a world hungry for evidence that God is real and present.

The Eternal Dimension of Temporal Strength

As you continue developing spiritual strength, remember that every choice to trust God rather than rely on human resources, every decision to seek His guidance rather than depend solely on your own wisdom, and every effort to serve His purposes rather than just your own agenda has eternal significance. You're not just building character for this life—you're preparing for responsibilities and relationships that will continue forever.

This eternal perspective transforms how you view spiritual disciplines, service opportunities, and faith challenges. The time you invest in prayer, Scripture study, and worship isn't just preparation for earthly effectiveness—it's relationship development that will continue in heaven. The character you build through faithful service isn't just for this life's impact—it's preparation for eternal responsibilities in God's kingdom.

Understanding the eternal dimension of spiritual strength provides motivation during seasons when faith feels difficult or costly. Even when spiritual growth requires sacrifice, patience, or perseverance, you can trust that you're investing in outcomes that transcend earthly limitations and last forever.

Your Spiritual Strength Assignment

As you move forward from this chapter, carry with you the Spiritual Strength Assessment from our practical applications. This week, honestly evaluate your current faith foundation and identify specific areas where God is calling you to deeper trust and dependence. Choose one daily spiritual practice from our toolkit and commit to it for the next 30 days, whether it's morning Scripture and prayer, midday presence awareness, or evening spiritual review.

Pay particular attention to opportunities to demonstrate spiritual strength in practical situations—workplace challenges, relationship conflicts, financial pressures, or health concerns. These real-life applications of faith principles are where spiritual strength becomes most evident and most effective.

Looking Ahead

In our next chapter, we'll explore how to cultivate gratitude and appreciation as expressions of spiritual strength that transform both our hearts and our service to others. You'll discover that the faith you're developing now provides the foundation for gratitude that transcends circumstances and creates joy that enhances every aspect of life and ministry.

But for now, embrace your calling to be a person of unshakeable faith in a shaking world. Trust that the God who called you to serve is faithful to provide all the spiritual strength you need for the journey. Believe that your faith, however small it may seem, has the power to move mountains and change lives when placed in the hands of an infinitely powerful and loving God.

14
Gratitude & Application

Gratitude is more than a fleeting feeling or a polite "thank you"—it is a powerful practice that transforms the way we lead, serve, and grow.

IN THE RUSH OF BUSINESS AND THE DEMANDS OF DAILY LIFE, it can be easy to overlook the gifts that surround us: the support of a colleague, the lessons hidden in challenges, or the simple beauty of ordinary moments. Yet, research and experience show that when we pause to notice and express appreciation, we unlock a wellspring of well-being, resilience, and connection.

For leaders and teams, gratitude is not just a nicety—it is a strategic advantage. Studies confirm that grateful leaders build stronger relationships, foster deeper trust, and inspire higher performance. When we take time to recognize the contributions of others, we create cultures where people feel valued and empowered to bring their best. As William Arthur Ward observed, "Feeling gratitude and not expressing it is like wrapping a present and not giving it." Gratitude is the foundation of authentic engagement, fueling collaboration, creativity, and a sense of belonging.

But gratitude is more than a leadership tool; it is a way of seeing the world. It shifts our focus from what is lacking to what is present and possible, helping us navigate uncertainty and adversity with hope and optimism. Even in seasons of challenge, gratitude does not deny hardship—it reframes it, allowing us to find meaning, growth, and even joy in the midst of difficulty. As Rev. Sheri D. Smith Clayborn writes, "Gratitude is both a centering practice and a lifestyle that should not be abandoned in difficult times". In faith communities, gratitude is a spiritual discipline—a way of acknowledging God's goodness and responding with acts of kindness, generosity, and service.

Practicing gratitude is not about ignoring problems or pretending everything is perfect. It is about choosing to notice the good, to celebrate progress, and to honor the people who journey with us. Leaders who cultivate gratitude create environments where everyone feels seen and appreciated, boosting morale, loyalty, and innovation. In your own life, gratitude can become a daily anchor—centering you in the present, reducing stress, and opening your heart to abundance.

The Science of Gratitude: How Appreciation Transforms the Brain

Modern neuroscience has revealed extraordinary insights about how gratitude affects our brains, bodies, and relationships, providing scientific validation for what ancient wisdom traditions have long taught about the transformative power of appreciation and thankfulness.

Neuroplasticity and Gratitude Circuits. Regular gratitude practice literally rewires the brain by strengthening neural pathways associated with positive emotions, social connection, and well-being. When we consistently notice and appreciate good things in our lives, we develop what researchers call "gratitude circuits"—interconnected brain networks that become increasingly sensitive to positive experiences while becoming less reactive to negative ones.

Brain imaging studies show that people who practice gratitude regularly have increased activity in the prefrontal cortex (associated with decision-making and emotional regulation) and decreased activity in the amygdala (associated with fear and stress response). This neurological shift creates a more optimistic default mode that enhances both mental health and relationship quality.

Memory consolidation research reveals that grateful people remember positive experiences more vividly and for longer periods while negative memories fade more quickly. This isn't about denying reality but rather about developing a more balanced and accurate perception of life experiences that includes appreciation for good alongside acknowledgment of difficulty.

Attention training through gratitude practice develops what psychologists call "benefit finding"—the ability to notice positive aspects of situations that might otherwise be overlooked. This enhanced appreciation sensitivity creates upward spirals of increasing happiness and life satisfaction.

Physical Health Benefits of Gratitude Cardiovascular health improvements include lower blood pressure, reduced inflammation, and stronger immune function among people who practice gratitude regularly. Sleep quality enhances through gratitude practices that calm the nervous system and reduce anxiety-driven insomnia. Pain management becomes more effective when appreciation practices shift attention from discomfort to things that are working well in the body.

Stress hormone regulation occurs as gratitude practices reduce cortisol levels while increasing production of serotonin, dopamine, and oxytocin—neurotransmitters associated with happiness, connection, and well-being. Energy levels typically increase as appreciation practices create positive emotional states that support rather than drain physical resources.

These physiological benefits mean that gratitude is not just emotionally beneficial but actually contributes to overall health and longevity, enabling more sustainable service and leadership over time.

Social and Relational Benefits Relationship quality improves significantly when partners, family members, or colleagues regularly express appreciation for each other. Trust building accelerates when people feel seen and valued through authentic gratitude expressions. Conflict resolution becomes easier when appreciation practices create positive emotional bank accounts that support working through disagreements.

Social connection deepens as gratitude practices increase empathy, compassion, and perspective-taking abilities. Leadership effectiveness enhances when appreciation becomes a regular practice that motivates and engages team members. Community building occurs naturally when gratitude creates cultures of mutual recognition and support.

Biblical Foundations of Gratitude and Praise

Scripture presents gratitude not as optional nicety but as fundamental spiritual discipline that reflects proper understanding of God's character and our relationship with Him. Biblical gratitude goes beyond positive thinking to encompass worship, trust, and responsive obedience to God's goodness.

Gratitude as Recognition of God's Character Divine provision acknowledgment recognizes that every good gift comes from God's hand, even when received through human instruments or natural processes. "Every good gift and every perfect gift is from above, and cometh down from the Father of lights" (James 1:17). This perspective transforms how we view success, resources, relationships, and opportunities.

God's faithfulness throughout history provides the foundation for gratitude that transcends current circumstances. Biblical gratitude draws on past evidence of God›s reliability and love as grounds for present appreciation and future hope. Creation beauty and natural provision reveal God›s care and creativity in ways that inspire worship and thanksgiving.

Redemptive work through Christ provides the ultimate reason for gratitude—forgiveness, reconciliation with God, and hope for eternal life that no earthly circumstance can diminish. Spiritual gifts and divine calling create appreciation for how God has uniquely equipped each person for specific service and contribution.

Gratitude as Spiritual Discipline Commanded gratitude appears throughout Scripture not as burdensome requirement but as pathway to blessing and spiritual health. "In every thing give thanks: for this is the will of God in Christ Jesus concerning you" (1 Thessalonians 5:18). This command suggests that gratitude serves our welfare rather than God's need for appreciation.

Worship integration combines gratitude with praise, creating holistic spiritual experiences that engage both emotion and will in response to God's character and actions. Prayer thanksgiving represents one of the primary ways believers express appreciation while also making requests and seeking guidance.

Sacrifice of praise (Hebrews 13:15) involves offering gratitude even during difficult circumstances as an act of faith and trust in God's ultimate goodness. Community thanksgiving creates shared experiences of appreciation that build corporate faith and mutual encouragement.

Lifestyle gratitude extends beyond formal religious settings to encompass daily recognition of God's involvement in ordinary experiences, relationships, and provision.

Gratitude in Suffering and Difficulty Contextual gratitude during hardship doesn't mean being grateful for the suffering itself but rather maintaining appreciation for God's presence, community support, lessons learned, or strength provided during difficult seasons. Perspective gratitude recognizes that current hardships are temporary while God's love and ultimate purposes are eternal.

Sacrificial gratitude offers thanksgiving as an act of faith when feelings don't naturally support appreciation, trusting that gratitude pleases God and serves spiritual health even when circumstances are challenging. Redemptive gratitude anticipates how God might use current difficulties for good purposes, even when specific benefits aren't yet visible.

The biblical approach to gratitude provides resources for maintaining appreciation during all seasons of life while connecting personal blessing to divine relationship and community responsibility.

Gratitude as Leadership and Service Strategy

Appreciation and recognition represent some of the most powerful tools available for inspiring others, building team effectiveness, and creating cultures where people thrive and contribute their best efforts willingly and enthusiastically.

Recognition Psychology and Motivation Intrinsic motivation research reveals that people's internal drive to excel increases significantly when their efforts are noticed and appreciated by others they respect. Effort validation through specific recognition encourages continued high performance more effectively than generic praise or purely financial rewards.

Autonomy support occurs when appreciation recognizes people's choices and initiative rather than just compliance with requirements. Competence confirmation builds confidence and motivation when recognition specifically acknowledges skills, growth, and effective contribution. Relatedness enhancement creates belonging and connection when appreciation comes from people whose opinion matters.

Behavioral reinforcement principles show that appreciated behaviors increase in frequency and quality while unrecognized efforts tend to diminish over time. Positive emotional contagion spreads appreciation throughout teams and organizations when leaders consistently model gratitude and recognition practices.

Types of Effective Recognition Specific appreciation identifies particular actions, qualities, or contributions rather than offering vague praise. Instead of "good job," effective recognition says "your thorough research and clear presentation helped our team make a much better decision about this project."

Timely recognition occurs as close to the appreciated behavior as possible while the action and its impact are still fresh and relevant. Personal relevance tailors appreciation to what each individual values—some prefer public recognition while others appreciate private acknowledgment.

Effort recognition acknowledges hard work and improvement attempt rather than just successful outcomes, encouraging continued effort even when results aren't perfect. Character appreciation recognizes integrity, kindness, perseverance, and other qualities that contribute to both individual and community health.

Value alignment connects recognition to organizational or team values, reinforcing cultural priorities while acknowledging individual contribution to shared goals.

Creating Cultures of Appreciation Systematic recognition involves establishing regular practices and structures that ensure appreciation happens consistently rather than sporadically. Peer recognition systems enable team members to appreciate each other rather than limiting recognition to hierarchical relationships.

Story sharing creates opportunities to tell stories about team members' contributions in ways that honor individuals while inspiring others. Celebration rituals mark milestones, achievements, and important transitions with appropriate recognition and community building.

Gratitude modeling by leaders creates permission and expectation for appreciation throughout the organization. Recognition training helps people develop skills for noticing and expressing appreciation effectively and authentically.

The Appreciation Mindset: Shifting from Scarcity to Abundance

Developing consistent gratitude requires transforming fundamental assumptions about life from scarcity-based thinking (focusing on what's lacking) to abundance-based thinking (recognizing what's available and possible).

Scarcity vs. Abundance Worldviews Scarcity mindset assumes that good things are limited and must be hoarded or competed for, creating anxiety, selfishness, and inability to appreciate what's currently available. Comparison focus measures personal success against others' achievements rather than celebrating individual progress and blessing.

Lack attention consistently notices what's missing, broken, or inadequate while overlooking what's working, beautiful, or sufficient. Fear-based decisions flow from worry about losing what you have rather than faith in continued provision and opportunity.

Abundance mindset recognizes that while some resources are finite, others (like love, creativity, knowledge, and meaning) can be shared and multiplied without diminishing their availability. Gratitude foundation enables generosity because appreciation for what you have creates confidence that more good things are possible.

Growth perspective sees challenges as opportunities for development rather than threats to security. Collaborative approach seeks ways to create mutual benefit rather than zero-sum competition.

Practical Abundance Cultivation Gratitude journaling involving daily writing about specific things you appreciate trains attention to notice positive aspects of ordinary experiences. Appreciation meditation focuses contemplative time on recognizing gifts, blessings, and positive qualities in your life and relationships.

Thank you practices involve regularly expressing appreciation to people who contribute to your welfare, learning, or opportunities. Blessing counting systematically reviews different life areas (health, relationships, work, home, community) to identify things often taken for granted.

Perspective practices compare current circumstances to earlier periods of your life or to global situations that provide context for appreciating your current situation. Service gratitude notices how opportunities to help others represent privileges rather than burdens.

Gratitude in Difficult Seasons: Finding Light in Darkness

One of the most challenging aspects of gratitude practice involves maintaining appreciation during seasons of loss, disappointment, failure, or overwhelming difficulty. Understanding how to practice authentic gratitude without denying reality creates resilience and hope that sustain service capacity during challenging times.

Contextual Gratitude Practices Present moment appreciation focuses on good things that exist even during difficult circumstances—supportive relationships, physical comfort, beauty in nature, or personal strengths that help navigate challenges. Historical gratitude draws on past experiences of God's faithfulness, human kindness, or personal growth through adversity.

Community gratitude recognizes how others' support, prayers, and practical help provide resources for enduring current difficulties. Learning gratitude appreciates lessons, character development, or insights gained through challenging experiences, even when the circumstances themselves aren't enjoyable.

Hope gratitude expresses appreciation for future possibilities and God's promises about ultimate outcomes, even when current circumstances are discouraging. Capacity gratitude recognizes the strength, faith, or resilience you've discovered in yourself during difficulty.

Avoiding Toxic Positivity Authentic gratitude acknowledges real pain, loss, and difficulty while also recognizing good things that remain present or possible. Balanced perspective includes both appreciation and honest assessment of challenges without requiring constant optimism or denial of negative realities.

Appropriate timing recognizes that gratitude practices may need to wait until acute grief, trauma, or crisis has been processed appropriately. Community discernment understands when to encourage gratitude and when to simply provide presence and support without trying to shift others' perspectives prematurely.

Grief integration allows appreciation for good memories, remaining blessings, and supportive relationships to coexist with sadness about losses rather than requiring gratitude to eliminate all negative emotions.

Gratitude as Spiritual Warfare Hope declaration through appreciation practices can counter despair and depression that undermine spiritual strength and service capacity. Truth focus emphasizes God's character and promises rather than allowing circumstances to define spiritual reality.

Praise warfare uses gratitude and worship to resist spiritual attacks of discouragement, fear, and hopelessness. Community strength draws on others' faith and appreciation when personal gratitude feels impossible or inadequate.

Future hope maintains confidence in God's ultimate goodness and purpose even when current experiences seem to contradict His character or promises.

Expressing Appreciation: The Art of Meaningful Recognition

Moving from internal gratitude to external expression requires skills for communicating appreciation in ways that genuinely encourage others while avoiding manipulation or superficial praise.

Elements of Effective Appreciation Specificity describes particular actions, qualities, or contributions rather than offering generic compliments. Impact description explains how the person's contribution affected you, the team, or others in meaningful ways. Personal connection shares how their action aligned with values you appreciate or how it made a difference in your experience.

Sincerity ensures that appreciation expressions reflect genuine feelings rather than obligatory social conventions or strategic manipulation. Appropriate intensity matches the level of appreciation to the significance of the contribution without overdoing or understating recognition.

Individual preferences consider how each person prefers to receive appreciation—some value public recognition while others prefer private acknowledgment, some want detailed feedback while others appreciate brief expressions.

Written Appreciation Practices Thank you notes provide tangible expressions of gratitude that people can save and review when they need encouragement. Email recognition creates records of appreciation that can be shared with supervisors or saved for performance reviews. Social media appreciation offers public recognition that honors individuals while inspiring others.

Letter writing for significant occasions or major contributions creates meaningful documents that express gratitude more thoroughly than brief notes. Card giving for birthdays, holidays, or achievements provides opportunities for regular appreciation expression.

Verbal Appreciation Skills Timing sensitivity chooses appropriate moments for appreciation expression when the person can receive and absorb recognition effectively. Setting consideration determines whether appreciation should be shared privately or publicly based on the individual and the situation.

Active listening ensures that appreciation expressions connect with what matters to the recipient rather than just what the giver wants to communicate. Follow-up questions invite conversation about their experience, motivation, or perspective on their contribution.

Body language awareness ensures that nonverbal communication supports verbal appreciation through eye contact, open posture, and engaged attention.

Gratitude and Generosity: The Natural Flow from Appreciation to Action

Authentic gratitude naturally motivates generous responses—giving back to those who have helped us, supporting others facing challenges we've overcome, and contributing to causes that serve human welfare and God's kingdom purposes.

The Gratitude-Generosity Connection Psychological research demonstrates that people who regularly practice gratitude tend to be more generous with time, money, and resources than those who don't maintain appreciation practices. Reciprocity motivation creates desire to give back when we recognize how much we've received from others and from God.

Abundance perception through gratitude practices increases willingness to share resources because appreciation reveals how much is actually available rather than focusing on scarcity and lack. Empathy development occurs as gratitude increases awareness of others' contributions, naturally leading to concern for their welfare and challenges.

Value alignment connects generosity to appreciation for what we've received, creating giving practices that reflect our values rather than just social pressure or guilt motivation.

Forms of Generous Response Financial giving to church, ministries, and charities represents one way to express gratitude for material provision while supporting others' welfare. Time volunteering offers skills and presence to serve causes and people who matter to you. Skill sharing teaches others abilities you've developed or connects them with opportunities for growth.

Resource sharing includes lending tools, providing space, or offering expertise that others need. Relationship investing involves introducing people to each other, providing references, or creating networking opportunities that serve others' advancement.

Creating Generosity Systems Planned giving establishes regular financial contributions to causes that align with your values and gratitude focus. Scheduled service commits specific time periods for volunteering or helping activities rather than waiting for convenient opportunities.

Relationship generosity creates regular practices for encouraging, supporting, and serving the people who contribute to your life and work. Resource allocation budgets time, money, and energy for generous giving rather than limiting generosity to leftover resources.

Impact assessment periodically reviews how your generous giving creates positive outcomes for recipients while also serving your own spiritual and emotional development through gratitude expression.

Building Gratitude Communities and Cultures

Individual gratitude practice becomes most powerful when embedded within communities and cultures that prioritize appreciation, recognition, and mutual support as normal aspects of relationship and organizational life.

Family Gratitude Practices Dinner table sharing creates regular opportunities for family members to share appreciation for good things that happened during their day or week. Gratitude traditions around holidays, birthdays, and special occasions focus celebration on appreciation rather than just gift-giving or entertainment.

Bedtime gratitude helps children (and adults) end days with appreciation practices that support positive sleep and emotional regulation. Challenge reframing teaches family members to look for learning opportunities and growth possibilities during difficult experiences.

Service projects provide shared experiences of giving back that demonstrate gratitude through action while building family bonds around generous values.

Workplace Appreciation Culture Regular recognition systems ensure that employee contributions are noticed and appreciated consistently rather than sporadically. Peer appreciation opportunities enable team members to express gratitude for each other's help, collaboration, and excellence.

Leadership modeling demonstrates consistent gratitude practices that set organizational tone and expectations for mutual appreciation. Customer appreciation practices recognize the people who make business success possible while building loyalty and positive relationships.

Community recognition celebrates the ways employees serve in volunteer activities and contribute to broader community welfare beyond their professional responsibilities.

Faith Community Gratitude Testimony sharing provides opportunities for community members to tell stories about God's faithfulness and provision in their lives. Prayer gratitude includes thanksgiving as regular component of corporate worship and intercessory prayer.

Service celebration recognizes how community members serve others within and beyond the church through various ministries and volunteer activities. Milestone recognition celebrates baptisms, graduations, anniversaries, and other significant events in members' lives.

Mutual appreciation creates opportunities for people to express gratitude for how others have contributed to their spiritual growth, practical support, or community connection.

PRACTICAL APPLICATIONS
The Gratitude Assessment:
Measuring Your Appreciation Capacity

Before developing deeper gratitude practices, it's important to honestly assess your current appreciation patterns and identify areas where cultivating thankfulness could enhance your well-being and service effectiveness.

Personal Gratitude Pattern Analysis

Daily Appreciation Awareness:

- How often do you notice positive things during ordinary activities and interactions?
- What percentage of your mental energy focuses on problems versus blessings?
- How frequently do you express appreciation to others versus keeping grateful thoughts to yourself?
- What types of experiences or gifts do you most easily appreciate versus take for granted?
- Rate your ability to find something to appreciate even during difficult days (1-10 scale)

Expression and Communication Assessment:

- How comfortable are you expressing appreciation verbally to family, friends, and colleagues?
- What barriers typically prevent you from sharing gratitude when you feel it?
- How specific and meaningful are your expressions of appreciation versus generic "thank you" statements?
- How often do others comment on feeling appreciated or valued by you?
- What methods of appreciation expression (verbal, written, acts of service) feel most natural to you?

Circumstances and Perspective Evaluation:

- How does your gratitude level change during stressful, disappointing, or challenging seasons?
- What situations or people consistently challenge your ability to maintain appreciation?
- How well do you balance honest acknowledgment of problems with recognition of blessings?
- What role does comparison with others play in your satisfaction and gratitude levels?
- How effectively do you use gratitude practices to shift your perspective during difficult times?

Community and Cultural Context Review:

- How well do your family, workplace, and social environments support or hinder gratitude practices?
- What appreciation practices exist in your communities versus what you might want to create?
- How do you contribute to cultures of appreciation versus waiting for others to initiate recognition?
- What opportunities do you have to model gratitude for others who might benefit from your example?
- How does your faith community integrate thanksgiving and appreciation into regular activities?

Daily Gratitude Practices: Building Your Appreciation Muscle

Developing consistent gratitude requires daily practices that train your attention to notice blessings while creating habits of appreciation expression that benefit both you and others.

Morning Gratitude Foundation (10 minutes)

The 3-3-3 Gratitude Practice:

- 3 Personal Blessings: Identify three things you're grateful for in your personal life (health, relationships, experiences, possessions, opportunities)
- 3 People Appreciations: Think of three people who contribute to your welfare and send brief mental appreciation their way
- 3 Daily Anticipations: Consider three things you're looking forward to today and express gratitude for the opportunities they represent

Gratitude Prayer Integration:

- Begin daily prayer with thanksgiving for God's character and faithfulness
- Thank God for specific provisions, relationships, and opportunities from yesterday
- Ask for eyes to see His blessings and heart to appreciate them throughout today
- Express gratitude for the ability to serve others through your daily activities and responsibilities

Intention Setting:

- Choose one person you'll express appreciation to today
- Identify one challenge from yesterday that taught you something valuable
- Set an intention to notice small blessings throughout ordinary activities
- Commit to ending the day with more gratitude than you started with

Midday Gratitude Check-in (5 minutes)

Appreciation Pause Practice:
- Stop current activity and take three deep breaths while looking around your environment
- Notice five things you can see that you appreciate (people, objects, beauty, opportunities)
- Recall one positive interaction or experience from earlier today
- Send mental appreciation to someone who has helped you today
- Adjust your perspective if you've been focusing primarily on problems or frustrations

Evening Gratitude Review (10-15 minutes)

Daily Gratitude Inventory:
- What three things went better today than they could have?
- Who showed you kindness, help, or consideration today?
- What challenges provided learning opportunities or character development?
- How did you see God's provision or faithfulness in ordinary experiences?
- What abilities, resources, or opportunities did you use today that deserve appreciation?

Gratitude Expression Planning:
- Choose one person who deserves appreciation and plan how you'll express it tomorrow
- Write a brief thank you note, text, or email to someone who helped you recently
- Identify one way you can show appreciation through actions rather than just words
- Plan how you'll share gratitude with family members during evening conversation
- Set intentions for how you want to demonstrate appreciation tomorrow

Appreciation Expression and Recognition Systems

Moving from internal gratitude to external expression requires specific strategies and skills for communicating appreciation in ways that genuinely encourage others while building relationships and community.

Effective Appreciation Communication

The IMPACT Appreciation Method:
- Identify the specific action, quality, or contribution you want to appreciate
- Mention the positive impact their action had on you, others, or the situation

- Personalize the appreciation by explaining why it matters to you specifically
- Acknowledge their character qualities that led to the positive action
- Connect their contribution to larger values or goals you both care about
- Thank them sincerely and specifically for their choice to contribute positively

Written Appreciation Strategies:

The Weekly Thank You Note Practice:

- Choose one person each week who deserves written appreciation
- Write a specific, detailed note explaining what they did and how it affected you
- Mention character qualities you observed through their actions
- Send the note within a week of the action you're appreciating
- Keep copies of appreciation notes you send to track your gratitude expression patterns

Digital Appreciation Tools:

- Use email to send specific appreciation messages that people can save and review
- Share public recognition on appropriate social media platforms when people would appreciate visibility
- Create photo or video messages that add personal touch to digital appreciation
- Use workplace communication tools to provide recognition that supervisors and colleagues can see
- Send calendar invitations for brief "appreciation meetings" when verbal recognition would be meaningful

Verbal Appreciation Skills:

The Appreciation Conversation Framework:

1. Get their attention and ensure they have time to receive appreciation fully
2. Share specific details about what they did that you want to acknowledge
3. Explain the impact their action had on you, others, or the situation
4. Connect to character by mentioning qualities like kindness, diligence, or creativity that you observed
5. Express genuine gratitude for their choice to act positively
6. Invite response if they want to share their perspective or motivation

Gratitude During Challenges: Maintaining Appreciation in Difficulty

Developing resilience through gratitude requires specific strategies for finding authentic appreciation during seasons of loss, disappointment, failure, or overwhelming stress.

Challenge-Specific Gratitude Approaches

During Health Challenges:
- Appreciate medical care, supportive relationships, and remaining physical capacities
- Find gratitude for lessons learned about priorities, mortality, and what truly matters
- Express appreciation for people who provide practical help, emotional support
- Practice gratitude for small improvements, good days, or effective treatments
- Thank God for strength to endure and hope for healing or peace

During Relationship Conflicts:
- Appreciate good aspects of the relationship that still exist despite current difficulties
- Find gratitude for lessons about communication, boundaries, or personal growth
- Express appreciation for people who provide perspective, mediation, or emotional support
- Practice gratitude for opportunities to develop patience, forgiveness, or conflict resolution skills
- Thank God for His love that remains constant regardless of human relationship challenges

During Financial Stress:
- Appreciate non-monetary resources like health, relationships, skills, and opportunities
- Find gratitude for lessons about priorities, contentment, and trust in God's provision
- Express appreciation for people who offer practical help, emotional support
- Practice gratitude for basic needs that continue to be met (food, shelter, safety)
- Thank God for past provision and trust in His continued faithfulness

During Career Setbacks:
- Appreciate skills, experience, and knowledge gained through work history
- Find gratitude for supportive relationships and opportunities to reassess priorities
- Express appreciation for people who provide networking, references, or encouragement
- Practice gratitude for the time to rest, learn new skills, or explore different directions

- Thank God for identity that transcends professional achievement and His plans for your future

The Gratitude Reframe Technique: When facing disappointment or setbacks, use this process to find authentic appreciation:

1. Acknowledge the difficulty honestly without minimizing or denying the challenge
2. Look for learning opportunities about yourself, others, or life priorities
3. Identify support you've received from people or circumstances during the challenge
4. Consider character development occurring through the experience of navigating difficulty
5. Find hope connections to future possibilities or God's larger purposes
6. Express specific gratitude for any positive aspects you can identify authentically

Building Gratitude Communities and Systems

Creating environments where appreciation thrives requires intentional development of practices and structures that make gratitude normal and expected rather than exceptional.

Family Gratitude Culture Development

Daily Family Gratitude Practices:

- Meal Gratitude: Begin family meals by sharing one thing each person appreciated during their day
- Bedtime Thankfulness: Help children end days by sharing three things they're grateful for
- Weekend Gratitude Review: Spend time during family breakfast or dinner discussing the week's blessings
- Monthly Appreciation Night: Dedicate one evening monthly to expressing specific appreciation for each family member
- Service Gratitude: After family service projects, discuss what you're grateful for about the opportunity to help others

Family Gratitude Traditions:

- Create annual gratitude journals where family members write appreciation notes to each other
- Establish holiday traditions focused on thanksgiving rather than just gift-giving
- Plan "gratitude field trips" to visit people who have helped your family over the years
- Develop family appreciation rituals for birthdays, achievements, and milestones
- Create photo albums or scrapbooks that focus on documenting blessings and positive memories

Workplace Appreciation Systems

Team Recognition Practices:

- Weekly Appreciation Rounds: Begin team meetings with team members sharing appreciation for colleagues

- Project Gratitude: End completed projects by acknowledging everyone's contributions specifically

- Peer Recognition Program: Create systems for team members to nominate colleagues for appreciation

- Customer Appreciation Sharing: Regularly share positive customer feedback with relevant team members

- Milestone Celebrations: Recognize work anniversaries, achievements, and personal milestones

Leadership Gratitude Modeling:

- Send weekly appreciation emails highlighting specific team member contributions

- Practice "gratitude leadership" by starting meetings with acknowledgment of recent positive developments

- Create appreciation rituals around performance reviews that balance feedback with recognition

- Share your own gratitude practices with team members as appropriate professional development

- Recognize team members publicly in front of supervisors, clients, or other departments

Faith Community Gratitude Enhancement

Corporate Thanksgiving Practices:

- Testimony Time: Regular opportunities for community members to share stories of God's faithfulness

- Prayer Gratitude: Include specific thanksgiving elements in corporate prayer and worship

- Service Appreciation: Recognize volunteers and their contributions to community welfare

- Life Milestone Celebration: Acknowledge baptisms, graduations, anniversaries, and achievements in members' lives

- Community Impact Recognition: Celebrate how the faith community serves the broader local community

Personal Gratitude Ministry:

- Volunteer to send appreciation notes to ministry leaders, volunteers, and community members

- Offer to create gratitude displays or presentations highlighting community blessings and achievements

- Organize appreciation events for pastors, staff members, or long-term volunteers

- Mentor others in developing personal gratitude practices as part of spiritual formation

- Share your gratitude journey and practices as appropriate testimony and encouragement

This comprehensive approach to gratitude development provides both personal practices for appreciation cultivation and community strategies for creating cultures where thankfulness enhances relationships, resilience, and service effectiveness.

CHAPTER CONCLUSION
The Transforming Power of a Grateful Heart

As we conclude this exploration of gratitude and appreciation, it's essential to understand the profound transformation that has occurred in your perspective. You haven't simply learned techniques for positive thinking or strategies for better relationships—you've discovered the transforming power of a grateful heart that sees abundance where others see scarcity, finds hope where others see despair, and creates joy where others experience only duty. Gratitude is not merely an emotional response to good circumstances; it is a chosen posture of the heart that transforms every aspect of life and service.

The most beautiful aspect of gratitude is its multiplying nature. When you appreciate what you have, you become more aware of additional blessings that were always present but previously unnoticed. When you express appreciation to others, you inspire them to notice good things in their own lives and relationships. When you maintain thanksgiving during difficulties, you model resilience that gives others hope for their own challenges. Your gratitude becomes a gift that keeps giving, creating ripple effects of appreciation that extend far beyond your immediate experience.

Gratitude as Worship and Service

Perhaps the most transformative understanding about gratitude is recognizing it as both worship and service. When you appreciate God's provision, character, and faithfulness, you offer Him the worship He deserves while positioning yourself to receive even greater awareness of His goodness. When you express appreciation to others, you serve their emotional and spiritual needs while reflecting God's love and recognition of their worth.

This understanding elevates every expression of gratitude from social nicety to sacred offering. The thank you note you write becomes a ministry of encouragement. The appreciation you express to a colleague becomes a reflection of how God values their contribution. The thanksgiving you maintain during hardship becomes a testimony to His faithfulness that strengthens others' faith. Your gratitude becomes a form of ministry that blesses both giver and receiver while honoring God.

When you approach gratitude as worship and service, you find motivation that transcends circumstances and emotions. You appreciate not just because you feel thankful but because appreciation honors God and serves others. You express gratitude not just when it's convenient but because it's a sacred responsibility to recognize good wherever it appears.

The Abundance Perspective

Remember that gratitude creates what researchers call an "abundance loop"—the more you appreciate what you have, the more you notice additional things to appreciate, creating ever-expanding awareness of blessing and possibility. This abundance perspective doesn't deny real challenges or pretend everything is perfect, but it provides a foundation of appreciation that supports resilience, generosity, and hope during any circumstances.

This perspective transforms how you view your resources, relationships, and opportunities. Instead of focusing on what's lacking, you become skilled at recognizing what's available. Instead of competing for limited good things, you discover that many of life's greatest gifts—love, kindness, wisdom, beauty, hope—multiply when shared rather than diminish. Instead of anxiously protecting what you have, you confidently invest in others because you trust that abundance is possible and blessing is available.

Years from now, people may not remember your specific achievements or possessions, but they will remember how your grateful spirit affected them. They'll recall how your appreciation made them feel valued, how your thanksgiving during difficulty gave them hope, and how your generous spirit inspired them to notice their own blessings. Your gratitude becomes a legacy that enriches lives long after specific expressions are forgotten.

The Grace Foundation of Gratitude

As you continue developing gratitude practices, remember that authentic appreciation is built on grace rather than performance. You don't need to earn God's blessings through perfect thankfulness, and you don't need to manufacture grateful feelings through willpower alone. Instead, you can choose grateful responses based on the evidence of God's goodness, regardless of your current emotional state or circumstances.

This grace foundation makes gratitude sustainable during difficult seasons when appreciation doesn't come naturally. You can express thanks as an act of faith rather than waiting for grateful feelings to motivate you. You can appreciate God's character based on His revealed nature rather than requiring perfect circumstances to feel thankful. You can maintain hope in His ultimate goodness even when immediate experiences seem to contradict His love.

The goal is not perfect gratitude but faithful appreciation that grows over time through practice and divine grace working within you. Every choice to notice blessing, every decision to express appreciation, and every effort to maintain thanksgiving during difficulty participates in God's transforming work in your heart and impact on others.

Your Gratitude Assignment

As you move forward from this chapter, carry with you the Gratitude Assessment from our practical applications. This week, honestly evaluate your current appreciation patterns and choose one daily gratitude practice to implement consistently. Whether it's the morning 3-3-3 practice, midday appreciation pauses, or evening gratitude review, begin building the muscle of appreciation that will transform your perspective and service capacity.

Pay particular attention to opportunities to express appreciation to others who contribute to your life and work. Use the IMPACT method to communicate specific, meaningful recognition that genuinely encourages others while building stronger relationships and community connections.

Looking Ahead

In our final chapter, we'll explore how to live in abundance mindset as the culminating expression of all the principles we've developed throughout this book. You'll discover that the gratitude you're cultivating now provides the foundation for abundant living that transforms both your experience and your service to others.

But for now, embrace your calling to be a person of extraordinary gratitude in an ordinary world. Trust that every choice to appreciate, every expression of thanksgiving, and every decision to notice blessing matters more than you can imagine. Believe that your grateful heart becomes a beacon of hope for others who struggle to see good in their circumstances.

15

Learning & Growth Mindset

The journey of serving and growing richly never truly ends, because at its core is a commitment to lifelong learning and the embrace of a growth mindset.

IN EVERY FIELD—BUSINESS, EDUCATION, FAITH, AND BEYOND—those who thrive are not those who know it all, but those who remain curious, humble, and willing to learn from every experience. A growth mindset is more than a motivational slogan; it is a way of seeing the world that transforms setbacks into stepping stones and challenges into opportunities for innovation and renewal.

At its essence, a growth mindset is the belief that our abilities, intelligence, and creativity can be developed through effort, practice, and learning—not fixed traits we are born with. This belief empowers us to step outside our comfort zones, pursue new skills, and view failure not as a verdict, but as valuable feedback on the path to mastery. In business, leaders with a growth mindset foster cultures of innovation, resilience, and continuous improvement. In faith and personal life, a growth mindset opens the door to deeper wisdom, greater empathy, and a willingness to be shaped by God's ongoing work in us.

Research shows that people with a growth mindset are more resilient, adaptable, and successful in the face of adversity. They are less afraid to try new things, more open to feedback, and better equipped to solve problems creatively. They understand that learning is a journey, not a destination, and that every experience—good or bad—can teach us something valuable. This perspective not only boosts self-esteem and reduces stress, but also leads to greater happiness and fulfillment.

Faith traditions echo these truths, inviting us to "grow in grace, and in the knowledge of our Lord and Saviour Jesus Christ" (2 Peter 3:18). The Bible teaches that wisdom is a lifelong pursuit, and that humility—a willingness to admit we don't have all the answers—is the beginning of true understanding (Proverbs 4:7). When we approach life with open hands and an open mind, we invite God to shape us, teach us, and use us in ways we could never have imagined.

Cultivating a growth mindset is a daily practice. It means welcoming challenges, seeking out new perspectives, and celebrating progress rather than perfection. It means asking questions, listening deeply, and being willing to start again when things don't go as planned. Most of all, it means believing that you—and those you serve—are always capable of learning, growing, and becoming more.

Practical Exercise: Think of an area in your life or work where you feel "stuck" or hesitant to try something new. Reflect on what beliefs or fears might be holding you back. This week, commit to learning one new skill or seeking feedback in that area. Approach it with curiosity and patience, reminding yourself that growth is a process, not an event. Consider journaling about what you learn and how your mindset shifts along the way.

Call to Action: As you close this chapter—and this book—remember that the richest lives are those marked by continual learning and a willingness to grow. Embrace each day as a classroom, every person as a teacher, and every challenge as an invitation to serve more deeply and grow more richly. Carry this mindset forward, and you will discover that the journey of serving and growing is truly endless—and endlessly rewarding.

The Neuroscience of Growth: How Learning Transforms the Brain

Understanding the biological foundation of learning and growth provides powerful motivation for embracing challenges and pursuing continuous development. Modern neuroscience has revealed that our brains remain remarkably plastic throughout our lives, capable of forming new neural pathways and strengthening existing connections through experience and practice.

Neuroplasticity and Lifelong Learning. The discovery of neuroplasticity has revolutionized our understanding of human potential. Unlike previous beliefs that brain development was largely fixed after childhood, we now know that the brain continues to adapt, reorganize, and grow throughout our entire lives. Every time we learn something new, practice a skill, or encounter novel experiences, we literally rewire our brains for enhanced capacity and performance.

Myelin development occurs when we repeatedly practice new skills, creating faster and more efficient neural pathways. Synaptic strengthening happens when we challenge ourselves intellectually, improving memory and cognitive processing. Neurogenesis research shows that new brain cells continue to form in areas associated with learning and memory, particularly when we engage in complex, challenging activities.

This scientific understanding validates the biblical teaching that we can be "transformed by the renewing of your mind" (Romans 12:2). The renewal process isn't just spiritual metaphor—it's biological reality that occurs when we consistently expose ourselves to truth, wisdom, and growth-producing experiences.

The Default Mode Network and Growth. Neuroscientists have identified a "default mode network" in the brain that activates when we're not focused on specific tasks. In people with fixed mindsets, this network often engages in self-protective thinking—rehearsing past failures, avoiding challenges, or comparing themselves negatively to others. In people with growth mindsets, the default mode network focuses on possibilities, learning opportunities, and creative problem-solving.

Meditation and prayer practices can actually reshape this default network toward more positive, growth-oriented patterns. Gratitude practices strengthen neural pathways associated with optimism and possibility. Challenge-seeking behaviors develop brain regions associated with resilience and adaptability.

The practical implication is profound: we can literally change our brains by changing our thinking patterns and learning behaviors. The person who consistently seeks growth opportunities, embraces challenges, and learns from failures develops a brain that naturally defaults to growth-oriented responses rather than fixed-mindset reactions.

Stress, Challenge, and Optimal Learning. The relationship between stress and learning is complex but crucial for understanding how to approach growth effectively. Positive stress (eustress) associated with appropriate challenges actually enhances learning and memory formation. Negative stress (distress) from overwhelming or threatening situations impairs cognitive function and reduces learning capacity.

The growth zone exists between our comfort zone (where no learning occurs) and the panic zone (where stress overwhelms learning capacity). Effective growth mindset development involves intentionally spending time in this growth zone—challenging ourselves enough to stimulate development without becoming overwhelmed or discouraged.

Flow states represent optimal learning conditions where challenge level perfectly matches skill level, creating experiences of deep engagement and accelerated learning. Deliberate practice involves structured, goal-oriented activity designed to improve performance through focused attention and feedback.

Understanding these principles helps us design learning experiences that maximize growth while maintaining motivation and enjoyment in the development process.

Biblical Foundations of Growth and Wisdom

Scripture presents a comprehensive framework for understanding learning and growth that goes far beyond intellectual development to encompass character formation, spiritual maturity, and service effectiveness. The biblical approach to growth mindset provides both motivation and methodology for lifelong development.

Wisdom as the Ultimate Learning Goal Biblical wisdom differs from mere knowledge or intelligence by integrating understanding, experience, and godly perspective into practical life application. "The fear of the Lord is the beginning of wisdom: and the knowledge of the holy is understanding" (Proverbs 9:10). This suggests that true wisdom begins with proper relationship to God and humble recognition of our need for His guidance.

Practical wisdom applies spiritual truth to daily decisions, relationships, and challenges. Relational wisdom enables us to love others well, resolve conflicts constructively, and build communities that reflect God's character. Leadership wisdom involves stewarding influence and authority in ways that serve others' development and advance God's purposes.

Experiential wisdom comes through navigating life's challenges with faith and integrity, extracting lessons that benefit both personal growth and service to others. Intergenerational wisdom involves both learning from those who have gone before us and sharing insights with those we can mentor and influence.

The Process of Spiritual Formation Spiritual growth involves progressive transformation into the likeness of Christ through the Holy Spirit's work in our lives. This process requires both divine initiative and human cooperation, creating a partnership between God's grace and our faithful response to His leading.

Character development occurs through the intersection of biblical truth, life experiences, and community relationships. Spiritual disciplines create conditions for growth by positioning us to receive God's grace while developing habits that support spiritual health. Service opportunities provide contexts for applying spiritual growth while contributing to others' welfare.

Community formation recognizes that spiritual growth happens primarily through relationships rather than individual effort. Mentoring relationships facilitate wisdom transfer while providing accountability and encouragement for continued development. Corporate worship creates shared experiences of encountering God that inspire and sustain individual growth.

Redemptive grace transforms failure into wisdom, weakness into strength, and brokenness into compassion for others facing similar struggles.

Confession and forgiveness create opportunities for learning and restoration rather than shame and condemnation. Community restoration involves others helping us learn from failures while maintaining relationship and support. Testimony development transforms personal failure and recovery into resources for helping others navigate similar challenges.

The biblical approach to failure emphasizes learning, growth, and redemption rather than perfectionism or shame, creating safe environments for the risk-taking that real growth requires.

Fixed vs. Growth Mindset in Leadership and Service

Understanding the difference between fixed and growth mindsets is crucial for developing leadership approaches and service strategies that facilitate development in ourselves and others rather than creating stagnation or defensiveness.

Fixed Mindset Characteristics in Leadership Talent assumption believes that effective leadership depends primarily on natural abilities rather than developed skills and learned wisdom. Defensive responses to criticism or challenges focus on protecting reputation rather than learning from feedback. Risk avoidance prevents leaders from attempting new strategies or admitting uncertainty about complex situations.

Competition orientation views other leaders as threats rather than potential collaborators or learning resources. Credit hoarding seeks recognition for successes while avoiding responsibility for failures or problems. Perfectionism pressure creates unrealistic expectations for both self and others that discourage honest communication about struggles or learning needs.

Static team assumptions treat team members' abilities as fixed rather than investing in their development and growth potential. Comfort zone leadership avoids challenges that might reveal limitations or require significant learning and adaptation.

Growth Mindset Characteristics in Leadership Development focus assumes that both personal and team effectiveness can be enhanced through learning, practice, and experience. Feedback seeking actively solicits input from others as valuable information for improvement rather than threat to self-image. Challenge embracing views difficult situations as opportunities to develop new skills and demonstrate faith in God's provision.

Collaboration mindset seeks to learn from other leaders while contributing to their development through shared experience and mutual support. Responsibility taking accepts accountability for both successes and failures as learning opportunities that inform future decision-making. Excellence pursuit maintains high standards while acknowledging that growth involves mistakes and imperfect performance.

Team development invests significantly in others' growth and capacity-building, viewing team success as reflection of leadership effectiveness. Innovation encouragement creates environments where experimentation, calculated risk-taking, and learning from failure are valued and supported.

Growth Mindset in Service and Ministry Service learning approaches helping others as opportunity to develop skills, wisdom, and character rather than just meeting others' needs. Feedback integration seeks input from those being served about effectiveness and areas for improvement in service approaches. Cultural humility recognizes that serving across cultural, economic, or social differences requires ongoing learning and adaptation.

Collaboration development works with others rather than for them when possible, respecting their capacity for growth and self-determination. Long-term perspective focuses on developing sustainable solutions and building others' capabilities rather than just addressing immediate needs. Resource multiplication looks for ways to increase impact through training others, developing systems, and creating ongoing opportunities rather than just individual service events.

Creating Learning Organizations and Communities

Implementing growth mindset principles at organizational and community levels requires intentional development of cultures, systems, and practices that support continuous learning and development for all participants.

Learning Organization Characteristics Psychological safety enables people to take risks, make mistakes, and share learning without fear of punishment or judgment. Shared vision aligns individual learning goals with organizational purposes and values. Team learning creates opportunities for collective problem-solving and knowledge sharing that benefits everyone involved.

Systems thinking helps people understand how their individual contributions connect to larger purposes and outcomes. Personal mastery encourages each person to pursue excellence in their areas of responsibility and interest. Mental model examination challenges assumptions and helps people see situations from multiple perspectives.

Experimentation culture supports trying new approaches while learning from both successful and unsuccessful attempts. Knowledge management creates systems for capturing, storing, and sharing learning across the organization. External learning seeks insights and best practices from other organizations, industries, and communities.

Building Learning Communities Diverse perspectives include people with different backgrounds, experiences, and viewpoints to enhance collective learning and problem-solving capacity. Mentoring networks connect experienced and developing members for mutual learning and support. Collaborative projects create opportunities for people to work together on meaningful challenges while developing new skills and relationships.

Reflection practices build regular opportunities for individuals and groups to process experiences and extract learning for future application. Celebration rituals acknowledge learning achievements and growth milestones to reinforce the value of continuous development. Resource sharing makes learning materials, opportunities, and expertise available to all community members.

Action learning approaches address real community challenges while building members' capacity for effective problem-solving and service. Storytelling traditions preserve and share wisdom gained through experience while inspiring others to pursue their own growth and development.

Learning from Failure: The Growth Catalyst

One of the most crucial aspects of growth mindset involves developing healthy relationships with failure that enable learning and development rather than discouragement and stagnation. Understanding how to process and extract value from setbacks transforms obstacles into opportunities.

Reframing Failure as Feedback Information processing treats unsuccessful attempts as data about what doesn't work rather than evidence of personal inadequacy or hopeless situations. Hypothesis testing approaches challenges as experiments where outcomes provide valuable information regardless of immediate success or failure. Course correction uses failure experiences to adjust strategies, improve preparation, or develop new approaches to similar challenges.

Skill development recognizes that failure often indicates areas where additional learning, practice, or resource development is needed. Resilience building understands that recovering from failure develops mental and emotional strength that serves future challenges. Empathy expansion through personal struggle creates greater compassion and understanding for others facing similar difficulties.

Wisdom cultivation extracts principles and insights from failure experiences that can benefit both personal growth and service to others who face comparable challenges.

The Failure Recovery Process Emotional processing allows appropriate time for disappointment, frustration, or discouragement without being overwhelmed or defined by these feelings. Responsibility assessment honestly examines personal contribution to failure without taking inappropriate blame for factors beyond individual control. Learning extraction systematically identifies lessons that can inform future decisions and actions.

Support seeking reaches out to mentors, friends, or advisors for perspective, encouragement, and guidance during recovery and planning phases. Action planning develops specific steps for applying lessons learned while moving forward with revised approaches or new opportunities. Sharing wisdom looks for appropriate ways to help others learn from your experience while maintaining healthy boundaries about privacy and timing.

Community support provides encouragement and practical help during failure recovery while celebrating the courage to take risks and learn from outcomes.

Building Failure Resilience Identity security maintains sense of worth and calling based on God's love and purpose rather than performance outcomes. Growth perspective views setbacks as normal parts of development rather than unexpected disasters or personal defects. Learning orientation focuses on gaining wisdom and skills rather than just achieving immediate success.

Risk calibration develops judgment about appropriate challenges that stretch capacity without overwhelming resources or commitment. Support systems build relationships and resources that provide encouragement and practical help during difficult seasons. Recovery practices establish routines and strategies for processing failure experiences constructively and moving forward with renewed energy and focus.

Lifelong Learning and Continuous Development

Maintaining growth mindset throughout different life seasons requires adapting learning approaches to changing circumstances, responsibilities, and opportunities while preserving curiosity and commitment to development.

Learning Across Life Stages Early career learning focuses on skill development, professional competence, and discovering strengths and interests that inform long-term direction. Mid-career learning often emphasizes leadership development, specialized expertise, and balancing professional growth with family and community responsibilities. Late career learning may involve mentoring others, developing wisdom for complex challenges, and preparing for transition to different types of contribution.

Retirement learning can include pursuing interests that were deferred during working years, developing new forms of service, and sharing accumulated wisdom with younger generations. Health challenge learning involves adapting to physical limitations while discovering new capacities and ways to contribute meaningfully.

Each life stage presents unique opportunities and constraints for learning that require flexibility and creativity to navigate effectively while maintaining growth orientation.

Integrating Learning with Service Service-learning approaches combine helping others with personal development, creating mutually beneficial experiences that serve community needs while building individual capacity. Reflective practice includes regular assessment of service experiences to identify learning opportunities and improve effectiveness over time.

Cross-cultural learning develops through service across economic, ethnic, or social boundaries that require humility, adaptation, and expanded perspective. Skill transfer shares abilities and knowledge with others while learning about different contexts and approaches to similar challenges.

Collaborative learning engages in mutual teaching and learning relationships where everyone contributes expertise while gaining new insights and abilities.

Creating Personal Learning Systems Learning goals establish specific objectives for growth and development that align with personal calling and service opportunities. Resource identification discovers books, courses, mentors, and experiences that support learning goals effectively. Practice opportunities create regular chances to apply new knowledge and skills in safe, supportive environments.

Feedback mechanisms establish ways to receive input about progress and areas for continued development. Reflection routines build regular time for processing learning experiences and planning next steps for growth. Community connections maintain relationships with others who share learning interests and can provide mutual encouragement and accountability.

Documentation practices preserve insights and lessons learned for future reference and potential sharing with others who might benefit from your experience and development.

PRACTICAL APPLICATIONS
The Growth Mindset Assessment:
Evaluating Your Learning Orientation

Before developing stronger growth mindset practices, it's important to honestly assess your current attitudes toward learning, challenges, and development. This assessment helps identify areas where fixed mindset thinking may be limiting your growth and service potential.

Learning Attitude Evaluation

Challenge Response Analysis:
- How do you typically react when facing tasks that feel difficult or beyond your cur-

rent abilities?

- What thoughts go through your mind when someone suggests you try something new or unfamiliar?
- How often do you avoid opportunities because you might not succeed immediately?
- When do you feel most comfortable: when demonstrating existing skills or when learning new ones?
- Rate your excitement level about challenges that require significant learning (1-10 scale)

Feedback and Criticism Reception:

- How do you respond emotionally when receiving constructive criticism about your performance?
- What is your first instinct when someone points out areas where you could improve?
- How often do you seek feedback versus waiting for others to offer it?
- Do you view criticism as attack on your character or information for your development?
- How well do you distinguish between your identity and your current performance level?

Failure and Setback Processing:

- What meaning do you typically assign to failures or unsuccessful attempts?
- How long does it usually take you to recover motivation after a significant setback?
- Do you tend to view mistakes as learning opportunities or evidence of inadequacy?
- How often do you share your failures and what you learned from them with others?
- What role does perfectionism play in your approach to new challenges or skills?

Learning Investment and Curiosity:

- How much time and energy do you regularly invest in learning new skills or knowledge?
- What motivates your learning: genuine curiosity, practical necessity, or external pressure?
- How often do you read books, take courses, or seek experiences outside your comfort zone?
- Do you believe your fundamental abilities can improve significantly through effort and practice?
- How excited do you get about others' successes and achievements in areas where you'd like to grow?

Daily Growth Mindset Practices: Building Your Learning Muscle

Developing consistent growth orientation requires daily practices that reinforce learning attitudes while creating opportunities for development and skill building.

Morning Growth Mindset Preparation (10 minutes)

Learning Intention Setting:
- Begin each day by identifying one area where you want to learn or improve today
- Ask yourself: "What opportunity for growth will I embrace today?"
- Set an intention to view challenges as learning opportunities rather than threats to your competence
- Remind yourself: "I am constantly learning and growing in wisdom and ability"
- Pray for humility to receive feedback and courage to attempt difficult things

Curiosity Activation Practice:
- Choose one person you'll encounter today and commit to learning something new about them
- Identify one task or responsibility where you can experiment with a different approach
- Plan to ask one thoughtful question during conversations rather than just sharing your own knowledge
- Look for one way to improve a routine activity through creative thinking or research
- Set an intention to notice what you can learn from any mistakes or setbacks today

Midday Learning Check-in (5 minutes)

Growth Opportunity Recognition:
- Pause and ask: "What have I learned so far today?"
- Identify any moments when you chose growth over comfort or learning over appearing knowledgeable
- Notice if you've been defending your ego versus staying open to new information
- Consider how you've responded to any challenges or feedback received today
- Adjust your approach if you've been operating from fixed mindset assumptions

Afternoon Intention Reset:
- Recommit to approaching remaining activities with curiosity and openness to learning
- If you've made mistakes, reframe them as valuable feedback rather than failures

- Look for ways to help others learn or grow through the rest of your day
- Ask: "How can I demonstrate growth mindset in my remaining interactions?"

Evening Growth Review (10-15 minutes)

Learning Harvest Reflection:
- What specific things did you learn today about yourself, others, or your work?
- How did you respond to challenges, feedback, or opportunities to try new approaches?
- Where did you demonstrate growth mindset versus where did fixed mindset thinking appear?
- What mistakes or setbacks provided valuable learning opportunities?
- How did your learning orientation affect your relationships and service to others?

Growth Planning and Gratitude:
- Identify one specific way you grew or learned today
- Plan one learning goal or experiment for tomorrow
- Express gratitude for people who taught you something or challenged you to grow
- Celebrate progress and effort rather than just achievements or outcomes
- Set intentions for how you want to approach tomorrow's learning opportunities

Challenge-Seeking and Skill Development Strategies

Growth mindset flourishes when we intentionally seek appropriate challenges that stretch our abilities while building new competencies through deliberate practice and strategic learning.

The Challenge Zone Navigation System

Comfort Zone Assessment:
- Identify activities, relationships, and responsibilities where you feel completely confident and competent
- List skills or knowledge areas where you haven't grown significantly in the past year
- Notice patterns in what you avoid due to fear of looking incompetent or making mistakes
- Evaluate whether staying in your comfort zone is limiting your service effectiveness or impact
- Consider how comfort zone living might be affecting your example to others

Growth Zone Identification:

- Choose challenges that stretch your abilities without overwhelming your capacity
- Look for opportunities to learn skills that would enhance your service to others
- Seek feedback or coaching in areas where you want to improve
- Join groups or activities where you'll be a beginner again
- Volunteer for projects that require you to develop new capabilities

Panic Zone Awareness:
- Recognize when challenges are too overwhelming for productive learning
- Develop skills for breaking large challenges into manageable steps
- Seek support, training, or resources when facing intimidating new responsibilities
- Practice saying no to opportunities that would create destructive stress levels
- Build capacity gradually rather than attempting dramatic capability leaps

Deliberate Practice Implementation

Skill Development Protocol:
1. Identify specific skills that would enhance your effectiveness in serving others
2. Find quality instruction through books, courses, mentors, or expert practitioners
3. Practice regularly with focused attention on improvement rather than just repetition
4. Seek feedback from knowledgeable people who can guide your development
5. Adjust approach based on what you learn about effective techniques and your learning style
6. Measure progress through objective criteria rather than just subjective feelings

Learning Project Management:
- Set specific, measurable goals for skill development with realistic timelines
- Create practice schedules that fit your other responsibilities and energy levels
- Track progress through journals, recordings, or other documentation methods
- Celebrate milestones and improvements rather than waiting for mastery achievement
- Share your learning journey with others who can provide encouragement and accountability

Failure Recovery and Learning Extraction Processes

Developing healthy responses to setbacks and mistakes transforms potentially discouraging experiences into valuable growth catalysts that strengthen both character and competence.

The Failure Learning Protocol

Immediate Response Framework: When experiencing failure or significant setbacks, use this structured approach:

1. Pause and breathe before reacting emotionally or making quick judgments
2. Acknowledge the disappointment without minimizing the setback or your feelings about it
3. Avoid immediate blame of yourself or others until you can think more clearly
4. Seek appropriate support from people who can provide perspective and encouragement
5. Postpone major decisions until emotional intensity has decreased and you can think strategically

Learning Extraction Process: After the initial emotional response has settled:

1. Analyze contributing factors including your preparation, decision-making, and external circumstances
2. Identify lessons learned about strategy, skill development needs, or environmental factors
3. Extract principles that could apply to future similar situations
4. Plan specific improvements in approach, preparation, or support systems
5. Share insights appropriately with others who might benefit from your experience

Recovery and Forward Movement:

- Forgive yourself for mistakes while taking responsibility for learning and improvement
- Adjust expectations about timelines or approaches based on new understanding
- Rebuild confidence through smaller successes and supportive relationships
- Apply lessons learned to new opportunities rather than avoiding similar challenges
- Help others who face comparable difficulties by sharing your experience and recovery

Creating Learning Communities and Support Systems

Sustaining growth mindset requires communities that support learning, celebrate development, and provide resources for continuous improvement and mutual encouragement.

Learning Partnership Development

Growth Accountability Partners: Find someone who shares your commitment to learning and development:

- Selection criteria: Choose someone who demonstrates growth mindset and shares your values

- Meeting structure: Meet regularly to share learning goals, challenges, and progress
- Mutual support: Provide encouragement during setbacks and celebration during breakthroughs
- Challenge invitation: Push each other toward appropriate stretch goals and new experiences
- Resource sharing: Exchange books, courses, opportunities, and insights that support growth

Mentoring Relationships for Learning:
- Seek mentors in areas where you want to develop expertise or wisdom
- Offer mentoring to others who could benefit from skills or knowledge you've developed
- Create learning exchanges where you teach others while learning from their expertise
- Join formal programs that facilitate mentoring relationships in your profession or interests
- Build intergenerational connections that enable wisdom transfer across age groups

Professional and Personal Learning Networks

Community Building Strategies:
- Join learning-focused groups in your profession, interests, or community service areas
- Participate in conferences, workshops, and training events that attract growth-oriented people
- Create study groups around books, topics, or skills you want to develop with others
- Engage in online communities that share resources and support learning in your interest areas
- Volunteer for challenging projects that require learning while serving meaningful causes

Family and Household Learning Culture:
- Model learning behavior for children and family members through your own growth pursuits
- Create family learning activities like reading together, taking classes, or working on projects
- Celebrate learning achievements rather than just performance outcomes in household conversations
- Share failure stories and what you learned from them to normalize growth through setbacks
- Support each other's learning goals through encouragement, resources, and practical assistance

Technology and Resources for Accelerated Learning

Leveraging modern tools and resources can significantly enhance your capacity for growth while providing flexible options that fit various schedules, learning styles, and budget constraints.

Digital Learning Platforms and Tools:

- Online courses through platforms like Coursera, edX, or specialized professional development sites
- Podcast learning during commutes, exercise, or routine activities to maximize learning time
- Video tutorials for visual learning of practical skills and techniques
- E-books and audiobooks for convenient access to vast knowledge resources
- Learning apps that provide micro-learning opportunities during brief free moments

Documentation and Reflection Systems:

- Learning journals to capture insights, progress, and lessons from various experiences
- Digital note-taking systems that organize and make searchable your accumulated learning
- Photo documentation of projects, experiments, and learning milestones
- Video reflection where you process learning experiences and track development over time
- Shared documentation with learning partners or communities for mutual benefit and accountability

Resource Planning and Investment:

- Learning budget allocation for books, courses, conferences, and other development resources
- Time blocking for regular learning activities that receive priority in your schedule
- Learning goal integration with professional development plans and personal growth objectives
- Resource sharing networks where you exchange materials and opportunities with others
- Sabbatical planning for extended learning experiences that require concentrated time and focus

This comprehensive approach to learning and growth mindset development provides both individual practices for continuous improvement and community strategies for creating environments where development flourishes and serves others' growth as well as your own.

CHAPTER CONCLUSION
The Endless Journey of Becoming

As we conclude this final exploration of learning and growth mindset, it's essential to understand the profound truth that has emerged throughout our entire journey together: serving and growing richly is not a destination to reach but a way of traveling through life. You haven't simply learned techniques for personal development or strategies for better service—you've discovered the endless journey of becoming the person God created you to be while blessing others through your continuous growth and faithful service.

The most beautiful aspect of a learning and growth mindset is that it transforms every experience into curriculum for your development. Every challenge becomes a classroom, every setback becomes a teacher, every success becomes preparation for greater service, and every person you encounter becomes both student and instructor in the magnificent school of life. When you embrace learning as a lifelong adventure, you never graduate from growth, never become too old to develop new capacities, and never exhaust the possibilities for deeper service and richer living.

The Integration of All Principles

This final chapter on learning and growth mindset serves as the capstone that integrates every principle we've explored throughout this book. Your mindset becomes anchored in growth possibilities rather than fixed limitations. Your action flows from continuous learning about what serves others most effectively. Your vision and goals evolve as you discover new capacities and opportunities through ongoing development.

Your courage to face fear and adversity grows as you understand that every challenge teaches valuable lessons. Your daily habits include learning practices that compound over time into extraordinary wisdom and skill. Your purpose and meaning deepen as you discover how your growth enables greater service to others. Your identity remains secure while continuously expanding through new understanding and capabilities.

Your resilience and endurance strengthen as you learn to extract value from every difficulty. Your relationships and influence flourish as you become someone others want to learn from and grow alongside. Your love and compassion expand as learning increases your understanding of others' experiences and needs. Your responsibility and ownership grow as learning enhances your capacity to steward greater opportunities and resources.

Your faith and spiritual strength deepen as you learn more about God's character and purposes through study and experience. Your gratitude and appreciation multiply as learning opens your eyes to blessings and possibilities you previously couldn't see. All of these elements work together when anchored in a learning and growth mindset that sees every aspect of life as opportunity for development and service.

The Legacy of Lifelong Learning

Remember that your commitment to learning and growth creates a legacy that extends far beyond your personal development. When you model curiosity, embrace challenges, learn from failures, and continuously develop your capacities, you give others permission to do the same. Your growth mindset becomes contagious, inspiring family members, colleagues, and community members to pursue their own development rather than settling for stagnation.

The children who observe your learning adventures learn that growth is possible at any age. The colleagues who watch you tackle new challenges gain courage to leave their own comfort zones. The friends who see you recover from setbacks with grace and wisdom discover resilience they didn't know they possessed. Your learning journey becomes a gift you offer to everyone whose life you touch, creating ripple effects of growth and development that continue long after your direct influence ends.

Years from now, people may not remember specific skills you developed or knowledge you acquired, but they will remember how your commitment to growth inspired their own journey of becoming. They'll recall how your humility in learning encouraged their honesty about their own limitations. They'll treasure how your excitement about discovery sparked their own curiosity and courage to explore new possibilities.

The Eternal Dimension of Temporal Growth

As you continue your learning journey, remember that every skill you develop, every insight you gain, and every character quality you cultivate has eternal significance. You're not just improving your effectiveness in this life—you're preparing for responsibilities and relationships that will continue forever. The wisdom you gain through learning becomes part of who you are eternally, and the service skills you develop prepare you for ways of contributing to God's kingdom that transcend earthly limitations.

This eternal perspective transforms learning from self-improvement project to sacred stewardship. Every book you read, every skill you develop, every lesson you extract from experience becomes part of your preparation for eternal service in God's kingdom. The character qualities you develop through growth challenges become permanent aspects of your identity that will serve others forever.

Understanding the eternal dimension of learning provides motivation during seasons when growth feels difficult or costly. Even when development requires sacrifice, patience, or perseverance, you can trust that you're investing in outcomes that transcend earthly limitations and contribute to purposes that will never end.

Your Lifetime Learning Assignment

As you close this book and continue your journey of serving and growing richly, carry with you the Practical Exercise from our opening section. This week, identify one area where you feel "stuck" and commit to learning something new in that domain. But more importantly, embrace the mindset that sees every day as a classroom, every person as a teacher, and every experience as curriculum for your continuing development.

Choose one daily learning practice from our toolkit and commit to it for the next 30 days. Whether it's morning growth intention setting, midday learning check-ins, or evening growth review, begin building the habit of intentional learning that will serve you for the rest of your life.

A Benediction for the Journey Ahead

As you continue serving and growing richly, may you always remain curious about what you don't yet know, humble about what you're still learning, and excited about who you're becoming. May every challenge you face become a teacher that strengthens your character and expands your capacity for service. May every success you achieve become preparation for greater opportunities to bless others through your gifts and growth.

May your learning journey inspire others to pursue their own development with courage and hope. May your growth mindset create communities where everyone feels safe to be vulnerable about their limitations while being encouraged to pursue their potential. May your commitment to lifelong learning become a legacy that blesses generations with the understanding that growth is always possible and that every person has unlimited potential for development and service.

And may you discover, as countless servants before you have found, that the journey of learning and growing in service to others is the richest, most rewarding, and most meaningful way to spend the precious gift of life that God has entrusted to your care.

The journey of serving and growing richly has no end—only new chapters waiting to be written through your continued learning, faithful service, and joyful growth. Step forward with confidence, knowing that the God who called you to this journey will provide everything you need for every lesson He wants to teach you and every service He wants to accomplish through you.

The adventure continues. The learning never ends. The growth is limitless. The service is eternal. And the richness of a life well-lived through continuous development and faithful service awaits your ongoing discovery.

www.ingramcontent.com/pod-product-compliance
Lightning Source LLC
Chambersburg PA
CBHW030451100526
44580CB00005B/85/J